College Degrees by Mail & Internet

8th edition

*100 Accredited Schools
That Offer Bachelor's,
Master's, Doctorates,
and Law Degrees
by Distance Learning*

*John Bear, Ph.D.
Mariah Bear, M.A.*

*Ten Speed Press
Berkeley   Toronto*

DEGREE.NET
A division of Ten Speed Press
P.O. Box 7123
Berkeley, California 94707
www.degree.net

Distributed in Australia by Simon & Schuster, in Canada by Ten Speed Press Canada, in New Zealand by Southern Publishers Group, in South Africa by Real Books, in Southeast Asia by Berkeley Books, and in the United Kingdom and Europe by Airlift Book Company.

Cover design by Cale Burr
Text design by Jeff Brandenburg (ImageComp) and Linda Davis (Star Type)

Disclaimer:
While the authors believe that the information in this book is correct as of the time of publication, it is possible we may have made errors, which we will correct at the first available opportunity. We, the publisher, are not responsible for any problems that may arise in readers' interactions with any schools described in the book.

Library of Congress Cataloging-in-Publication Data on file with publisher.

First printing this edition, 2001
Printed in Canada

1 2 3 4 5 6 7 8 9 10 — 05 04 03 02 01

Dedication

John's:
For Marina, for 37 years of love and help.

Mariah's:
For Joe, who's all that.

Table of Contents

Introduction

Four Essential Assumptions

Here are the four basic assumptions upon which this book is built. You already know the first, you probably know the second, you probably don't know the third, and the fourth is the reason to buy this book.

There is often no connection whatsoever between ability and degrees.

There are extremely talented and capable people who never went to college for a single day. And, as everyone knows, some of the most incompetent boobs on our planet have degrees from prestigious universities.

A degree is often more useful than a good education or valuable skills in your field.

You may be the best business manager, teacher, or pilot in three counties, but if you don't have a piece of imitation parchment that certifies you as an Associate, Bachelor, Master, or Doctor, you are somehow perceived as less worthy and are often denied the better jobs and higher salaries that go to degree-holders, regardless of their competence.

It is easier than it ever has been to earn a degree.

Since the mid-1970s, there has been a virtual explosion in what is now called "alternative" or "nontraditional" or "external" or "off-campus" education—ways and means of getting an education or a degree (or both, if you wish) without sitting in classrooms day after day, year after year.

But it is not always easy to find the right school.

Many of the good schools never advertise or promote themselves, either because they don't know how or because they think it unseemly. And most of the bad schools, the illegal or barely legal diploma mills, advertise all the time in national newspapers and magazines.

Let this book be your guide, your starting point, and your road map. Of course, it will require effort on your part to end up with the degree you want. Still, we think it is safe to say that if you cannot find what you are looking for or hoping for in this book, it probably doesn't exist.

College Degrees by Distance Learning

The Two Ideas That Make It All Possible

There are two very clever ideas that make it possible to earn good, usable college degrees by distance learning. Surprisingly, both ideas have been around for a long time, although many people in the degree-granting business are just beginning to pay attention to them.

Idea Number One:

If you've *already* done it, you don't have to do it again.

When Aristotle arrived to train Alexander T. Great, it was clear to the old boy that his student already had learned a great deal, which did not have to be taught again, and so they could get on with studying the arts of war and diplomacy. Compare that with many of today's students who "learn" the exports of Brazil and the parts of speech every year for eight consecutive years. As John's mentor, Dr. Elizabeth Drews, wrote, "It is immoral to teach someone something he or she already knows."

Fortunately, more and more colleges and universities are giving credit for the things one already knows. If you can speak a second language—it doesn't matter whether you learned it from your grandmother or out of a book or by living in another country—you'll get credit for it. If you learned journalism by working on a newspaper, you'll get credit for it. If you learned meteorology while studying for your pilot's license, you'll get credit for it. That sort of thing. (How do you get that credit? Read on. That's what much of this book is about.)

Idea Number Two:

Meaningful learning can take place outside the classroom.

Abraham Lincoln studied law at night, by the fire, in his home. We have always known that learning can take place anywhere, anytime, although for years most universities have pretended that the only worthwhile learning, the only *degree-worthy* learning, takes place in classrooms and lecture halls. But now, more and more schools are not only acknowledging the learning that took place before you enrolled, they are making their own courses available in a multitude of ways, including

- courses by correspondence, or home study
- courses offered over cable television (or by videotape)
- courses through guided independent study at your own pace
- courses offered over home computers linked to the university computer, most often via the Internet
- courses offered in your neighborhood by schools that are actually located in another state or country

Important Issues

College Degrees

What Are They?

A degree is a title conferred by a school to show that a certain course of study has been successfully completed. A diploma is the actual document or certificate that is given to the student as evidence of the awarding of the degree. The following six kinds of degrees are awarded by colleges and universities in the United States:

The associate's degree

The associate's degree is a relatively recent development, reflecting the tremendous growth of two-year community colleges (which is the new and presumably more respectable name for what used to be known as junior colleges).

Since many students attend these schools for two years, but do not continue on to another school for the bachelor's degree, a need was felt for a degree to be awarded at the end of these two years of full-time study (or their equivalent by nontraditional means). More than two thousand two-year schools now award associate's degrees, and a small but growing number of four-year schools also award them to students who leave after two years.

The two most common associate's degrees are the A.A. (Associate of Arts) and the A.S. (Associate of Science). But more than one hundred other titles have been devised, ranging from the A.M.E. (Associate of Mechanical Engineering) to the A.D.T. (Associate of Dance Therapy).

An associate's degree typically requires 60 to 64 semester hours of credit, which normally takes two academic years (four semesters, or six quarters) to complete in a traditional program.

The bachelor's degree

In most places in the world, the bachelor's is the first university degree earned. (The associate's is little used outside the United States.) The traditional bachelor's degree in America is widely believed to require four years of full-time study (120 to 128 semester units). However, a rather alarming report recently revealed that, because more students are attending on a part-time basis, and because of difficulties getting into overcrowded classes, the average time is closer to six years! But through nontraditional approaches, some people with a good deal of prior learning have earned bachelor's degrees in as short a time as two or three months.

More than three hundred different bachelor's degree titles have been used in the last hundred years, but the great majority of the million-plus bachelor's degrees awarded in the United States each year are either the B.A. (Bachelor of Arts) or the B.S. (Bachelor of Science), sometimes with additional letters to indicate the field (e.g., B.S.E.E. for electrical engineering, B.A.B.A. for business administration, and so on). Other common bachelor's degree titles include the B.B.A. (business administration), B.Mus. (music), B.Ed. (education), and B.Eng. (engineering). Some nontraditional schools or programs award their own degrees: B.G.S. (general studies), B.I.S. (independent studies), B.L.S. (liberal studies), and so on. (Incidentally, in the late nineteenth century, educators felt that the title of "Bachelor" was inappropriate for young ladies, so some schools awarded female graduates titles such as Mistress of Arts or Maid of Science.)

The master's degree

The traditional master's degree requires one to two years of on-campus work after the bachelor's. Some nontraditional master's degrees may be earned entirely through nonresident study, while others require anywhere from a few days to a few weeks on campus.

There are several philosophical approaches to the master's degree. Some schools regard it as a sort of advanced bachelor's, requiring only the completion of one to two years of advanced-level studies and courses. Other schools see it as a junior doctorate, requiring creative, original research and culminating in the writing of a thesis, or original research paper. Some programs give students the option of choosing either approach: they may choose either to take, for example, ten courses and write a thesis, or thirteen courses with no thesis, to earn the master's degree.

Master's degree titles tend to follow closely those of bachelor's degrees. The M.A. (Master of Arts) and M.S. (Master of Science) are by far the most common, along with the standby of American business, the M.B.A. (Master of Business Administration). Other common master's degrees include the M.Ed. (education), M.Eng. (engineering), M.L.S. (library science), and M.J. (either journalism or jurisprudence).

The doctorate

The academic title of "Doctor" (as distinguished from the professional and honorary titles, to be discussed shortly) is awarded for completion of an advanced course of study that culminates in a piece of original research in one's field, known as the doctoral thesis, or dissertation.

The total elapsed time can be anywhere from 3 to 12 years. The trend has been for doctorates to take longer and longer. A typical Ph.D. now takes 6 or 7 years, not all of it necessarily spent in residence on campus.

Some doctoral programs permit the use of work already done (books written, symphonies composed, business plans created, etc.) as partial (or, in a few cases, full) satisfaction of the dissertation requirement. But many schools insist on all, or almost all, new work.

The most common doctorate is the Doctor of Philosophy (Ph.D. in North America, D.Phil. in many other countries), which need not have anything to do with philosophy. It is awarded for studies in dozens of fields, ranging from chemistry to communication to agriculture. There are more than 500 other doctorate titles in the English language alone. After the Ph.D., the most common include the Ed.D. (education), D.B.A. (business administration), D.P.A. (public administration), D.A. (art or administration), Eng.D. (engineering), and Psy.D. (psychology).

Finally, it should be mentioned that several American schools, concerned with what one called the "doctoral glut," are reported to be seriously considering instituting a new degree, *higher* than the doctorate, presumably requiring more years of study and a more extensive dissertation. The name "Chancellorate" has been bandied about. Indeed, the prestigious *Chronicle of Higher Education* devoted a major article to this possibility in 1990. It may well be that holders of a Chancellorate (Ph.C.?) would not appreciably affect the job market, since most of them will be on Social Security by the time they complete this degree.

The professional degree

Professional degrees are earned by people who intend to enter what are often called "the professions"—medicine, dentistry, law, the ministry, and so forth. In the United States, these degrees are almost always earned *after* completing a bachelor's degree, and almost always carry the title of "Doctor" (e.g., Doctor of Medicine, Doctor of Divinity).

In many other countries, it is common to enter professional school directly from high school, in which case the first degree earned is a bachelor's. (For instance, there is the British Bachelor of Medicine, whose holders are invariably called "Doctor" unless they have earned the advanced degree of "Doctor of Medicine." Then they insist on being called "Mister." No one ever said the British were easy to understand.)

Honorary degree

The honorary degree is the stepchild of the academic world, and a most curious one at that. It has no more relationship or connection with academia than bandleader Doc Severinson has with the world of medicine. It is, purely and simply, a title that some institutions (and some scoundrels) have chosen to bestow from time to time, and for a wide variety of reasons, upon certain people. These reasons often have to do with the donation of money or with attracting celebrities to a commencement ceremony.

The honorary doctorate has no academic standing whatsoever and yet, because it carries with it the same title, "Doctor," that is used for the earned degree, it has become an extremely desirable commodity for those who covet titles and the prestige they bring. For respectable universities to award the title of "Doctor" via an honorary doctorate is as peculiar as if the Army were to award civilians the honorary title of "General"—a title the honorees could then use in their everyday lives.

More than one thousand traditional colleges and universities award honorary doctorates (anywhere from 1 to 50 per year each), and a great many Bible schools, spurious schools, and degree mills hand them out with wild abandon to almost anyone willing to pay the price. And that is why we have Doctor Michael Jackson, Doctor Ed McMahon, Doctor Frank Sinatra, Doctor Ella Fitzgerald, Doctor Mister Rogers, Doctor Captain Kangaroo, Doctor Dr. Seuss, Doctor Jane Pauley, Doctor Bob Hope, Doctor Robert Redford, Doctor Stevie Wonder, Doctor Dan Rather, and thousands of other doctors.

Checking Out Schools

Two Problems, Two Questions to Ask

A degree program is, for many people, one of the most expensive and time-consuming things they will do in their lives. And yet some people will spend more time and energy choosing a refrigerator or a television set than they will selecting a school. For such people, one of two major problems may later set in:

Problem One: The school turns out to be less than wonderful

Some people enroll in a questionable school and then, when they see their alma mater exposed on *60 Minutes* or *Inside Edition,* they wail, "But I didn't know; they had such a lovely catalog." Now clearly, if you apply to one of the schools listed in this book, that won't be a problem. All of these schools have proper accreditation, whether regional, national, or international (see "Accreditation," starting on page 16, for an explanation of these terms). Still, it's our experience that some people will buy a book such as this, note all of the accredited schools, and still end up studying at a less-than-wonderful institution. Why? Well, maybe it was less expensive, or seemed easier to do, or swore that it was just as good as the schools in this book.

In addition, there's the fact that good, accredited programs will almost certainly debut after this book does (distance learning being such an active, growing field). So, you may well be faced with advertisements or Web sites for interesting-looking degree programs that aren't listed here, and need to know how to evaluate them.

Problem Two: There are unpleasant surprises down the road

Some people enroll in good, legitimate schools, but then discover that the program just doesn't suit their needs. For instance, while most MBA programs have an analytical or mathematical bent, others are more focused on people management or leadership. There's also the possibility that the program your heart is set on isn't exactly what you need—perhaps another program would serve the same purpose as well or better. Or maybe the school's sales reps said the program could be finished in two years, but a closer reading of the catalog shows that only a full-time, nonworking student could accomplish this.

Thus there are two kinds of "checking out" to do: Is the school legitimate? And will the school meet my needs?

Question One: Is the school legitmate?

If you have any doubts, concerns, worries, or hunches about any school, whether in this book or not, you have every right to check it out. It's a buyer's market.

You can ask any questions you want about accreditation, number of students, credentials of the people in charge, campus facilities (some schools with very impressive-looking catalogs are operated from mail-forwarding services), and so on. Of course, the school has the right not to answer, whereupon you have the right not to enroll.

You may also want to confirm what a school tells you about its accreditation or legal status. Recognized accrediting agencies are more than happy to tell you what schools they accredit; we list the contact information for accreditors starting on page 18. To check whether a school is operating legally or not, inquire with the appropriate state or government agency; you'll find a list of these higher education agencies in Appendix E.

The information in this book is as complete and current as we could make it. But things change: schools change their policies, bad schools get better, good schools get worse, new schools appear, old schools disappear. For ways and means of getting more information, see Appendices B and C.

Question Two: Will it meet my needs?

You'd think people would know this before spending thousands of dollars and years of their lives. But we have received hundreds of letters from people who had very unpleasant surprises after enrolling, and some even after they had graduated. It is essential that you satisfy yourself that a given school will meet your needs before you spend any money. Make sure you know exactly what it will cost (no hidden "graduation fees," for instance), whether your employer will accept (and perhaps pay for) your degree, whether any relevant licensing agencies will accept the work, and so on.

Applying to Schools

How Many Schools Should You Apply To?

There is no single answer to this question that is right for everyone. Each person will have to determine his or her own best answer. The decision should be based on the following four factors:

1. Likelihood of admission

Some schools are extremely competitive or popular and admit fewer than 10 percent of qualified applicants. Some have an "open admission" policy and admit literally everyone who applies. Most are somewhere in between.

If your goal is to be admitted to one of the highly competitive schools (for instance, Harvard, Yale, Princeton, or Stanford), where your chances of being accepted are not high, then it is wise to apply to at least four or five schools that would be among your top choices and to at least one "safety valve," an easier one, in case all else fails.

If you are interested in one of the good, but not world-famous, nonresident programs, your chances for acceptance are probably better than nine in ten, so you might decide to apply to only one or two.

2. Cost

There is a tremendous range of possible costs for any given degree. For instance, a respectable Ph.D. could cost around $3,000 at a good nonresident school or more than $80,000 at a prestigious university—not even taking into account the salary you would lose by taking the time to do such a degree in residence.

3. What they offer you

Shopping around for a school is a little like shopping for a new car. Many schools either have money problems or operate as profit-making businesses. In either case, they are most eager to enroll new students. Thus it is not unreasonable to ask the schools what they can do for you. Let them know that you are a knowledgeable "shopper" and that you have this book. Do they have courses or faculty advisors in your specific field? If not, will they get them for you? How much credit will they give for prior life-experience learning? How long will it take to earn the degree? Are there any scholarships or tuition reduction plans available? Does tuition have to be paid all at once, or can it be spread out over time? If factors like these are important to you, then it could pay to shop around for the best deal.

You might consider investigating at least two or three schools that appear somewhat similar because there will surely be differences.

CAUTION: Remember that academic quality and reputation are probably the most important factors—so don't let a small financial savings be a reason to switch from a good school to a less-good school.

4. Your own time

Applying to a school can be a time-consuming process—and it costs money, too. Many schools have application fees ranging from $25 to $100. Some people get so carried away with the process of applying to school after school that they never get around to earning their degree!

Of course, once you have prepared a good and detailed resumé, curriculum vitae, or life-experience portfolio, you can use it to apply to more than one school.

Another time factor is how much of a hurry you are in. If you apply to several schools at once, the chances are good that at least one will admit you, and you can begin work promptly. If you apply to only one, and it turns you down, or you experience long delays, then it can take a month or two to go through the admission process again elsewhere.

Speeding Up the Admission Process

The admission process at most traditional schools is very slow; most people apply nearly a year in advance and do not learn whether their application has been accepted for four to six months. The schools in this book vary immensely in their policies in this regard. Some will grant conditional acceptance within a few weeks after receiving the application. ("Conditional" means that they must later verify the prior learning experiences you claim.) Others take just as long as traditional programs.

The following three factors can result in a much faster admission process:

1. Selecting schools by admission policy

A school's admission policy should be stated in its catalog. Since you will find a range among schools of a few weeks to six months for a decision, the simple solution is to ask and then apply to schools with a fast procedure.

2. Asking for speedy decisions

Some schools have formal procedures whereby you can request an early decision on your acceptance. Others do the same thing informally for those who ask. In effect, this puts you at the top of the pile in the admission office, so you will have the decision in perhaps half the usual time. Other schools use what they call a "rolling admissions" procedure, which means, in effect, that each application is considered soon after it is received instead of being held several months and considered with a large batch of others.

3. Applying pressure

As previously indicated, many schools are eager to have new students. If you make it clear to a school that you are in a hurry and may consider going elsewhere if you don't hear from them promptly, they will usually speed up the process. It is not unreasonable to specify a time frame. If, for instance, you are mailing in your application on September 1, you might enclose a note saying that you would like to have their decision mailed or phoned to you by October 1. (Some schools routinely telephone their acceptances, others do so if asked, some will only do so by collect call, and others will not, no matter what.)

How to Apply to a School

The basic procedure is essentially the same at all schools, traditional or nontraditional:

1. You write (or telephone) for the school's catalog, bulletin, or other literature, and admission form.

2. You complete the admission form and return it to the school with the application fee, if any.

3. You complete any other requirements the school may have (exams, transcripts, letters of recommendation, etc.).

4. The school notifies you of its decision.

It is step three that can vary tremendously from school to school. At some schools, all that is required is the admission application. Others require various entrance examinations to test your aptitude or knowledge level, transcripts, three or more letters of reference, a statement of financial condition, and possibly a personal interview, either on the campus or with a local representative in your area.

Luckily, the majority of schools in this book have relatively simple entrance requirements. All schools should tell you exactly what they expect you to do in order to apply. If it is not clear, ask. If the school does not supply prompt, helpful answers, then you probably don't want to deal with them anyway. Remember, it's a buyer's market.

It is advisable, in general, *not* to send a whole bunch of stuff to a school the very first time you write to them. A short note asking for their catalog should suffice. You may wish to indicate your field and degree goal ("I am interested in a master's and possibly a doctorate in psychology") in case they have different sets of literature for different programs. It probably can do no harm to mention that you are a reader of this book; it might get you slightly prompter or more personal responses. (On the other hand, we have gotten more than a few grouchy letters from readers who say, "I told them I was a personal friend of yours, and it still took six months for an answer." Oh, dear. Well, if they hadn't said that, it might have been even longer. Or perhaps shorter. Who knows?)

The Matter of Entrance Examinations

Many nonresident degree programs, even at the master's and doctoral levels, do not require any entrance examinations. On the other hand, the majority of residential programs *do* require them. The main reason for this appears to be that nonresidential students do not contribute to overcrowding on the campus, so more of them can be admitted. A second reason is that nonresidential students tend to be more mature, and schools acknowledge they have the ability to decide which program is best for them.

There are, needless to say, exceptions. If you have particular feelings about examinations—positive or negative—you will be able to find schools that meet your requirements. Do not hesitate to ask any school about their exam requirements if they are not clear from the catalog.

Bachelor's admission examinations

Most residential schools require applicants to take the SAT test, developed and distributed by the College Board (*www.collegeboard.com*). The general test, also known as the SAT I, measures verbal and math ability. There are also subject-specific tests (SAT II's) focused on such fields as biology, U.S. history, and French. These examinations are given at centers all over North America several times each year for modest fees, and by special arrangement in many foreign localities.

A competing private organization, ACT (*www.act.org*), offers a similar general aptitude test, covering English, reading, mathematics, and science reasoning. Virtually all schools accept the ACT in place of the SAT I, though some express a preference for the SAT.

The important point is that very few schools have their own exams; virtually all rely on either the SAT or the ACT.

Graduate admission examinations

Again, many nonresidential schools do not require any entrance examinations. When an exam is required for admission to a graduate program, it is often the GRE, or Graduate Record Examination, administered by the Educational

Testing Service (*www.gre.org*). The basic GRE consists of a 3½-hour aptitude test with verbal, quantitative, and analytical sections. Some schools also require one or more GRE subject exams, which test knowledge in a variety of specific fields (chemistry, computer science, psychology, etc.).

Professional school admission examinations

Most medical schools require applicants to take the MCAT (Medical College Admission Test; *www.aamc.org/stuapps/admiss/mcat*). Law schools generally require the LSAT (Law School Admission Test; *www.lsat.org*).

Exam preparation

There are many excellent books available at most libraries and larger bookstores on how to prepare for these various exams, complete with sample questions and answers. Also, the testing agencies themselves sell literature on their tests as well as copies of previous years' examinations.

The testing agencies used to deny vigorously that either cramming or coaching could affect one's scores. In the face of overwhelming evidence to the contrary, they no longer make those claims. Some coaching services have documented score increases of 25 to 30 percent. Check the Yellow Pages or the bulletin boards on high school or college campuses.

Accreditation

Accreditation is one of the most complex and confusing issues in higher education. It is also one of the most misused concepts—both intentionally and unintentionally. Let us try to make some sense out of the situation.

What is Accreditation?

Quite simply, it is a validation—a statement by a group of persons who are, theoretically, impartial experts in higher education, that a given school, or department within a school, has been thoroughly investigated and found worthy of approval.

It is important to know these things about accreditation:

- It is voluntary. No school is required to be accredited.

- It is not a government process. Accrediting agencies are private, independent organizations. The U.S. government does have a small role in recognizing accreditors (more on that to come), but that's the extent of it.

- It is a peculiarly American concept. In every other country in the world, all colleges and universities are either operated by the government, or given the right to grant degrees directly by the government, so there is no need for an independent agency to say that a given school is OK.

- There are hundreds of accrediting agencies. Some are generally recognized as legitimate; others are not. (The rest of this section shows you how to tell the difference.)

- Many acceptable schools (or departments within schools) are not accredited, either by their own choice (since accreditation is a totally voluntary and often very expensive procedure), or because they are too new (all schools were unaccredited at one time in their lives) or too experimental (many would say too innovative) for the generally conservative accreditors.

- Some less-than-wonderful schools are legitimately accredited, but not many.

- Many very bad schools claim to be accredited—but it is always by unrecognized, sometimes nonexistent, accrediting associations, often of their own creation.

- Accreditation is a controversial topic in higher education. The last two U.S. secretaries of education have stated in no uncertain terms that the accrediting agencies are not doing their jobs, especially with respect to "nontraditional" schools, such as some of the distance-learning institutions described in this book.

- Accreditation is not the same thing as being licensed, chartered, approved, authorized, or recognized.

How Important Is Accreditation?

That all depends on what you're using your degree for. If it is only for your personal knowledge and edification—it's not for career advancement, you're never listing it on your resume, you're not pursuing a higher degree—then accreditation is really not that important. Most of us, however, invest time and money into a degree not merely for the knowledge it bestows but also for the doors it will open as we move onward and upward in our lives. And in the

United States, particularly in the realms of business and academia, doors generally only open to degrees that are *legitimately* accredited.

So if you want your degree to be useful—for job hunting, for pursuing graduate studies, etc.—then you should pay attention to accreditation, and not simply to whether a school has got it, but to whether that accreditation is generally accepted.

GAAP: the Generally Accepted Accreditation Principles

In the world of accounting, there is the concept of GAAP: Generally Accepted Accounting Principles. Not absolutely, not always, not universally, but generally. The same concept makes just as much sense in the world of accreditation—GAAP: Generally Accepted Accreditation Principles.

We first heard the term used, informally, at the national convention of registrars and admissions officers (AACRAO) in Reno, a few years ago. It made good sense to us, and we have adopted it.

In the U.S., there is near-unanimous agreement on this among the relevant key decision-makers, especially university registrars, admissions officers, corporate human resource officers, and government agencies. Not everyone calls it "GAAP," but the concept is the same: If a school meets certain criteria, they will probably accept its credits or degrees; if not, they probably won't.

What are the criteria for GAAP?

- For schools based in the U.S., there is no disagreement: accreditation by an accrediting agency recognized either by the U.S. Department of Education, and/or by the Council for Higher Education Accreditation (CHEA).

- For schools in Great Britain and the British Commonwealth, it is membership in the Association of Commonwealth Universities and a listing in the *Commonwealth Universities Yearbook*.

- For schools in Australia, it is recognition by the Australian Qualifications Framework.

- For schools in other countries, it is an appropriate listing in the *International Handbook of Universities* (published by UNESCO), or an appropriate description in the *World Education Series* (published by PIER, Projects in International Education Research, a joint venture of AACRAO, NAFSA [the Association of International Educators] with the participation of the College Board); or a listing in the *Countries Series*, published by NOOSR, the Australian National Office for Overseas Skills Recognition.

All of the schools profiled in this book meet the standards of GAAP.

The Recognized Accrediting Agencies

There are six regional accrediting associations (each covering a particular region of the United States and its territories), several national accrediting agencies, and about 80 professional associations (accrediting specific departments or programs within a school). What makes these agencies "recognized"? They have been evaluated and approved by either the **U.S. Department of Education** (*www.ed.gov*) or the **Council for Higher Education Accreditation** (*www.chea.org*).

If an accredited degree is important to you, the first question to ask is, "Has the school been accredited by the relevant national accreditor or one of the six regional accreditors?" The next question is, "Has the department in which I am interested been accredited by its relevant professional association?"

It may be the case, for instance, that the North Central Association (one of the six regional accreditors) has accredited Dolas University. This means that the entire school is accredited, and all its degrees may be called accredited degrees or, more accurately, degrees from an accredited institution.

Or it may be that just the art department of Dolas University has been accredited by the relevant professional association—in this case, the National Association of Schools of Art. Then only the art majors at Dolas University can claim to have accredited degrees.

There are some jobs (psychology and nursing are two examples) in which professional accreditation may be more important than regional accreditation. In other words, even if a school is accredited by its regional association, unless its psychology department is also accredited by the American Psychological Association, its degree will be less useful for psychology majors. (One of the persistent legends about accreditation—the belief that Harvard is not accredited—has arisen because of this distinction. Harvard University is duly accredited by its regional agency, but its psychology department—and many others—are not accredited by the relevant professional agencies.)

All of the approved accreditors will gladly supply lists of all the schools (or departments within schools) they have accredited and those that are candidates for accreditation. They will also answer questions pertaining to any school's status (or lack of status) with them.

The six regional accrediting agencies

The most important accreditors are the six regional agencies, each with responsibility for dealing with all schools in the states over which it has jurisdiction.

Middle States Association of Colleges and Schools
Commission on Higher Education
3624 Market Street
Philadelphia, PA 19104
(215) 662 5606 • Fax: (215) 662 5501 • Web site: www.msache.org
Delaware, District of Columbia, Maryland, New Jersey, New York, Pennsylvania, Puerto Rico, Virgin Islands

New England Association of Schools and Colleges
209 Burlington Road
Bedford, MA 01730
(781) 271 0022 • Fax: (781) 271 0950 • Web site: www.neasc.org
Connecticut, Maine, Massachusetts, New Hampshire, Rhode Island, Vermont

North Central Association of Colleges and Schools
30 North La Salle Street, Suite 2400
Chicago, IL 60602
(800) 621 7440 • Fax: (312) 263 7462 • Web site: www.ncacihe.org
Arizona, Arkansas, Colorado, Illinois, Indiana, Iowa, Kansas, Michigan, Minnesota, Missouri, Nebraska, New Mexico, North Dakota, Ohio, Oklahoma, South Dakota, West Virginia, Wisconsin, Wyoming

Northwest Association of Schools and Colleges
11300 NE 33rd Place, Suite 120
Bellevue, WA 98004
(425) 827 2005 • Fax: (425) 827 3395 • Web site: www.cocnasc.org
Alaska, Idaho, Montana, Nevada, Oregon, Utah, Washington

Southern Association of Colleges and Schools
1866 Southern Lane
Decatur, GA 30033
(404) 679 4500 • Fax: (404) 679 4558 • Web site: www.sacs.org
Alabama, Florida, Georgia, Kentucky, Louisiana, Mississippi, North Carolina, South Carolina, Tennessee, Texas, Virginia

Western Association of Schools and Colleges
985 Atlantic Ave., Suite 100
Alameda, CA 94501
(510) 748 9001 • Fax: (510) 748 9797 • Web site: www.wascweb.org
California, Hawaii, Guam, Trust Territory of the Pacific

The relevant national accrediting agency

The only recognized agency with responsibility for distance-learning schools
everywhere in the United States is the Distance Education and Training
Council (DETC). While many of the schools it accredits are vocational (truck
driving, small-engine repair, real estate, etc.), the council is empowered to
accredit distance-learning academic schools offering associate's, bachelor's, and
master's degrees; it cannot deal with schools offering doctorates.

Distance Education and Training Council (DETC)
1601 18th Street NW
Washington, DC 20009
(202) 234 5100 • Fax: (202) 332 1386 • Web site: www.detc.org

The professional accrediting agencies

There are more than 80 specialized agencies with responsibility for accrediting
programs in architecture, art, Bible education, business, chiropractic, and scores
of other fields. Lists of them can be found in many standard reference books
(including our own *Bears' Guide to Earning Degrees by Distance Learning*,
described in Appendix C), or by contacting either the Department of Education
or CHEA (see page 17).

Unrecognized Accrediting Agencies

There are a great many accrediting agencies that are not approved or recognized
either by CHEA or by the Department of Education. A very small number are
clearly sincere and legitimate, many others are not; none will meet the needs of
a person who requires an accredited degree. Here are some of the more prominent ones:

Accrediting Commission for Specialized Colleges (ACSC)
According to their literature, the accrediting procedures of ACSC seem super-
ficial at best. The only requirement for becoming a candidate for accreditation
was to mail in a check for $110.

Accrediting Commission International for Schools, Colleges and Theological Seminaries (ACI)
See "International Accrediting Commission for Schools, Colleges and Theological Seminaries" in this section. After the IAC was fined and closed down by
authorities in Missouri in 1989, Dr. Reuter retired and turned his work over to
a colleague, who juggled the words in the name and opened up one state over,
in Arkansas. All IAC schools were offered automatic accreditation by the ACI;
we are not aware of any that turned it down. ACI refuses to make public a list of
schools they have accredited. We have noted more than 130 schools that claim
ACI accreditation, most of them apparently evangelical Bible schools, but more
than a few nonreligious schools as well.

Alternative Institution Accrediting Association
Allegedly in Washington, DC, and the accreditor of several phony schools.

American Council of Private Colleges and Universities (ACPCU)
A fake accrediting agency set up by the Wyoming-based diploma mill, Hamilton University.

APIX Institute
Claimed by the probably-phony Horizons University, whose campus is either a driving school or a hairdresser in Paris.

Arizona Commission of Non-Traditional Private Postsecondary Education
Established in the late 1970s by the proprietors of Southland University, which claimed to be a candidate for their accreditation. The name was changed after a complaint by the real state agency, the Arizona Commission on Postsecondary Education.

Association for Online Academic Excellence
An unrecognized accrediting agency claimed by Trinity College & University (in the U.S.).

Association Internationale des Educateurs pour la Paix Mondiale
Many schools claim a "diploma of recognition" from this organization, supposedly affiliated with UNESCO. It's not hard to get one. In fact, if you are "interested in the promotion of international understanding and world peace through education, the protection of the environment from man-made pollution, and/or the safeguard of human rights everywhere," you can have one too!

Association of Accredited Private Schools
This unrecognized agency wrote to many schools in 1997, inviting them to send a $1000 application fee.

Association of Career Training Schools
A slick booklet sent to schools says, "Have your school accredited with the Association. Why? The Association Seal . . . could be worth many $ $ $ to you! It lowers sales resistance, sales costs, [and] improves image." Nuff said.

Association of Private Colleges and Universities (APCU)
Before a school can buy the APCU "seal of approval," it must provide three student email addresses and show that it delivers the student's diploma within 30 days of graduation. The APCU says it is "not an accreditation agency, and makes no claims to be so"; considering such "tough" standards for gaining approval, we're glad they make no such claims.

Association of World Universities and Colleges
An unrecognized accreditor, allegedly from Switzerland, that has been claimed by the University of Asia. The Web site happens to be registered to the president of the University of Asia. Not to be confused (though perhaps that was intended) with the also-unrecognized World Association of Universities and Colleges (WAUC).

Correspondence Accreditation Association
Created by and the accreditor for Trinity College & University (the British version).

Council for National Academic Accreditation
In 1998, they wrote to schools from Cheyenne, Wyoming, offering the opportunity to be accredited on payment of a fee up to $1,850.

Council for the Accreditation of Correspondence Colleges
Several curious schools claimed their accreditation; the agency is supposed to be in Louisiana.

Council on Postsecondary Alternative Accreditation
An accreditor claimed in the literature of Western States University. Western States never responded to requests for the address of their accreditor.

Distance Education Council of America
Quite reminiscent in name and literature to the recognized Distance Education and Training Council, this agency arose in Delaware in 1998, offering schools the opportunity to pay $200 or more for accreditation and $150 more for an "Excellence" rating.

Distance Graduation Accrediting Association (DGAA)
An unrecognized agency claimed by Capitol University and Concordia College & University.

Integra Accreditation Association
We somehow intercepted an email from this agency, sent June 2000, offering its accrediting services to a who's who list of nonwonderful schools.

International Accreditation and Recognition Council
An unrecognized accreditor based in Australia.

International Accreditation Association of Nontraditional Colleges and Universities
Unrecognized accreditor allegedly located in the British West Indies. Web site (*www.iaancu.nu*) does not list its accredited members.

International Accrediting Association
The address in Modesto, California, is the same as that of the Universal Life Church, an organization that awards doctorates of all kinds, including the Ph.D., to anyone making a "donation" of $5 to $100.

International Accrediting Commission for Schools, Colleges and Theological Seminaries (IAC)
More than 150 schools were accredited by this organization. In 1989, the attorney general of Missouri conducted a clever "sting" operation, in which he created a fictitious school, the "East Missouri Business College," which rented a one-room office in St. Louis and issued a typewritten catalog with such school executives as "Peelsburi Doughboy" and "Wonarmmd Mann." The Three Stooges were all on the faculty. Their marine biology text was *The Little Golden Book of Fishes*. The school's motto, translated from Latin, was "Education is for the birds." Nonetheless, Dr. George Reuter, Director of the IAC, visited the school, accepted their money, and duly accredited them. Soon after, the IAC was enjoined from operating and slapped with a substantial fine, and the good Dr. Reuter decided to retire. (But the almost identical "Accrediting Commission International" [see above] immediately arose in Arkansas, offering instant accreditation to all IAC members.)

International Association of Non-Traditional Schools
The claimed accreditor of several British degree mills and one now-defunct nonwonderful Mexican school; allegedly located in England.

International Association of Schools, Colleges, and Universities (IASCU)
Antwerp, Belgium. The accreditor for Newport University International, which happens to own IASCU's email domain name. Other schools claiming accreditation from IASCU include Westbrook University, American Pacific University, and e Online University.

International University Accreditation Foundation
The Web domain name for this accreditor is owned by St. George University International. And guess who is the accreditor for St. George University International?

International University Accrediting Association (IUAA)
One of two unrecognized accrediting agencies (the other is the Virtual University Accrediting Association) founded and operated by Dr. Chief Swift Eagle of the Cherokee Western Federation Church and Tribe. The only accredited member we know of is International Theological University, also founded by Dr. Chief Swift Eagle.

Life Experience Accreditation Association (LEAF)
Unrecognized agency claimed by Earlscroft University. No address or URL ever found.

Middle States Accrediting Board
A nonexistent accreditor, made up by Thomas University and other degree mills, for the purpose of self-accreditation. The name was chosen, of course, to be confused with the Middle States Association of Colleges and Schools, in Philadelphia, one of the six regional associations.

National Accreditation Association
In a mailing to presidents of unaccredited schools, the NAA offered full accreditation by mail, with no on-site inspection required.

National Association of Private, Nontraditional Schools and Colleges (NAPNSC)
A serious effort to establish an accrediting agency specifically concerned with alternative schools and programs. It was established in Grand Junction, Colorado, in the 1970s by a group of educators associated with Western Colorado University, a nontraditional school that has since gone out of business. Although NAPNSC's standards for accreditation have grown more rigorous over the years, their application for recognition has been turned down many times by the U.S. Department of Education, but they plan to keep trying. Formerly the National Association for Schools and Colleges.

United Congress of Colleges
Another unrecognized agency claimed by Earlscroft University. No address or URL ever found.

West European Accrediting Society
Established from a mail-forwarding service in Liederbach, Germany, by the proprietors of a chain of diploma mills such as Loyola, Roosevelt, Lafayette, Southern California, and Cromwell universities, for the purpose of accrediting themselves.

Western Association of Schools and Colleges
This is the name of the legitimate regional accreditor for the West coast. However, it is also the name of a fake accreditor with a Los Angeles address set up by the proprietors of such diploma mills as Loyola, Roosevelt, Lafayette, Southern California, and Cromwell universities.

Western Council on Non-Traditional Private Post Secondary Education
An accrediting agency started by the founders of Southland University, presumably for the purpose of accrediting themselves and others.

World Association of Universities and Colleges (WAUC)
Established in 1992 by Dr. Maxine Asher, and run from a secretarial service in Nevada. Accredits a long list of nonwonderful institutions, including, not surprisingly, American World University, which is also operated by Dr. Asher. In February 1995, the national investigative publication *Spy Magazine* ran a most unflattering article on WAUC. Dr. Asher also operates the Ancient Mediterranean Research Association, which has produced a film that "clearly demonstrates the existence of Atlantis off the coast of Spain."

World Council of Excellence in Higher Education
Shares all of its addresses—mail, email, and URL—with Intercultural Open University (based in the Netherlands), the only school we know of that claims this accreditor.

World Council of Global Education
As part of the World Natural Health Organization, issues accreditation to institutions that provide an education in the natural health-care field.

World Organization of Institutes, Colleges, and Universities
Omega University "enjoys" their international accreditation, but a fairly thorough Internet search suggests that they must be the only one doing so.

Worldwide Accrediting Commission
Operated from a mail-forwarding service in Cannes, France, for the purpose of accrediting various American-run degree mills.

Ways of Earning Credit

Correspondence Courses

More than 100 major universities and teaching institutions in the United States and dozens more in other countries offer academic correspondence (or email) courses—more than 13,000 courses in hundreds of subjects, from accounting to zoology. Virtually all of these courses can be counted toward a degree at almost any college or university.

Most schools have a limit on the amount of correspondence credit they will apply to a degree. This limit is typically around 50 percent, but the range is from zero to 100 percent. Through such schools such as Excelsior College, Thomas Edison State College, and Western Illinois University, it is possible to earn an accredited bachelor's degree entirely through correspondence study.

Every school publishes or offers online a catalog or bulletin listing their available correspondence courses—some offer just a few, others have hundreds. All of the schools accept students living anywhere in the United States, although some charge more for out-of-state students. Most accept foreign students.

Correspondence courses range from 1 to 6 semester hours worth of credit, and can cost anywhere from less than $40 to more than $150 per semester hour. The average is just over $80, so that a typical 3-unit course would cost about $250. Because of the wide range in costs, it pays to shop around.

A typical correspondence course will consist of from 5 to 20 lessons, each one requiring a short written paper, answers to questions, or an unsupervised test graded by the instructor. There is almost always a supervised final examination. These can usually be taken anywhere in the world where a suitable proctor can be found (usually a high school or college teacher).

People who cannot go to a testing center because, for instance, they are handicapped, live too far away, or are in prison, can usually arrange to have a test supervisor come to them. Schools can be extremely flexible. One correspondence program administrator told us he had two students—a husband and wife—working as missionaries on a remote island where they were the only people who could read and write. He allowed them to supervise each other.

Many schools set limits on how quickly and how slowly you can complete a correspondence course. The shortest time is generally three to six weeks, while the upper limit ranges from three months to two years. Some schools limit the number of courses you can take at one time, but most do not. Even those with limits are concerned only with courses taken from their own institution. There is no cross-checking, so in theory one could take simultaneous courses from all 100+ institutions.

Where To Find Them

Peterson Publishing used to publish an excellent compendium of all the 13,000+ correspondence courses in a book called *The Independent Study Catalog*. But there hasn't been a new edition for several years.

What has risen in its place are a group of Web sites—so-called higher education "portals"—that have put vast databases of correspondence courses online. Search engines allow you to browse these databases by subject, whether it's introductory astronomy, management information systems, or home ice cream making (the legendary one taken from Penn State University by Ben and Jerry cost them five bucks).

Here are some of the leading portals at the time we went to press—with the warning, perhaps needless to say, that dot-com companies come and go with the morning dew:

www.hungrymindsuniversity.com

www.mindedge.com

www.cyberu.com

www.lifelonglearning.com

www.dlcoursefinder.com

Some Schools That Offer Lots of Correspondence Courses

We don't have enough space to list all of the hundreds of schools that offer correspondence courses, but we will prime the pump for you by identifying a couple of dozen with a wide range of available courses, undergraduate and graduate.

United States

Brigham Young University
Independent Study
206 Harman Building,
     P.O. Box 21514
Provo, UT 84602
(801) 378 2868 • (800) 914 8931
ce.byu.edu/is

Charter Oak State College
55 Paul J. Manafort Dr.
New Britian, CT 06053-2142
(860) 832 3800
www.cosc.edu

Colorado State University
Division of Educational Outreach
Spruce Hall
Fort Collins, CO 80523-1040
(970) 491 5288 • (877) 491 4336
www.csu2learn.colostate.edu

Indiana University
School of Continuing Studies
Owen Hall 002
Bloomington, IN 47405
(812) 855 2292 • (800) 334 1011
scs.indiana.edu

Louisiana State University
Office of Independent Study
E106 Pleasant Hall
Baton Rouge, LA 70803
(225) 388 3171 • (800) 234 5046
www.is.lsu.edu

Ohio University
Office of Independent Study
302 Tupper Hall
Athens, OH 45701
(740) 593 2910 • (800) 444 2910
www.cats.ohiou.edu/independent

Pennsylvania State University
Department of Distance Education
207 Mitchell Building
University Park, PA 16802
(814) 865 5403 • (800) 252 3592
www.cde.psu.edu/de

Stephens College
School of Graduate and
     Continuing Education
Campus Box 2083
Columbia, MO 65215
(573) 876 7125 • (800) 388 7579
www.stephens.edu

University of California-Berkeley
UC Extension Online
2000 Center St., Suite 400
Berkeley, CA 94704
(510) 642 4124
learn.berkeley.edu

University of Iowa
Guided Correspondence Study
116 International Center
Iowa City, IA 52242
(319) 353 2575 • (800) 272 6430
www.uiowa.edu/~ccp

University of Minnesota
Independent and Distance Learning
150 Wesbrook Hall
77 Pleasant St. SE
Minneapolis, MN 55455
(612) 624 4000 • (800) 234 6564
www.uc.umn.edu/idl

University of Missouri
    Center for Distance and
        Independent Study
    136 Clark Hall
    Columbia, MO 65211-4200
    (572) 882 6431 • (800) 609 3727
    cdis.missouri.edu

University of Wisconsin
    Independent Learning
    505 South Rosa Rd., Suite 200
    Madison, WI 53719-1257
    (800) 442 6460
    learn.wisconsin.edu/il

U.S. Department of Agriculture
    Graduate School
    Correspondence and Online Program
    Room 1112, South Building
    1400 Independence Avenue, SW
    Washington, DC 20250-9911
    (202) 314 3670
    www.grad.usda.gov

Canada

Acadia University
    Division of Continuing and
        Distance Education
    Wolfville, Nova Scotia B0P 1X0
    www.acadiau.ca

Athabasca University
    1 University Drive
    Athabasca, Alberta T95 3A3
    www.athabascau.ca

McGill University
    Centre for Continuing Education
    688 Sherbrooke Street West
    Montreal, Quebec H3A 3R1
    www.mcgill.ca

University of Manitoba
    Distance Education Program
    188 Continuing Education Complex
    Winnipeg, Manitoba R3T 2N2
    www.umanitoba.ca/coned

University of New Brunswick
    P.O. Box 4400
    Fredericton, New Brunswick
        E3B 5A3
    www.unb.ca/coned

University of Toronto
    School of Continuing Studies
    158 St. George St.
    Toronto, Ontario M5S 2V8
    www.continuallyuoft.utoronto.ca

University of Waterloo
    Continuing Education
    Waterloo, Ontario N2L 3G1
    dce.uwaterloo.ca

Australia

Curtin University of Technology
    GPO Box U 1987
    Perth, Western Australia 6845
    www.curtin.edu.au

Deakin University
    221 Burwood Highway
    Burwood, Victoria 3125
    www.deakin.edu.au

Edith Cowan University
    Pearson St., Churchlands,
    Western Australia 6018
    www.cowan.edu.au

James Cook University
    Townsville, Queensland 4811
    www.jcu.edu.au

University of South Australia
    Underdale Campus, External Studies
    Holbrooks Road
    Underdale, South Australia 5032
    www.unisa.edu.au

South Africa

University of South Africa
    P. O. Box 392
    Unisa 0003, South Africa
    www.unisa.ac.za

University of Cape Town
    Rondebosch 7701, South Africa
    www.uct.ac.za

Equivalency Examinations

Most of the schools in this book would agree that if you have knowledge of an academic field, then you should get credit for that knowledge, regardless of how or where you acquired the knowledge. The simplest and fairest way (but by no means the only way) of assessing that knowledge is through an examination.

More than 3,000 colleges and universities in the United States and Canada award students credit toward their bachelor's degrees (and, in a few cases, master's and doctorates) solely on the basis of passing examinations.

Many of the exams are designed to be equivalent to the final exam in a typical college class, and the assumption is that if you score high enough, you get the same amount of credit you would have gotten by taking the class—or, in some cases, a good deal more.

While there are many sources of equivalency exams, including a trend toward schools developing their own, two national testing agencies are dominant in this field: the College-Level Examination Program (CLEP) and Excelsior College Examinations. Together, they administer more than 70 equivalency exams that are given at hundreds of testing centers all over North America. By special arrangement, many of them can be administered almost anywhere in the world.

CLEP Tests

CLEP is offered by the College Entrance Examination Board, known as "the College Board" (45 Columbus Avenue, New York, NY 10023-6992; phone: (212) 713 8064; fax: (212) 713 8063; email: *clep@info.collegeboard.org*; Web site: *www.collegeboard.org/clep*). Military personnel who want to take CLEP exams should see their education officer or contact DANTES/CLEP at P.O. Box 6604, Princeton, NJ 08541; (609) 720 6740.

CLEP tests are given at more than 1,200 centers, most of them on college or university campuses. Each center sets its own schedule for frequency of testing, so it may pay to "shop around" for convenient dates. After July 1, 2001, the tests are only offered on computer.

The exams are designed to correspond to typical one-semester or full-year introductory-level courses offered at a university, and they are titled accordingly. Test takers are given 90 minutes to answer multiple-choice questions at a computer terminal. The Composition and Literature exams have an optional essay section (required by some colleges). It costs about $50 to take any test in one of the following fields:

Business

- Information Systems and Computer Applications
- Principles of Management
- Principles of Accounting
- Introductory Business Law
- Principles of Marketing

Composition and Literature

- English Composition
- Humanities
- American Literature
- Analyzing and Interpreting Literature
- Freshman College Composition

Languages Other than English

- College-Level French
- College-Level German
- College-Level Spanish

History and Social Sciences

- Social Sciences and History
- American Government
- History of the U.S.: Early Colonizations to 1877
- History of the U.S.: 1865 to the Present
- Human Growth and Development
- Introduction to Educational Psychology
- Principles of Macroeconomics
- Principles of Microeconomics
- Introductory Psychology
- Introductory Sociology
- Western Civilization: Ancient Near East to 1648
- Western Civilization: 1648 to the Present

Science and Mathematics

- General Mathematics
- Natural Sciences
- Calculus with Elementary Functions
- College Algebra
- College Algebra-Trigonometry
- General Biology
- General Chemistry
- Trigonometry

Excelsior College Examinations

Excelsior College Examinations are developed by Excelsior College (Test Administration Office, 7 Columbia Circle, Albany, NY 12203-5159; (888) 723 9267; Web site: *www.excelsiorcollege.edu*). (Note: Excelsior College was formerly known as Regents College, and the exam program, respectively, was known as Regents College Examinations. Before that, and in the last edition of this book, it was called the Proficiency Examination Program, or PEP.)

Excelsior College Examinations are administered at Sylvan Technology Centers (*www.educate.com*) at more than 200 locations throughout the U.S. and Canada. Persons living more than 250 miles from a test center may make special arrangements for the test to be given nearer home.

While CLEP tests generally correspond to introductory-level college courses, Excelsior College Examinations are more geared toward the intermediate to advanced college-level. The tests are three hours long, but a few are four hours. Ranging in price from $70 to $370 per exam, they are offered in the following fields:

Art and Science

- Abnormal Psychology
- American Dream
- Anatomy & Physiology
- English Composition
- Ethics: Theory & Practice
- Foundations of Gerontology
- History of Nazi Germany
- Life Span Developmental Psychology
- Microbiology
- Pathophysiology
- Psychology of Adulthood and Aging
- Religions of the World
- Research Methods in Psychology
- Statistics

- Structure & Change: Our Place in the World
- Values & Responsibility: The Individual & Society
- World Population

Education

- Reading Instruction in the Elementary School

Business

- Business Policy & Strategy
- Human Resource Management
- Labor Relations
- Organizational Behavior
- Production/Operations Management

Nursing

- 18 specialized exams, ranging from professional strategies in nursing to maternity nursing

How Exams Are Scored and Credited

Each college or university sets its own standards for passing grades, and also decides for itself how much credit to give for each exam. Both of these factors can vary substantially from school to school. Take, for example, the Excelsior exam in anatomy and physiology, a three-hour multiple-choice test that hundreds of schools give credit for passing. But the amount of credit given, as well as the score required to pass, is different for almost every school:

- Central Virginia Community College requires a score of 45 (out of 80), and awards nine credit hours for passing.
- Edinboro University in Pennsylvania requires a score of 50 to pass, and awards six credit hours for the same exam.
- Concordia College in New York requires a score of 47, but awards only three credit hours.

Similar situations prevail on most of the exams. There is no predictability or consistency, even within a given school. For instance, at the University of South Florida, a three-hour multiple-choice test in maternal nursing is worth 18 units while a three-hour multiple-choice test in psychiatric nursing is worth only 9.

So, with dozens of standard exams available, and with about 3,000 schools offering credit, it pays to shop around a little and select both the school and the exams that will give you the most credit.

How Hard Are These Exams?

This is, of course, an extremely subjective question. However, we have heard from a great many readers who have attempted CLEP and Excelsior exams, and the most common response is "Gee, that was a lot easier than I had expected." This is especially true with more mature students. The tests are designed for 18- to 20-year-olds, and there appears to be a certain amount of factual knowledge, as well as experience in dealing with testing situations, that people acquire in ordinary life situations as they grow older.

There is no stigma attached to poor performance on these tests. In fact, if you wish, you may have the scores reported only to you, so that no one but you and the computer will know how you did. Then, if your scores are high enough, you can have them sent on to the schools of your choice. CLEP allows exams to be taken every 6 months; you can take the same Excelsior College exam twice in any 12-month period.

Preparing (and Cramming) for Exams

Both testing agencies issue detailed syllabuses describing each test and the specific content area it covers. They both sell an "official study guide" that gives sample questions and answers from each examination. On its Web site, CLEP also offers practice tests with sample questions.

The testing agencies create their exam questions from college textbooks, so for studying they recommend that you go to the source. At the bookstore of a local college, browse the textbook selection for the course that corresponds to the test you'll be taking.

At least four educational publishers have produced series of books on how to prepare for such exams, often with full-length sample tests. These can be found in the education or reference section of any good bookstore or library.

For years, the testing agencies vigorously fought the idea of letting test-takers take copies of the test home with them. But consumer legislation in New York has made at least some of the tests available, and a good thing, too. Every so often, someone discovers an incorrect answer or a poorly phrased question that can have more than one correct answer, necessitating a recalculation and reissuance of scores to all the thousands of people who took that test.

In recent years, there has been much controversy over the value of cramming for examinations. Many counseling clients report having been able to pass four or five CLEP exams in a row by spending an intensive few days (or weeks) cramming for them. Although the various testing agencies used to deny that cramming can be of any value, in the last few years there have been some extremely persuasive research studies that demonstrate the short-term effectiveness of intensive studying.

These data have vindicated the claims made by people and agencies that assist students in preparing for examinations. Such services are offered in a great many places, usually in the vicinity of college campuses, by graduate students and moonlighting faculty. The best place to find them is through the classified ads in campus newspapers, on bulletin boards around the campus, and through on-campus extension programs. Prices vary widely, so shop around.

But buyer beware: Test prep services are an unregulated industry and quality varies widely. Some make promises that that they simply cannot keep. We have heard reports of a growing number of fraudulent test prep services; many of them seem to be targeting members of the military and their families. Watch out for demands of large payments up front, strange-looking credit agreements, outdated preparation materials, book lists that include dictionaries or encyclopedias, or claims to be representing one of the testing agencies such as CLEP. The people who make the tests don't make sales calls.

Often the best strategy is to take a self-scoring test from one of the guidebooks. If you do well, you may wish to take the real exam right away. If you do badly, you may conclude that credit by examination is not your cup of hemlock. And if you score in between, consider studying (or cramming) on your own, or with the help of a paid tutor or tutoring service.

Other Examinations

Here are some other examinations that can be used to earn substantial credit toward many nontraditional degree programs.

Graduate Record Examination

The GRE is administered by the Educational Testing Service (P.O. Box 6000, Princeton, NJ 08541; (609) 771 7670; email: *gre-info@ets.org*; Web site: *www.gre.org*). There is a general test, which is more of an aptitude test, which is now given on demand at more than 600 computer centers throughout North America. On completing this exam by computer, the student is given the choice of either erasing the exam entirely and walking out (no harm, no foul), or pressing another button, and being given an instantaneous (but still unofficial) score.

The GRE Subject Tests are still given in written form, although this may change in the near future. It is a three-hour multiple-choice test, designed to test knowledge that would ordinarily be gained by a bachelor's degree-holder in that given field. The exams are available in the fields of:

- Biochemistry
- Biology
- Chemistry
- Computer science
- English literature
- Mathematics
- Physics
- Psychology

This menu changes often, so check GRE's Web site for the latest list.

Few schools give credit for the general GRE. Schools vary widely in how much credit they will give for each subject-area GRE; for some schools it even depends on your score. The range is from none at all to 30 semester units (in the case of Excelsior College).

A National Guard sergeant once crammed for, took, and passed three GRE exams in a row, thereby earning 90 semester units in ten and a half hours of testing. Then he took five CLEP exams in two days, and earned 30 more units, which was enough to earn an accredited bachelor's degree (from what is now Excelsior College), start to finish, in 18 hours, starting absolutely from scratch with no college credit.

DANTES

The Defense Activity for Non-Traditional Education Support tests, or DANTES, were developed for the Department of Defense, but are available to civilians as well. The tests were developed by the Educational Testing Service, and are offered by hundreds of colleges and universities nationwide. While there is some overlap with CLEP and Excelsior exams, there are also many unique subjects. DANTES information is available from the DANTES Program, P.O. Box 6604, Princeton, NJ 08541; (609) 720 6740; *www.chauncey.com/dantes*.

Tests include, among others:

- Anthropology
- Art of the Western World
- Astronomy
- Business Law
- Civil War and Reconstruction
- College Algebra
- Criminal Justice
- Drug & Alcohol Abuse
- Ethics in America
- Geography
- History of the Vietnam War
- Human Resource Management
- Modern Middle East
- Organizational Behavior
- Physical Geology
- Physical Science
- Principles of Finance
- Principles of Financial Accounting
- Public Speaking
- Rise & Fall of the Soviet Union
- Statistics
- Technical Writing
- World Religions

University End-of-Course Exams

Several schools offer the opportunity to earn credit for a correspondence course solely by taking (and passing) the final exam for that course. One need not be enrolled as a student in the school to do this. Two schools with especially large programs of this kind are Ohio University (Independent Study, 302 Tupper Hall, Athens, OH 45701; *www.cats.ohiou.edu/independent*) and the University of North Carolina (UNC Division of Continuing Education, CB# 1020 The Friday Center, Chapel Hill, NC 27599-1020; *www.fridaycenter.unc.edu*).

Advanced Placement Examinations

The College Board (45 Columbus Avenue, New York, NY 10023-6992; (212) 713 8066; *ap@collegeboard.org*) offers subject-specific exams specifically for students who wish to earn college credit while still in high school. For a list of the available subjects, go to *www.collegeboard.org/ap/students*.

What If You Hate Exams or Don't Do Well on Them?

Don't despair. There are two other less threatening ways to get credit for life-experience learning: special assessments and preparation of a life-experience portfolio. These are discussed in the following section.

Life-Experience Learning

The philosophy behind credit for life-experience learning can be expressed very simply: Academic credit is given for what you know without regard for how, when, or where the learning was acquired.

Consider a simple example: Quite a few colleges and universities offer credit for courses in typewriting. For instance, at Western Illinois University, Business Education 261 is a basic typing class. Anyone who takes and passes that class is given three units of credit.

An advocate of credit for life-experience learning would say: "If you know how to type, regardless of how and where you learned, even if you taught yourself at the age of nine, you should still get those same three units of credit, once you demonstrate that you have the same skill level as a person who passes Business Education 261."

Of course not all learning can be converted into college credit. But many people are surprised to discover how much of what they already know is, in fact, creditworthy. With thousands of colleges offering hundreds of thousands of courses, it is a rare subject indeed that someone hasn't determined to be worthy of some credit. There is no guarantee that a given school will honor a given learning experience, or even accept another school's assessment for transfer purposes. Yale might not accept typing credit. But then again, the course title often sounds much more academic than the learning experience itself, as in "Business Education" for typing, "Cross-Cultural Communication" for a trip to China, or "Fundamentals of Applied Kinesiology" for golf lessons.

Eight Kinds of Creditworthy Life Experience

Here are eight major types of life experience that may be worth college credit, especially in nontraditional degree-granting programs:

1. **Work.** Many of the skills acquired in paid employment are also skills that are taught in colleges and universities. These include, for instance, typing, filing, shorthand, accounting, inventory control, financial management, map reading, military strategy, welding, computer programming or operating, editing, planning, sales, real estate appraisals, and literally thousands of other things.

2. **Homemaking.** Home maintenance, household planning and budgeting, child rearing, child psychology, education, interpersonal communication, meal planning and nutrition, gourmet cooking, and much more.

3. **Volunteer work.** Community activities, political campaigns, church activities, service organizations, volunteer work in social service agencies or hospitals, and so forth.

4. **Noncredit learning in formal settings.** Company training courses, in-service teacher training, workshops, clinics, conferences and conventions, lectures, courses on radio or television, noncredit correspondence courses, etc.

5. **Travel.** Study tours (organized or informal), significant vacation and business trips, living for periods in other countries or cultures, participating in activities related to other cultures or subcultures.

6. **Recreational activities and hobbies.** Musical skills, aviation training and skills, acting or other work in a community theater, sports, arts and crafts, fiction and nonfiction writing, public speaking, gardening, visiting museums, designing and making clothing, attending plays and concerts, and many other leisure-time activities.

7. **Reading, viewing, listening.** This may cover any field in which a person has done extensive or intensive reading and study, and for which college credit has not been granted. This category has, for instance, included viewing various series on public television.

8. **Discussions with experts.** A great deal of learning can come from talking to, listening to, and working with experts, whether in ancient history, carpentry, or theology. Significant, extensive, or intensive meetings with such people may also be worth credit.

The Most Common Error People Make

The most common error most people make when thinking about getting credit for life experience is confusing *time spent* with *learning*. Being a regular church-goer for 30 years is not worth any college credit in and of itself. But the regular churchgoer who can document that he or she has prepared for and taught Sunday school classes, worked with youth groups, participated in leadership programs, organized fund-raising drives, studied Latin or Greek, taken tours to the Holy Land, or even engaged in lengthy philosophical discussions with a clergyman, is likely to get credit for those experiences. Selling insurance for 20 years is worth no credit—unless you describe and document the learning that took place in areas of marketing, banking, risk management, entrepreneurial studies, etc.

It is crucial that the experiences can be documented to a school's satisfaction. Two people could work side by side in the same laboratory for five years. One might do little more than follow instructions—running routine experiments, setting up and dismantling apparatus, and then heading home. The other, with the same job title, might do extensive reading on the background of the work being done, get into discussions with supervisors, make plans and recommendations for other ways of doing the work, propose or design new kinds of apparatus, or develop hypotheses on why the results were turning out the way they were.

It is not enough just to say what you did, or to submit a short resumé. The details and specifics must be documented. The two most common ways this is done are by preparing a life-experience portfolio (essentially a long, well-documented, annotated resumé) or by taking an equivalency examination to demonstrate knowledge gained.

Presenting Your Learning: The Life-Experience Portfolio

Most schools that give credit for life-experience learning require that a formal presentation be made, usually in the form of a life-experience portfolio. Each school will have its own standards for the form and content of such a portfolio, and many, in fact, offer either guidelines or courses (some for credit, some not) to help the nontraditional student prepare the portfolio.

The Council for Adult and Experiential Learning offers for sale a number of books designed to help people prepare life-experience portfolios. For a list of current publications, contact them at CAEL, 55 East Monroe Street, Suite 1930, Chicago, IL 60603; (312) 499 2600; *www.cael.org*.

The following list should help to get you thinking about the possibilities by presenting a sampling of some 24 other means by which people have documented life-experience learning, sometimes as part of a portfolio, sometimes not:

- Official commendations
- Audiotapes
- Slides
- Course outlines
- Bills of sale
- Exhibitions
- Programs of recitals and performances
- Videotapes
- Awards and honors
- Mementos
- Copies of speeches made
- Licenses (pilot, real estate, etc.)
- Certificates
- Testimonials and endorsements
- Interviews with others
- Newspaper articles
- Official job descriptions
- Copies of exams taken
- Military records
- Samples of arts or crafts made
- Writing samples
- Designs and blueprints
- Works of art
- Films and photographs

How Life Experience is Turned into Academic Credit

It isn't easy. In a perfect world, there would be universally accepted standards, and it would be as easy to measure the credit value in a seminar on refrigeration engineering as it is to measure the temperature inside a refrigerator. Some schools and national organizations are striving to create extensive "menus" of nontraditional experiences, to ensure that anyone doing the same thing would get the same credit.

There continues to be progress in this direction. Many schools have come to agree, for instance, on aviation experience: a private pilot's license is worth four semester units, an instrument rating is worth six additional units, and so forth.

The American Council on Education (ACE), a private organization, regularly publishes a massive multivolume set of books, in two series: *The National Guide to Educational Credit for Training Programs* and *Guide to the Evaluation of Educational Experiences in the Armed Forces*, which many schools use to assign credit directly; others use them as guidelines in doing their own evaluations. A few examples will demonstrate the sort of thing that is done:

- A nine-day Red Cross training course called The Art of Helping is evaluated as worth 2 semester hours of social work.

- The John Hancock Mutual Life Insurance Company's internal course in technical skills for managers is worth 3 semester hours of business administration.

- Portland Cement Company's five-day training program in kiln optimization, whatever that may be, is worth 1 semester hour.

- The Professional Insurance Agents' 3-week course in basic insurance is worth 6 semester units: 3 in principles of insurance and 3 in property and liability contract analysis.

- The U.S. Army's 27-week course in ground surveillance radar repair is worth 15 semester hours: 10 in electronics and 5 more in electrical laboratory.

- The Army's legal-clerk training course can be worth 24 semester hours, including 3 in English, 3 in business law, 3 in management, etc.

There are hundreds of additional business and military courses that have been evaluated already, and thousands more that will be worth credit for those who have taken them, whether or not they appear in these ACE volumes.

Some Inspiration

There are always some people who say, "Oh, I haven't ever done anything worthy of college credit." We have yet to meet anyone with an IQ higher than room temperature who has not done at least some creditworthy things. Often it's just a matter of presenting them properly in a portfolio. Just to inspire you, then, here is a list of 100 things that could be worth credit for life-experience learning. The list could easily be 10 or 100 times as long. Please note the "could." Some reviewers in the past have made fun of this list, suggesting that we were saying you can earn a degree for buying Persian rugs. Not so. We suggest, however, that a person who made a high-level study of Persian art and culture, preparatory to buying carpets, and who could document the reading, consultations, time spent, sources, etc., could probably earn some portfolio credit for this out-of-classroom endeavor. Here, then, the list:

- Playing tennis
- Preparing for natural childbirth
- Leading a church group
- Taking a body-building class
- Speaking French
- Selling real estate
- Studying gourmet cooking
- Reading *War and Peace*
- Building model airplanes
- Touring through Belgium
- Learning shorthand
- Starting a small business
- Navigating a small boat
- Writing a book
- Buying a Persian carpet
- Watching public television
- Decorating a home or office
- Attending a convention
- Being a camp counselor
- Playing in a punk-rock band
- Bicycling across Greece
- Interviewing senior citizens
- Living in another culture
- Writing advertisements
- Throwing a pot
- Repairing a car
- Performing magic
- Attending art films
- Welding and soldering
- Designing and weaving a rug
- Negotiating a contract
- Editing a manuscript
- Planning a trip
- Steering a ship
- Appraising an antique
- Writing a speech
- Studying first aid or CPR
- Organizing a union
- Researching international laws
- Listening to Shakespeare's plays on tape
- Designing a playground
- Planning a garden
- Devising a marketing strategy
- Reading the newspaper
- Designing a home
- Attending a seminar
- Playing the piano
- Studying a new religion
- Visiting Civil War battlegrounds
- Taking ballet lessons
- Helping a dyslexic child
- Riding a horse
- Pressing flowers
- Keeping tropical fish
- Writing public relations releases
- Writing for the local newspaper
- Running the PTA
- Acting in a community theater
- Flying an airplane
- Designing a quilt
- Taking photographs

- Building a table
- Developing an inventory system
- Programming a home computer
- Helping in a political campaign
- Playing a musical instrument
- Painting a picture
- Playing political board games
- Serving on a jury
- Volunteering at the hospital
- Visiting a museum
- Attending a "great books" group
- Designing and sewing clothes
- Playing golf
- Having intensive talks with a doctor
- Teaching the banjo
- Reading the Bible
- Leading a platoon
- Learning Braille
- Operating a printing press
- Eating in an exotic restaurant
- Running a store
- Planning a balanced diet
- Reading *All and Everything*
- Learning American Sign Language
- Teaching Sunday school
- Training an apprentice
- Being an apprentice
- Hooking a rug
- Learning yoga
- Laying bricks
- Making a speech
- Being Dungeon Master
- Negotiating a merger
- Developing film
- Learning calligraphy
- Applying statistics to gambling
- Doing circle dancing
- Taking care of sick animals
- Reading this book

Special Assessments

There is a middle ground between taking an exam and preparing a portfolio. For people whose knowledge is both extensive and in an uncommon field (or at least one for which no exams have been developed), some schools are willing to conduct special assessments for a single student. At Excelsior College, both for its students and for Excelsior Credit Bank depositors (see the chapter in this section on the Credit Bank), this takes the form of an oral examination. They will find at least two experts in your field, be it Persian military history, paleontology, French poetry, or whatever. Following a three-hour oral exam, conducted at everyone's mutual convenience in Albany, New York, the examiners decide how many credits to award for that particular knowledge area.

Foreign Academic Experience

There are many thousands of universities, colleges, technical schools, institutes, and vocational schools all over the world whose courses are at least the equivalent of work at American universities. In principle, most universities are willing to give credit for work done at schools in other countries.

Can you imagine the task of an admissions officer faced with the student who presents an advanced diploma from the Wysza Szkola Inzynierska in Poland or the degree of Gakushi from the Matsuyama Shoka Daigaku in Japan? Are these equivalent to a high school diploma, a doctorate, or something in between?

Until 1974, the U.S. Office of Education helped by evaluating educational credentials earned outside the United States and translating them into approximately comparable levels of U.S. achievement. This service is no longer available. There have arisen, to fill this gap, quite a few private independent credential and transcript evaluation services. Some deal exclusively with credentials and transcripts earned outside the United States and/or Canada, while others also consider experiential learning wherever it took place (such as military courses, aviation credentials, company training programs, and the like).

These services are used mostly by the schools themselves to evaluate applicants from abroad or with foreign credentials, but individuals may deal with them directly.

The costs run from $50 to $200 or more, depending on the complexity of the evaluation. The services operate quickly; less than two weeks for an evaluation is not unusual. Typical reports from the services will give the exact U.S. equivalents of non-U.S. work, both in terms of semester units earned and of any degrees or certificates received. For instance, they would report that the Japanese degree of Gakushi is almost exactly equivalent to the American bachelor's degree.

While many schools will accept the recommendations of these services, others will not. Some schools do their own foreign evaluations. It may be wise, therefore, to determine whether a school or schools in which you have interest will accept the recommendations of such services before you invest in them.

Also, it is important to remember that these services are independent, unregulated, and often inconsistent. Work that one agency valuates as master's level may be regarded as bachelor's level (or even less) by another. So if you feel one agency's evaluation is inappropriate or incorrect, it may be wise to seek a second (and even third) opinion.

Here is a list of some of the organizations performing these services, both in the U.S. and Canada.

Those with a "*" are approved by the state of California's Commission on Teacher Credentialing (*www.ctc.ca.gov*).

Those with a "#" are members of the industry's trade association, the National Association of Credential Evaluation Services: (414) 289 3412; email: *margit@ece.org*; Web site: *voled.doded.mil/dantes/refpubs/ftr.htm*.

American Education Research Corporation*
P.O. Box 996
West Covina, CA 91793-0996
Phone: (626) 339 4404
Fax: (626) 339 9081
Email: aerc@cyberg8t.com
Web site: www.aerc-eval.com

Educational Credential Evaluators, Inc.*#
P.O. Box 92970
Milwaukee, WI 53217
Phone: (414) 289 3400
Fax: (414) 289 3411
Email: eval@ece.org
Web site: www.ece.org

Education Evaluators International, Inc.

P.O. Box 5397
Los Alamitos, CA 90720
Phone: (562) 431 2187
Fax: (562) 493 5021
Email: garyeei@ix.netcom.com

Educational Records Evaluation Service*

777 Campus Commons Road, #200
Sacramento, CA 95825
Phone: (916) 565 7475
Fax: (916) 565 7476
Email: edu@eres.com
Web site: www.eres.com

Foreign Academic Credential Service, Inc.

P.O. Box 400
Glen Carbon, IL 62034
Phone: (618) 288 1661
Fax: (618) 288 1691
Email: facs@aol.com
Web site: www.facsusa.com

Global Education Group

407 Lincoln Rd., Suite 2H
Miami Beach, FL 33139
Phone: (305) 534 8745
Fax: (305) 534 3487
Email: global@globaledu.com
Web site: www.globaledu.com

International Consultants of Delaware, Inc.

109 Barksdale Professional Center
Newark, DE 19711
Phone: (302) 737 8715
Fax: (302) 737 8756
Email: icd@icdel.com
Web site: www.icdel.com

International Credential Evaluation Service

4355 Mathissi Place
Burnaby, BC V5G 4S8, Canada
Phone: +1 (604) 431 3402
Fax: +1 (604) 431 3382
Email: icesinfo@ola.bc.ca
Web site: www.ola.bc.ca/ices

International Credentialing Associates, Inc.

7245 Bryan Dairy Rd.
Largo, FL 33777
Phone: (727) 549 8555
Fax: (727) 549 8554
Email: info@icaworld.com
Web site: www.icaworld.com

International Education Research Foundation*

P.O. Box 3665
Culver City, CA 90231-3655
Phone: (310) 390 6276
Fax: (310) 397 7686
Email: info@ierf.org
Web site: www.ierf.org

International Qualifications Assessment Service

Department of Learning, Government
of Alberta
4th Floor, Sterling Place, 9940 - 106 St.
Edmonton, Alberta T5K 2N2, Canada
Phone: +1 (780) 427 2655
Fax: +1 (780) 422 9734
Email: iqas@aecd.gov.ab.ca
Web site: www.aecd.gov.ab.ca/iqas

Joseph Silny & Associates, Inc.

P.O. Box 248233
Coral Gables, FL 33124
Phone: (305) 666 0233
Fax: (305) 666 4133
Email: info@jsilny.com
Web site: www.jsilny.com

World Education Services*

P.O. Box 745
Old Chelsea Station
New York, NY 10013
Phone: (212) 966 6311 • (800) 937 3895
Fax: (212) 966 6395
Email: info@wes.org
Web site: www.wes.org

The Credit Bank Service

A lot of people have very complicated educational histories. They may have taken classes at several different universities and colleges, taken some evening or summer-school classes, perhaps some company-sponsored seminars, some military training classes, and possibly had a whole raft of other informal learning experiences. They may have credits or degrees from schools that have gone out of business, or whose records were destroyed by war or fire. When it comes time to present a cohesive educational past, it may mean assembling dozens of transcripts, certificates, diplomas, job descriptions, and the like, often into a rather large and unwieldy package.

There is, happily, an ideal solution to this problem: the Excelsior College Credit Bank, operated by the enlightened Excelsior College in New York, and available to people anywhere in the world. (Note: Excelsior College was formerly known as Regents College, and the credit bank service, respectively, was known as the Regents College Credit Bank.)

Excelsior College Credit Bank

Excelsior College
7 Columbia Circle
Albany, NY 12203
Phone: (518) 464 8500
Web site: www.excelsiorcollege.edu

The Credit Bank is an evaluation and transcript service for people who wish to consolidate their academic records, perhaps adding credit for nonacademic career and learning experiences (primarily through equivalency examinations). The Credit Bank issues a single widely accepted transcript on which all credit is listed in a simple, straightforward, and comprehensible form.

The Credit Bank works like a money bank, except that you deposit academic credits, as they are earned, whether through local courses, correspondence courses, equivalency exams, or other methods.

Seven Kinds of Deposits That Can Be Made

There are seven basic categories of learning experiences that can qualify to be "deposited" in a Credit Bank account, and, of course, various elements of these seven can be combined as well:

1. College courses taken either in residence or by distance learning from regionally accredited schools in the U.S., or their equivalent in other countries.

2. Scores earned on a wide range of equivalency tests, both civilian or military.

3. Military service schools and military occupational specialties that have been evaluated for credit by the American Council on Education.

4. Workplace-based learning experiences, such as company courses, seminars, or in-house training from many large and smaller corporations, evaluated by the American Council on Education or the New York National Program on Noncollegiate Sponsored Instruction.

5. Pilot training licenses and certificates issued by the Federal Aviation Administration.

6. Approved nursing performance examinations.

7. Special assessments of knowledge gained from experience or independent study.

The first six categories have predetermined amounts of credit. The CLEP basic science exam will always be worth 6 semester units. Fluency in Spanish will always be worth 24 semester units. Xerox Corporation's course in repairing the 9400 copier will always be worth 2 semester units. The army course in becoming a bandleader will always be worth 12 semester units. And so forth, for thousands of already evaluated nonschool learning experiences.

The seventh category can be extremely flexible and variable. Special assessment is a means of earning credit for things learned in the course of ordinary living or job experience. The Credit Bank assesses this learning by appointing a panel of two or more experts in the field. Except in rare cases, it is necessary to go to Albany, New York, to meet with this panel.

The panel may wish to conduct an oral, a written, or, in the case of performers, a performance examination. They may wish to inspect a portfolio of writing, art, or documentation. Following the evaluation, whatever form it may take, the panel makes its recommendations for the amount of credit to be given. This has, in practice, ranged from 0 to more than 80 semester units, although the typical range for each separate assessment is probably from 15 to 30 credits.

The Credit Bank has, for example, conducted special assessments in journalism, ceramics, Hebrew, electronics engineering, aircraft repair and maintenance, and Japanese culture studies, among many others.

There is a $200 fee to set up a Credit Bank account. There is a $25 fee each time a new "deposit" is made. (These rates are dramatically lower than those charged a few years ago.)

Work that is, for whatever reason, deemed not creditworthy may still be listed on the transcript as "noncredit work." Further, the Credit Bank will only list those traditional courses from other schools that the depositor wishes included. Thus any previous academic failures, low grades, or other embarrassments may be omitted from the Credit Bank report.

Students who enroll in Excelsior College automatically get Credit Bank service, and do not need to enroll separately.

One Hundred Accredited Schools Offering Degrees Entirely or Almost Entirely by Distance Learning

Information on 100 accredited schools follows. We think it is all self-explanatory.

Information in this book, especially the school listings, changes fast: new names, new area codes, new degree programs, etc. We do our best to stay on top of things; updates and corrections are posted on our Web site at *www.degree.net/updates/mailandinternet*. But remember, our readers play a huge role in this ongoing process. Please, whether it's a defunct email address or a hot new distance-learning program, bring it to our attention at *johnandmariah@degree.net* or Bears' Guide, P.O. Box 7123, Berkeley CA 94707.

If a school is listed in the next 100 pages, but you can't get in touch with them, see Appendix B.

If a school is not listed in the next 100 pages, and you want to know about them, see Appendix C.

American College

American offers degrees and credentials for insurance professionals, employee benefit professionals, and financial consultants through distance learning plus two 1-week residency sessions in Pennsylvania.

270 South Bryn Mawr Avenue
Bryn Mawr, PA 19010

Web site	www.amercoll.edu
Email	studentservices@amercoll.edu
Telephone	(610) 526 1490 • (888) AMERCOLL
Fax	(610) 526 1465
Year established	1927
Ownership status	Nonprofit, independent
Residency	Two weeks per year
Cost	Average
Degree level	Master's
Fields of study or special interest	Professional, mostly financial planning
Other information	American College offers an external Master of Science in financial services through a combination of distance-learning courses and two 1-week intensive residency sessions. It also offers the Certified Financial Planner (CFP), Chartered Life Underwriter (CLU), Chartered Financial Consultant (ChFC), Registered Health Underwriter (RHU), and Registered Employee Benefits Counselor (REBC) designation programs. Courses are developed by resident faculty and taken by students around the world. Students study independently or in classes sponsored by local chapters, as well as by other universities and professional associations. Examinations of the Society of Financial Service Professionals are given online whenever possible.

The college operates an office of student services with counselors available to give advice by phone or email. The purpose is to eliminate some of the problems that arise in distance education by providing a stronger relationship between the student and the college.

The American College accepts up to 9 credits in transfer. Most students are fully employed adults. The average student takes two and a half to three years to complete a program.

Antioch University

Student-designed Master of Arts, M.F.A. in writing, and Ph.D. in leadership and professional studies from one of America's higher education pioneers.

800 Livermore Street
Yellow Springs, OH 45387

Web site	www.antioch.edu
Email	admiss@antioch.edu
Telephone	(937) 767 6321
Fax	(937) 767 6461
Year established	1852
Ownership status	Nonprofit, independent
Residency	Short residency
Cost	High average
Degree level	Master's, Doctorates
Fields of study or special interest	Individualized; leadership and professional studies; writing

Other information   The individualized M.A. is based around a student-designed, faculty-approved program of study. All U.S. students are required to come to Antioch's Yellow Springs, Ohio, campus for a five-day orientation seminar during the first quarter they're enrolled, and a four-day thesis seminar toward the end of their program. Foreign students need only come to Yellow Springs for the thesis seminar; their orientation seminar is held in Germany.

Each student develops an individualized curriculum under the direction of two degree committee members who are recruited by the student and approved by Antioch University. Students then complete the coursework in their own community. Coursework may include independent study, research, practicums, workshops, conferences, tutorials, and traditional courses at other institutions. A thesis is required. Popular fields include counseling, applied psychology, creative writing, environmental studies, women's studies, education, peace studies, performing arts, visual arts, and organizational development. A maximum of 15 quarter credits from prior learning experiences can be applied to this program.

The Master of Fine Arts in writing takes place primarily over the Internet, with five required 10-day intensive workshops in Los Angeles.

Antioch also offers a low-residency (four seminars per year) Ph.D. in leadership and professional studies. Students may fulfill residency requirements at any of Antioch's campuses (Los Angeles and Santa Barbara, CA; Keene, NH; Yellow Springs, OH; and Seattle, WA).

Athabasca University

More than 20,000 students worldwide are earning recognized degrees through this Canadian school's many sophisticated home-study programs.

1 University Drive
Athabasca, AB T9S 3A3
Canada

Web site	www.athabascau.ca
Email	auinfo2@athabascau.ca
Telephone	+1 (780) 675 6100 • (800) 788 9041
Fax	+1 (780) 675 6145
Year established	1970
Ownership status	Nonprofit, independent
Residency	No residency
Cost	Average
Degree level	Bachelor's, Master's
Fields of study or special interest	Administration, arts and sciences, business administration, commerce, computing and information systems, counseling, distance learning, general studies, health studies, integrated studies, nursing
Other information	Athabasca University offers bachelor's degrees in administration, arts, commerce, general studies, nursing (for registered nurses), professional arts (with emphasis in communications or criminal justice), science, and computing and information systems, as well as certificates in a number of fields from accounting to labor studies to public administration.

Distance-learning master's degrees include an M.A. in integrated studies, MBA (requiring three short campus visits), Master of Counseling, Master of Distance Education, and Master of Health Studies. Advanced diplomas are offered in community nursing practice, health studies (with emphasis in advanced nursing practice or leadership), and information technology management.

Distance education courses are offered through sophisticated home-study packages. Students can register any month throughout the year for undergraduate courses. All students are assigned telephone tutors (with tollfree access for students in North America) with whom they can discuss course content. Some courses are also supplemented by radio, television, audio- and videocassettes, computer components, seminars, laboratories, or teleconference sessions. Many courses are now offered electronically, and all university services can be contacted through email.

Auburn University

Almost entirely nonresident master's degrees in business-related and engineering-related fields.

Graduate Outreach Program
106 Hargis Hall
Auburn, AL 36849-5122

Web site	www.auburn.edu
Email	gradadm@mail.auburn.edu
Telephone	(334) 844 4700
Fax	(334) 844 4348
Year established	1856
Ownership status	Nonprofit, state
Residency	1–3 days, depending on program
Cost	Average
Degree level	Master's
Fields of study or special interest	Accounting, business administration, computer science, and many engineering-related fields

Other information Auburn offers an almost totally nonresident Master of Accounting, an MBA (with concentrations in finance, health care administration, human resource management, marketing, operations management, management of information systems, and management of technology), and a Master of Engineering (in aerospace engineering, chemical engineering, civil and environmental engineering, computer science, industrial engineering, materials science and engineering, or mechanical engineering). Graduate courses are taped in on-campus classrooms and mailed to distance students, who must keep the same pace as resident students. Class assignments and group work are facilitated by Internet interaction.

Faculty members set aside special telephone "office hours" for external students. They generally answer the questions over the phone and then restate those questions and the answers in the next videotaped class for the benefit of all students.

Limited credit is available for prior learning. A student must earn at least 35 quarter hours, or half of the total hours required for a master's degree, whichever is greater, at Auburn University. A program that requires only 45 hours of credit will be limited to 10 quarter hours of transfer credit. No course on which a grade lower than B was earned may be transferred. The program is limited to U.S. and Canadian residents and overseas U.S. military personnel.

The MBA requires three days on campus for group presentation; the engineering degrees require one or two days for exams.

Students generally complete the program in two and a half years, but they have up to five years to earn their degree. Career counseling and job placement assistance are available.

Baker College

Degrees in business administration—associate's, bachelor's, and master's—entirely through online study.

1050 West Bristol Road
Flint, MI 48507-5508

Web site	www.baker.edu
Email	adm-ol@baker.edu
Telephone	(800) 469 4062
Year established	1888
Ownership status	Nonprofit, independent
Residency	None
Cost	High average
Degree level	Associate's, Bachelor's, Master's
Fields of study or special interest	Business administration (ABA/BBA/MBA)

Other information   Part of Michigan's largest private, not-for-profit college (13 campuses), Baker On-Line offers an Associate of Business Administration (ABA), a Bachelor of Business Administration (BBA), and an MBA, entirely through online study. MBA specializations include accounting, computer information systems, finance, health care management, human resource management, industrial management, international business, leadership studies, and marketing.

Each class takes place in a "virtual classroom," and every student is provided with 24-hour access to their "classes," as well as a private mailbox. Interaction between students and instructors occurs through Web-based bulletin boards. Each course takes six weeks to complete. The master's can be completed in 18 months.

Bellevue University

Undergraduate and graduate programs in business, computing, and criminal justice, through an interactive online site.

1000 Galvin Road South
Bellevue, NE 68005

Web site	www.bellevue.edu
Email	online-u@scholars.bellevue.edu
Telephone	(402) 291 8100 • (800) 756 7920
Fax	(402) 293 3730
Year established	1965
Ownership status	Nonprofit, independent
Residency	None
Degree level	Bachelor's, Master's
Fields of study or special interest	Business administration, business information systems, criminal justice administration, e-business, leadership, management, management information systems, management of human resources
Other information	Bellevue University Online is the distance education component of this otherwise traditional university. The university is dedicated to providing an online classroom community and support. Internet students can open the online classroom, interact with professors and other students, use online library services, and receive online advising. To demo this environment, just go to the school's Web site.

At the undergraduate level, Bellevue offers the Bachelor of Science in business information systems, criminal justice administration, e-business, leadership, management, management information systems, and management of human resources.

At the graduate level, an online MBA and M.A. in leadership are offered, both requiring 36 credit hours and about 18 months of study.

Credit can also be earned through self-study, life experience assessment, video courses, and examination.

Brigham Young University

Bachelor of General Studies through independent study.

315 Harman Building
P.O. Box 21515
Provo, UT 84602-1515

Web site	ce.byu.edu/bgs
Email	bgs@byu.edu
Telephone	(801) 378 4351 • (888) 298 3137
Year established	1875
Ownership status	Nonprofit, church
Residency	11 weeks
Cost	High average
Degree level	Bachelor's
Fields of study or special interest	Independent studies

Other information
Brigham Young University's Bachelor of General Studies (B.G.S.) is a flexible, external program that uses the same BYU curriculum that is offered on campus. Up to 90 of the required 120 credits can be earned through independent study. Though the major is in general studies, the student must emphasize in one of eight study areas: American studies, English and American literature, family history, family life, history, management, psychology, or writing.

The 120 semester hours required for graduation are roughly broken down as follows: general education requirements (30–60 hours), general electives (10–40 hours), religious education (14 hours), and emphasis (30 hours). Transfer credits from other accredited colleges and universities are accepted and will be evaluated upon application.

Eleven weeks of residency are required: five 2-week residency sessions and a one-week "closure seminar" at the end of the program.

BYU is owned and operated by the Church of Jesus Christ of Latter-Day Saints, but admission is open to all who will abide by BYU's nonsectarian Code of Honor and receive an annual ecclesiastical endorsement.

Burlington College

Bachelor's degrees in the liberal arts, almost entirely by independent study.

95 North Avenue
Burlington, VT 05401

Web site	www.burlcol.edu/distance.htm
Email	admissions@burlcol.edu
Telephone	(802) 862 9616 • (800) 862 9616
Fax	(802) 660 4331
Year established	1972
Ownership status	Nonprofit, independent
Residency	Four days per semester
Cost	Average
Degree level	Bachelor's
Fields of study or special interest	Cinema studies, fine arts, individualized major, literature, psychology, transpersonal psychology, writing

Other information Burlington offers a liberal arts–centered B.A. through the school's primarily nonresident Independent Degree Program (IDP). Applicants to the IDP must have already completed 45 college credits, have "strong writing skills," and be able to spend four days on the Vermont campus at the beginning of each semester.

Those 45 credits can come from prior traditional college learning, proficiency exams, or experiential learning. In addition to the required units, students can transfer in a maximum of 90 credits. All students must complete a minimum of 30 credits through the program, regardless of prior experience.

Although Burlington's programs are highly individualized, the school specifically encourages applicants whose interests fall in the fields of fine arts, humanities, psychology, transpersonal psychology, or "almost any liberal area(s) of study."

During the four-day residency, the student works with faculty to plan out the semester of independent study, then returns home to carry out the plan, communicating with faculty by telephone, mail, fax, or modem.

Formerly Vermont Institute of Community Involvement.

Caldwell College

Bachelor's degrees in a wide range of fields, with only one day per semester on campus.

9 Ryerson Avenue
Caldwell, NJ 07006-6195

Web site	www.caldwell.edu/adult-ed
Email	agleason@caldwell.edu
Telephone	(973) 618 3385 • (888) 864 9518
Fax	(973) 618 3660
Year established	1939
Ownership status	Nonprofit, church
Residency	First Saturday of each semester
Cost	High average
Degree level	Bachelor's
Fields of study or special interest	Accounting, art, business administration, computer information systems, communication arts, criminal justice, English, French, history, international business, management, marketing, political science, psychology, religious studies, social studies, sociology, Spanish
Other information	Caldwell's mission statement speaks of "a commitment to assist adult learners in their pursuit of lifelong learning," and the school prides itself on its flexibility in meeting the needs of fully employed students. Bachelor's degrees are offered in the above fields.

This is primarily an off-campus, independent study program that utilizes tutorial relationships with professors. Students spend one day per semester on campus (the computer information systems major may also require a few on-campus workshops). The school estimates that part-time students will take five to seven years to complete the bachelor's degree. Applicants must be 23 years of age or older.

Up to 75 credits of prior learning can be applied towards the degree; these credits can come from prior schooling, exams (CLEP, DANTES, and other standardized subject examinations), and life experience. Credit is granted for military and nonacademic training through portfolio assessment.

A wide range of student support services is offered, including assistance with financial aid, academic and career counseling, and tutoring in a range of subjects.

California College for Health Sciences

Associate's, bachelor's, and master's degrees in a variety of health and human service disciplines, entirely through distance learning.

2423 Hoover Avenue
National City, CA 91950

Web site	www.cchs.edu
Email	cchsinfo@cchs.edu
Telephone	(619) 477 4800 • (800) 221 7374
Fax	(619) 477 4360
Year established	1979
Ownership status	Proprietary
Residency	None
Cost	Average
Degree level	Associate's, Bachelor's, Master's
Fields of study or special interest	Health and human services

Other information   With no residency requirements, California College's degree programs in the health and human service disciplines are geared toward adults juggling work, family, and community commitments.

Associate's degrees are available in business, early childhood education, electroencephalographic technology, medical transcription, and respiratory therapy. Bachelor's degrees are available in business, health services management, and respiratory care.

Master's programs—in health care administration, health services, and public health, as well as an MBA specializing in health care—are designed particularly for those already employed in a health care setting. The core of each program is a series of correspondence courses. Texts and syllabuses are mailed to students, who complete assignments and mail them back. Students are expected to complete 1 credit per month; thus, a 3-credit course is expected to take three months, and normally must be completed within six months. Exams can be taken anywhere, but must be supervised by an approved proctor.

In addition to the college's many student services, students have instant access to the college's Web site 24 hours a day, and can visit the student services tutorial help center, quickly get feedback from faculty online, and review the course catalogs at any time.

California College for Health Sciences is a division of Harcourt Higher Learning; the school's accreditation comes from the Distance Education and Training Council (DETC).

California State University—Dominguez Hills

A variety of nonresident degrees (including an M.A. in humanities) offered through a state university.

Division of Extended Education
1000 East Victoria Street
Carson, CA 90747

Web site	www.csudh.edu
Email	info@csudh.edu
Telephone	(310) 243 3741
Fax	(310) 516 3971
Year established	1960
Ownership status	Nonprofit, state
Residency	None
Cost	Low to average
Degree level	Bachelor's, Master's
Fields of study or special interest	Applied studies, business administration, humanities, negotiation & conflict management, nursing, quality assurance
Other information	Dominguez Hills's Division of Extended Education offers eight nonresidential degree programs through online study, correspondence, or a combination of the two.

Three bachelor's degrees are available: the B.S. in applied studies (an interdisciplinary program geared toward working professionals), a B.S. completion program in nursing (for registered nurses), and a B.S. in quality assurance. These programs can be completed through a mix of online coursework and prior study.

The school also offers an M.A. in the humanities via correspondence: a rare opportunity to earn an accredited, nonresidential master's degree in art, history, literature, music, or philosophy. (We are biased. The authors' wife and mother, respectively, Marina Bear, completed her M.A. here in 1985 while living in a remote location and taking care of three young children.) This M.A. requires 33 semester hours of credit (including a 4–6 hour thesis or creative project). No credit is awarded for equivalency exams or life-experience learning, and only 9 credits can be transferred into the program. Communication with faculty is by mail, fax, email, telephone, and the Web.

Other master's degrees offered nonresidentially include an MBA, M.A. in behavioral science (focusing on negotiation and conflict management), M.S. in quality assurance (specializing in health care, manufacturing, or service), and an M.S. in nursing.

Some programs may not be available until late 2001; contact the school for details.

Capella University

Online degrees, including doctorates, in business, education, human services, information technology, and psychology, from a school dedicated entirely to adult learners.

222 South 9th Street, 20th Floor
Minneapolis, MN 55402-3389

Web site	www.capellauniversity.edu
Email	info@capella.edu
Telephone	(612) 339 8650 • (888) 227 3552
Fax	(612) 337 5396
Year established	1993
Ownership status	Proprietary
Residency	None for bachelor's and most master's programs; short residency sessions for doctorates
Cost	High average
Degree level	Bachelor's, Master's, Doctorates
Fields of study or special interest	Business, education, human services, information technology, psychology

Other information   Capella University began as the Graduate School of America, a major, well-funded, and ambitious effort to create an important nontraditional institution that meets the needs of busy professionals seeking a master's or doctoral degree. It now offers degree programs at all levels, as well as a number of certificates.

Online master's and doctoral programs are offered by the schools of business, education, human services, psychology, and technology. A wide range of specializations are available in each of these fields. All of the doctoral programs require some residency; none of the master's degrees do, except for the more clinically oriented specializations within the M.S. programs in psychology and human services.

The B.S. completion program in information technology is designed for students who have already earned 60 semester hours through another regionally accredited institution; the remaining coursework (including the IT major) is completed online through Capella. Students may specialize in e-business, project management, or Web application development.

Graduate certificate programs are available in most of the degree specialization areas; an undergraduate certificate in information technology is also available.

Capital University

Bachelor's degrees in an array of fields through a venerable private university.

Columbus Center
2199 East Main Street
Columbus, OH 43209-2394

Web site	www.capital.edu
Email	rashbroo@capital.edu
Telephone	(614) 236 6996
Fax	(614) 236 6171
Year established	1850
Ownership status	Nonprofit, independent
Residency	None
Cost	High average
Degree level	Bachelor's

Fields of study or special interest

Accounting, computer science, criminology, economics, English, general studies, international studies, management, nursing, organizational communications, philosophy, political science, psychology, public relations, religion, social work, sociology

Other information

This University Without Walls program began in 1976 under the auspices of the Union for Experimenting Colleges and Universities (now the Union Institute), and was taken over in 1979 by the venerable Capital University. Bachelor's degrees are available in the above fields, or (with faculty approval) an individualized field of the student's choice.

Students must complete 124 semester hours' worth of course requirements, largely through guided independent study and online coursework. All students must complete a senior project in his or her field showing bachelor's-level abilities and serving as a capstone learning experience. Some transfer credit is accepted, and credit for experiential learning is available through portfolio assessment.

Central Michigan University

Off-campus bachelor's, master's, and doctorates in various fields.

CMU-DDL
CEL-North
Mt. Pleasant, MI 48859

Web site	www.ddl.cmich.edu
Telephone	(517) 774 3505 • (800) 688 4268
Fax	(517) 774 3491
Year established	1892
Ownership status	Nonprofit, state
Residency	Short or no residency
Cost	Low average to average, depending on program
Degree level	Bachelor's, Master's, Doctorates
Fields of study or special interest	Administration, audiology, community development, industrial administration, health sciences, nutrition & dietetics

Other information   Central Michigan University offers degrees at all levels through online study and other nontraditional methods.

The B.S. is available in administration, community development, health sciences, or industrial administration. The program requires 124 semester hours of credit; up to 94 hours may consist of prior learning (transfer credit and/or portfolio evaluation). Students may fulfill remaining requirements through residential coursework, courses taken at off-campus sites (CMU will consider setting up a corporate extension site whenever the demand justifies it), online classes, telecourses, or correspondence.

The M.S. programs in administration and in nutrition and dietetics each involve 36 semester hours of credit; 21 hours must be taken through CMU, but the remaining 15 can consist of transfer credit and evaluation of prior work. A full-time student can finish the program in about two years.

The online Doctor of Audiology (Au.D.), designed in consultation with Vanderbilt University, is a course-based program designed for professional audiologists. No dissertation is required, and the program can usually be completed in about three years.

Charles Sturt University

Australia's largest distance-learning provider offers hundreds of rigorous, inexpensive programs to students worldwide.

International Division
Locked Bag 676
Wagga Wagga, NSW 2678
Australia

Web site	www.csu.edu.au
Email	inquiry@csu.edu.au
Telephone	+61 (2) 6933 2666
Fax	+61 (2) 6933 2799
Year established	1989
Ownership status	Nonprofit
Residency	No residency for most programs
Cost	Low
Degree level	Bachelor's, Master's, Doctorates, Law
Fields of study or special interest	See below

Other information In 1989, Mitchell College of Advanced Education and Riverina-Murray Institute of Higher Education merged to form Charles Sturt University, now the largest distance education provider in Australia.

Bachelor's programs are completed through a mix of online and correspondence courses, and take an average of six years for a part-time student to complete (or 3–4 years for a full-time student). Offerings include psychology, a variety of agriculture and food-related fields (such as agriculture, ecotourism, environmental agriculture, equine studies, food science, parks and heritage, or viticulture), business (with several specializations, including accounting), education (early childhood, primary, or vocational), health and medicine (complementary medicine, gerontology and aged care, mental health, nursing, pre-hospital care, and other fields), information technology (or spatial information systems), natural science fields (such as analytical chemistry, biotechnology, mathematics, and many others), social sciences (such as emergency management, justice studies, leisure, policing, social work, and other fields), and theology (Th.B.).

Master's degrees tend to involve a series of six to ten modules focusing on a specific area of study within the major; some culminate in a thesis or project, while others do not. The master's is available in a variety of fields related to business (including accounting, applied finance, human resources, and marketing; an MBA is also available with three specializations, including one in global business), education (with numerous specializations), health (including aged services management, asthma education, genetic counseling, medical imaging, medical laboratory science, medical ultrasound, and nursing; an M.Psy. is also available), religion (both the M.Min. and Th.M.), and social sciences (such as cultural heritage studies, journalism, and organizational communication). Perhaps the widest range of offerings are in the general area of law enforcement, where students may choose from programs in child protection investigations, criminal intelligence, ethics and legal studies, fraud investigations, police nego-tiation, or other related fields.

At the doctoral level, Sturt offers the following professional doctorates: the Doctor of Business Administration (which can be done by coursework alone), the Doctor of Psychology, and the Doctor of Public Policy. CSU also offers research doctorates in the following fields: agricultural economics, agriculture, Australian history, business management, communication and culture, drama, education, environmental and information science, environmental studies, finan-cial and managerial accounting, fine arts, health studies, industry and resource economics, information studies, information technology, justice studies and police studies, professional and applied ethics, psychology, rural social studies, science and technology, social welfare and social policy, social work, and wine and food sciences.

Charter Oak State College

Associate's and bachelor's degrees through any combination of nontraditional credit-earning opportunities.

55 Paul J. Manafort Drive
New Britain, CT 06053-2142

Web site	www.cosc.edu
Email	info@cosc.edu
Telephone	(860) 832 3855
Fax	(860) 832 3999
Year established	1973
Ownership status	Nonprofit, state
Residency	None
Cost	Low
Degree level	Associate's, Bachelor's
Fields of study or special interest	Anthropology, applied arts, art history, biology, business, chemistry, child study, communication, computer science studies, criminal justice, economics, engineering studies, fire science technology, French, geography, geology, German, history, human services (specializing in administration, applied behavioral science, or health studies), individualized studies, information systems, information technology, liberal studies, literature, mathematics, music history, music theory, optical business management, organizational management, philosophy, physics, political science, psychology, religious studies, sociology, Spanish, technology studies
Other information	Operated by the Connecticut Board for State Academic Awards, Charter Oak offers associate's and bachelor's in general studies with concentrations in the above fields.

Charter Oak accepts an unlimited number of transfer credits from other regionally accredited schools, regardless of when they were earned. Students can earn remaining credits to fulfill degree requirements through a variety of means: classroom-based or distance-learning courses taken at any regionally accredited school, military training, standardized college-level examinations such as CLEP or DANTES, portfolio assessment of life experience, and contract learning. With this array of options, including some distance-learning courses and independent study offered through Charter Oak itself, students can complete their degree in a manner that suits their lifestyles

Enrollment is open to anyone over the age of 16 who has completed 9 college-level credits. Foreign students must show evidence of fluency in English, contract to have foreign credits evaluated by a service chosen by Charter Oak, and earn at least 30 U.S. credits while enrolled.

Originally known as the Connecticut Board for State Academic Awards; later, as Charter Oak College.

City University

Nonresident bachelor's and master's degrees through online study or traditional correspondence.

335 116th Avenue SE
Bellevue, WA 98004

Web site www.cityu.edu

Email info@cityu.edu

Telephone (425) 637 1010 • (800) 426 5596

Fax (425) 277 2437

Year established 1973

Ownership status Nonprofit, independent

Residency None

Cost High average

Degree level Bachelor's, Master's

Fields of study or special interest See below

Other information Nonresident bachelor's degrees in accounting, business administration, commerce, computer systems (with emphasis in computer programming, internetworking, networking and telecommunications, networking technologies, or student-defined selected studies), e-commerce, general studies, humanities, management, marketing, quantitative studies, and social sciences. Up to 135 of the 180 quarter hours for the bachelor's degree may be transferred in. These credits may come from prior schooling, standardized college-level exams, departmental exams, and military and/or other life-experience learning. Some corporate training may be considered for credit on a case-by-case basis.

City University also offers an MBA (emphasis in financial management, information systems, managerial leadership, marketing, or personal financial planning); an M.P.A. (Master of Public Administration); M.A.'s in counseling psychology, executive leadership, and management; M.S.'s in computer systems and project management; and M.Ed.'s in curriculum and instruction, educational leadership and principal certification, educational technology, guidance and counseling, and reading and literacy. A Master of Teaching completion program is also available to residents of Washington and California. Up to 12 quarter hours may be transferred into a City University master's program, with faculty approval.

City University also offers a variety of extension programs in ten Washington cities, as well as San Jose, California; Vancouver, British Columbia, Canada; Zurich, Switzerland; Frankfurt, Germany; and two locations in Slovakia.

Some university-sponsored scholarships are available.

Clarkson College

Nonresident bachelor's degrees in health care fields, as well as a low-residency master's degree in nursing.

101 South 42nd Street
Omaha, NE 68131

Web site	www.clarksoncollege.edu
Email	admiss@clrkcol.crhsnet.edu
Telephone	(402) 552 3041 • (800) 647 5500
Fax	(402) 552 6057
Year established	1888
Ownership status	Nonprofit, independent
Residency	None for bachelor's; some for master's
Cost	High average
Degree level	Bachelor's, Master's
Fields of study or special interest	Business administration (health care–related), medical imaging, nursing
Other information	Clarkson offers a B.S. in business administration with a concentration in health service management entirely through distance-learning methods. The bachelor's degree may be completed entirely through Clarkson, or by building on an associate's degree in science, or on courses taken for another bachelor's degree.

Bachelor's degree completion programs are available in medical imaging (for registered technicians) and nursing (for registered nurses). Credit is available for a range of life-experience learning through portfolio evaluation, assessment of military training, and standardized college-level tests. Clarkson's own courses are delivered through a range of media including the Internet, fax, video- and audiocassettes, and teleconferencing.

In addition, Clarkson offers a distance-learning M.S. in nursing with a concentration in administration, education, or family nurse practice. A post-master's family nurse practitioner certificate is also available for students who have already earned an MSN. Students must come to campus for three weekends total for clinical evaluation, and to defend a thesis or complete comprehensive exams (depending on the track chosen).

Students must live at least 75 miles from Omaha to qualify for Clarkson's distance-learning programs.

Colorado State University

Graduate programs in scientific, business, education, engineering, and computer fields through Internet study or videocassette-based classes.

Division of Educational Outreach
Spruce Hall
Fort Collins, CO 80523-1040

Web site	www.colostate.edu
Email	questions@learn.colostate.edu
Telephone	(970) 491 5288 • (800) 525 4950
Fax	(970) 491 7885
Year established	1870
Ownership status	Nonprofit, state
Residency	None for master's programs; variable for doctorates
Cost	High average
Degree level	Master's, Doctorates
Fields of study or special interest	Agriculture, business-related fields, computer science, engineering and industrial fields, statistics
Other information	Established in 1967, the Distance Degree Program (formerly called SURGE) was the first video-based graduate education program of its kind in America. Today, courses are delivered through videotape, the Internet, or a combination of the two.

An average of 80 courses are taught at a distance each semester, representing the College of Agricultural Sciences, Applied Human Sciences, Business, Engineering, Natural Sciences, and Veterinary Medicine & Biomedical Sciences. Live Colorado State courses are recorded and sent with available materials to a participating site, or directly to a student on videocassette or through Internet streaming video. The student must find a proctor for exams and is not required to return tapes.

Master's degrees are available in agriculture, business administration (MBA), engineering (agricultural, civil, electrical, environmental, industrial, or mechanical), computer science, human resources, industrial hygiene, management, and statistics. Doctoral degrees (which require a variable amount of campus residency) are available in electrical engineering, industrial engineering, mechanical engineering, and systems engineering.

Colorado State's Distance Degree Program is available to residents of the U.S. and Canada, as well as to overseas U.S. military personnel.

Columbia Union College

Bachelor's degrees in many fields entirely through correspondence courses.

7600 Flower Avenue
Wilkinson Hall, Room 336A
Takoma Park, MD 20912-7796

Web site	www.cuc.edu
Email	hsi@cuc.edu
Telephone	(301) 8 91 4124 • (800) 835 4212
Year established	1904
Ownership status	Nonprofit, church
Residency	No residency (except for the respiratory therapy program)
Cost	High average
Degree level	Bachelor's
Fields of study or special interest	Business administration, general studies, information systems, psychology, religion, respiratory care, theology
Other information	Columbia Union College offers bachelor's in general studies, psychology, religion, business administration, and theology entirely through correspondence study. A maximum of 90 credits (out of the 120 required) can be transferred into the program based on prior study. These credits can come from courses taken at or through other schools, standardized examinations, and life-experience evaluation (portfolio credit).

Remaining credit is earned through Columbia Union's correspondence courses. For each course, the student is sent a syllabus, textbook, and assignments. All courses require proctored examinations, which can be taken anywhere. Contact is maintained between students and instructors by mail, phone, and email, and through ongoing progress evaluations.

The school is owned and operated by the Seventh-Day Adventist Church, but nonmembers are welcome. Students may live anywhere in the world, but all work must be done in English.

Columbia University

Nonresidential master's, specialist, and certificate programs in many engineering and technology fields from one of the most prestigious schools in the United States.

540 Mudd, MC 4719
500 West 120th Street
New York, NY 10027

Web site	www.cvn.columbia.edu
Email	cvn@columbia.edu
Telephone	(212) 854 6447
Fax	(212) 854 2325
Year established	1754
Ownership status	Nonprofit, independent
Residency	None
Cost	High average to high
Degree level	Master's
Fields of study or special interest	A good variety of engineering and technology-related fields

Other information

Columbia University offers a solid assortment of degree and certificate programs through the Columbia Video Network (CVN); students watch taped lectures through videoconferencing, videocassette, and/or streaming Internet media. Class notes, homework assignments, and syllabi are accessed through the Web. Programs tend to be highly flexible and can generally be tailored to the student's professional and research interests.

M.S. programs are available in computer science, electrical engineering, engineering and management systems, materials science, and mechanical engineering. Each program concludes with a capstone project; a thesis is optional. The M.S. involves an estimated three to five years of part-time study.

The Professional Degree (P.D.) is a specialist-level credential designed for students who already hold an appropriate master's degree. Students must complete at least two full semester loads (30 semester hours) of approved coursework beyond the master's to earn this credential. No capstone thesis or project is required. Students may major in computer science, electrical engineering, or mechanical engineering. The P.D. can be expected to involve two to three years of part-time study beyond the master's.

The Certificate of Professional Achievement involves 12 semester hours of graduate-level coursework and is available in the following fields: computer science, earth and environmental science, electrical engineering, financial engineering, genomic engineering, industrial engineering and operation research, material science, and mechanical engineering. Students must complete the program within two years.

De Montfort University

Degrees at all levels from a British university, with minimal time required on campus in England.

Centre for Independent Study
The Gateway
Leicester LE1 9BH
United Kingdom

Web site	www.dmu.ac.uk
Email	enquiry@dmu.ac.uk
Telephone	+44 (116) 255 1551
Fax	+44 (116) 257 7533
Year established	1897
Ownership status	Nonprofit, state
Residency	Short or no residency
Cost	Average
Degree level	Bachelor's, Master's, Doctorates, Law
Fields of study or special interest	See below
Other information	

De Montfort University (formerly Leicester Polytechnic) offers a variety of programs through independent study, with minimal residence required on the campus in England. Most programs are based on a learning contract, an agreement negotiated between the student and the university. When a student is accepted into the program, she is assigned a mentor or supervisor (usually a member of the university staff) who will guide her through the program and assist in the formulation of a research or study proposal. Normally the mentor meets with the student once during each term; for foreign (non-U.K.) students, the school generally requires the student to have a local mentor as well as the university mentor.

At the undergraduate level, De Montfort offers B.A. and Honours B.A. programs in business; B.S. and Honours B.S. programs are available in chemistry, waste and environmental management, and water and environmental management. Undergraduate diplomas are also available in environmental protection and legal practice.

Master's can be earned in health and community development, clinical pharmacy, conservation science, environmental quality management, industrial data modeling, lubricant and hydraulic technology, polymer technology, and law (advanced legal practice, business law, countryside and agriculture law, environmental law, or food law). In lieu of formal examinations, the university conducts continuous assessment through a variety of coursework assignments plus a major project or thesis which will account for at least 40 percent of the total. An oral examination is held in the U.K. at the end of each program.

De Montfort may also negotiate a research Ph.D. in fine art practice on a nonresidential or low-residency basis. Contact the school for details.

Deakin University

Nonresidential and low-residency degrees at all levels from one of Australia's top universities.

Deakin International
336 Glenferrie Road
Malvern, Victoria 3144
Australia

Web site	www.deakin.edu.au
Telephone	+61 (3) 9244 5095
Fax	+61 (3) 9244 5094
Year established	1974
Ownership status	Nonprofit
Residency	Short or no residency
Cost	Low average
Degree level	Bachelor's, Master's, Doctorates, Law
Fields of study or special interest	See below
Other information	Deakin University offers programs to students worldwide through Deakin International, its overseas student office. Most instruction takes place online or via correspondence, although the majority of courses also require proctored final examinations (which may be taken anywhere).

Bachelor's degrees are available in international development studies, international relations, journalism, law (LL.B.), and public relations.

Master's degrees are available in aquaculture, commerce (specializing in accounting, economics, law, management information systems, or marketing), computing studies, distance education, education (focusing on curriculum and administration studies or TESOL), environmental engineering, health science (emphasis human nutrition or nursing), international and community development, international relations, international trade and investment law, law (LL.M.), professional education and training, science and technology studies, and TESOL.

A research-based Doctor of Health Science (D.H.Sc.) is available almost completely nonresidentially, and it may be possible to fulfill the residency requirements through one of Deakin's many partner universities located worldwide. Contact the school for details.

Eastern Illinois University

Bachelor of Arts that can be earned completely through distance-learning methods.

School of Adult and Continuing Education
600 Lincoln Avenue
Charleston, IL 61920

Web site	www.eiu.edu/~adulted
Email	lkwoodward@eiu.edu
Telephone	(217) 581 5618
Year established	1895
Ownership status	Nonprofit, state
Residency	None
Cost	Low average
Degree level	Bachelor's
Fields of study or special interest	Individualized program of study

Other information
This nontraditional program is designed to allow working adults with family and other responsibilities the chance to complete their degree requirements off campus. No major for the Bachelor of Arts need be declared.

A maximum of 105 of the 120 required credits can be transferred into the program. Those credits can come from prior schooling; correspondence courses; many sorts of life-experience learning, including but not limited to military and job-related training; and ACT, CLEP, DANTES, and departmental exams. The university stresses that skills and knowledge acquired by nonacademic means can be evaluated for academic credit. Applicants without a high school degree or G.E.D. will be considered on a case-by-case basis.

Fifteen credits must be completed through coursework at Eastern Illinois University, Chicago State University, Governors State University, Northeastern Illinois University, or Western Illinois University. Of these, Governors State and Western Illinois specialize in correspondence courses.

The time to complete the B.A. depends on the amount of prior credit, but it is not uncommon for students to graduate within one semester of enrolling. In other cases, however, the process may take several years.

Eastern Oregon University

A number of wholly nonresident undergraduate degrees for students anywhere, as well as two low-residency master's programs for Oregon residents.

Division of Distance Education (DDE)
1 University Boulevard
La Grande, OR 97850-2889

Web site	www2.eou.edu/dde
Email	jhart@eou.edu
Telephone	(541) 962 3614 • (800) 452 8639
Fax	(541) 962 3627
Year established	1929
Ownership status	Nonprofit, state
Residency	None for bachelor's programs; short residencies for master's
Cost	Low average
Degree level	Associate's, Bachelor's, Master's
Fields of study or special interest	Business, economics, fire services administration, liberal studies, philosophy, physical education, politics, social work, teacher education
Other information	Eastern Oregon offers wholly nonresident B.A.'s and B.S.'s in business and economics, fire services administration, liberal studies (with a concentration in virtually anything), philosophy/politics/economics (combined program), and physical education and health. An A.S. in office administration is also available. Credit is given for independent study, cooperative work experience, assessment of prior learning, weekend college, and examination. Coursework is accomplished via correspondence courses (with video- and audiotapes), computer conferencing courses, Web-based courses, and weekend classes.

An M.S. in social work and a Master of Teacher Education (M.T.E.) are available by distance learning to Oregon residents.

The school currently limits itself to working with English-speaking students in North America because of the logistics involved in negotiating postage costs, delays, and test proctoring for students in other countries.

Eastern does not charge additional tuition to out-of-state students, but does require that they have full Internet communication capabilities (email and Web access).

Edith Cowan University

Many nonresidential degrees from a major university named after the first woman to serve in Australia's parliament.

International Students Office
Claremont, WA 6010
Australia

Web site	www.cowan.edu.au
Email	extstudi@echidna.cowan.edu.au
Telephone	+61 (9) 273 8681
Year established	1990
Ownership status	Nonprofit, state
Residency	Short or no residency
Cost	Low average
Degree level	Bachelor's, Master's, Doctorates
Fields of study or special interest	See below

Other information
Edith Cowan University (formerly Western Australian College of Advanced Education) offers programs through a variety of distance-learning methods, including guided independent research, correspondence, audio-visual materials, online study, and other appropriate instructional media.

Bachelor's degrees are offered in aboriginal studies, accounting, addiction studies, advertising, applied anthropology and sociology, applied women's studies, children and family studies, disability studies, education (with optional specialization in special education), gerontology, health promotion, human services, indigenous studies, information systems, justice studies, leisure studies, management, marketing, nursing (for registered/licensed nurses), police studies, psychology, and youth work.

Master's degrees are offered in accounting, applied linguistics, business administration (MBA) with an optional specialization (in health services management, justice administration, or sports management), education (M.Ed.) with optional specialization (in any of the fields listed for the Ed.D; see below), health science (with optional emphasis in health promotion or occupational safety and health), information science, medicine (M.Med.) for practicing physicians (in family medicine, palliative care, or sports medicine), nursing, public health, social science (with optional emphasis in development studies or leisure studies), and sports management.

Research Ph.D.'s are available in development studies, education, interdisciplinary studies, nursing, and occupational health and safety. An Ed.D. is also available with specialization in one of the following fields: career education, children with special needs, early childhood studies, educational computing, educational policy and administrative studies, interactive multimedia, language and literacy, mathematics education, music education, religious education, science education, society and environmental education, teaching and learning, or technology and enterprise education.

Empire State College

Associate's, bachelor's, and master's degrees from a longtime leader in individualized academic programs.

Center for Distance Learning
3 Union Avenue
Saratoga Springs, NY 12866-4391

Web site	www.esc.edu
Email	cdl@esc.edu
Telephone	(518) 587 2100 • (800) 847 3000
Fax	(518) 587 2660
Year established	1971
Ownership status	Nonprofit, state
Residency	None for bachelor's degrees; some for master's degrees
Cost	Low
Degree level	Associate's, Bachelor's, Master's
Fields of study or special interest	Accounting, business, criminal justice, emergency management, fire service, health services, human services, interdisciplinary studies, labor studies, management, public affairs
Other information	Part of the State University of New York (SUNY), Empire State College offers totally nonresident associate's and bachelor's degrees and several low-residency master's programs.

Through its Center for Distance Learning, students can develop an individualized bachelor's or associate's degree program that builds upon their interests, life experiences, needs, and goals in one of the general areas listed above. The primary mode of study is independent study guided by faculty mentors. Credit is given for CLEP, DANTES, and other exams, as well as for college-level learning gained from work and other life experience (the school provides help in creating a life-experience portfolio for evaluation). In addition, Empire State offers structured online and correspondence courses.

At the graduate level, Empire State offers an MBA that allows distance learners to test out of almost half of the required credits through assessment of prior knowledge, workplace training, and managerial experience. Remaining credits are earned through Internet courses, independent studies, and two weekend residencies in New York.

Empire State also offers M.A. programs in business and policy studies, labor and policy studies, liberal studies, and social policy. These programs are primarily earned through independent study, with three weekend residencies per year at one of 45 locations across New York state.

Excelsior College

Undergraduate and graduate degrees from a pioneer in nontraditional education.

7 Columbia Circle
Albany, NY 12203-5159

Web site	www.excelsiorcollege.edu
Email	info@excelsiorcollege.edu
Telephone	(518) 464 8500 • (888) 647 2388
Fax	(518) 464 8777
Year established	1971
Ownership status	Nonprofit, independent
Residency	None
Cost	Low to low average
Degree level	Associate's, Bachelor's, Master's
Fields of study or special interest	Business, liberal arts, liberal studies, science, nursing, technology

Other information

Among the largest and most popular nonresident degree programs in the U.S., Excelsior College (formerly Regents College) has no campus and offers no undergraduate courses of its own; rather, it evaluates work done elsewhere and awards its own degrees to students who have accumulated sufficient credits by a broad variety of means.

Those means include course credit from any regionally accredited college (both correspondence- and classroom-based); many equivalency exams (CLEP, DANTES, GRE, etc.), including, of course, Excelsior's own nationally recognized exam program (see the "Equivalency Examinations" chapter); and life-experience portfolios as evaluated through partnerships with Ohio University, Charter Oak State College, and Empire State College. Excelsior offers credit for many noncollege learning experiences, including corporate training programs, military training, and professional licenses. (For example, the technology degree program offers credit for Microsoft certifications.) If nonschool learning experiences cannot be assessed easily at a distance, or by exam, the student may go to Albany, New York, for an oral examination.

Excelsior offers associate's and bachelor's degrees in arts, science, business (including accounting, finance, management, and marketing), nursing, and technology (including computer information systems, nuclear engineering, and electronics engineering).

At the graduate level, Excelsior does offer some of its own courses, for an M.A. in liberal studies and an M.S. in nursing.

Excelsior was formerly known as Regents College. It began as an integral part of the University of the State of New York, and the degrees were awarded by the latter. In a controversial move in 1998, Regents College purchased its independence and became a private institution. As part of the separation, it was required to change its name: thus the switch from Regents to Excelsior.

Fielding Institute

Offers a variety of social science–oriented master's and doctoral programs, including the only APA-approved distance learning Ph.D. in clinical psychology.

2122 Santa Barbara Street
Santa Barbara, CA 93105

Web site	www.fielding.edu
Email	admissions@fielding.edu
Telephone	(805) 687 1099 • (800) 340 1099
Year established	1974
Ownership status	Nonprofit, independent
Residency	Short residency
Cost	High average
Degree level	Master's, Doctorates
Fields of study or special interest	Clinical psychology, educational leadership and change, human and organizational development, neuropsychology, organizational management, psychopharmacology
Other information	Fielding's flexible, student-centered distance-learning format is founded on the principles of adult learning. Its competency-based scholar-practitioner model is designed to serve midcareer professionals who must maintain multiple commitments to family, work, and community while earning an advanced degree. An electronic virtual learning community known as the Fielding Electronic Information Exchange (FELIX) is supplemented with periodic face-to-face events at various locations throughout the United States.

The Ph.D. in clinical psychology is the only distance-learning Ph.D. program in its field to be approved by the American Psychological Association (APA). Other programs offered include the Ph.D. in human and organizational development, the Ed.D. in educational leadership and change, and the M.A. in organizational design and effectiveness. Graduate-level certificate programs are also available in neuropsychology and psychopharmacology. Fielding also offers a special clinical psychology "retooling" program for students who hold a non-APA-approved Ph.D. and would like to fulfill remaining curricular requirements.

For the psychology and organizational development programs, students must attend a five-day orientation workshop in Santa Barbara (held each March and September) before enrolling. Students must also attend regional research sessions and academic seminars, held throughout the year in various parts of the country.

Coursework is competency-based, individualized, and accomplished through academic study, research, and practical field experience and training, according to an approved learning contract.

George Washington University

Nonresidential and low-residency programs in educational technology, health sciences, and project management.

GWTV – Distance Learning
801 22nd Street NW, Suite 350
Washington, DC 20052

Web site	www.gwu.edu/~distance
Email	webmaster@gwtv.gwu.edu
Telephone	(202) 994 8233
Fax	(202) 994 5048
Year established	1821
Ownership status	Nonprofit, independent
Residency	Short or no residency
Cost	High average
Degree level	Bachelor's, Master's
Fields of study or special interest	Educational technology, health sciences (with four specializations), project management
Other information	George Washington University offers a totally nonresident degree through its Graduate School of Education and Human Development: the M.A. in educational technology. Instruction takes place through a range of nontraditional learning methods including cable television, the Internet, and videocassettes.

For working professionals in health-related fields, a bachelor's program in health sciences is available with the following specializations: clinical health sciences, clinical management and leadership, clinical research administration, and EMS management. An M.S. in health sciences (specializing in clinical leadership) is also offered for certified Physician Assistants.

A low-residency M.S. in project management is also available. Students attend a one-week residency in Washington, DC, at the beginning of the program, and complete all remaining work via distance learning.

Georgia Institute of Technology

Technology-oriented degrees from a highly respected institution.

Center for Distance Learning
Atlanta, GA 30332

Web site	www.conted.gatech.edu/distance
Email	cdl@conted.gatech.edu
Telephone	(404) 894 8572
Fax	(404) 894 8924
Year established	1885
Ownership status	Nonprofit, state
Residency	None
Cost	Moderately high
Degree level	Master's
Fields of study or special interest	Engineering, health physics

Other information   Georgia Tech is one of the more highly respected schools of its kind in the United States and is consistently ranked as one of the top five engineering schools in the country by *U.S. News and World Report*. The Georgia Tech distance-learning program, started in 1977, is as rigorous as its on-campus counterpart, but the effort has been worth it for the many working professionals who have completed it. If you are interested, look into whether your company is one of the many that offer their employees tuition reimbursement plans.

The school's Internet-based instruction system allows people who are working in technological fields to earn an M.S. in electrical and computer engineering, environmental engineering, health physics, radiological engineering, industrial engineering, or mechanical engineering entirely through online courses (or videotaped classes that can be sent anywhere in the United States and, in some cases, to other countries as well).

Proctored examinations are required, and may be taken in a student's local area with a school-approved proctor supervising.

Goddard College

Student-designed bachelor's and master's degrees in a range of innovative fields.

123 Pitkin Road
Plainfield, VT 05667

Web site	www.goddard.edu
Email	admissions@goddard.edu
Telephone	(802) 454 8311
Year established	1938
Ownership status	Nonprofit, independent
Residency	Short (twice per year)
Cost	Average to moderately high, depending on program
Degree level	Bachelor's, Master's
Fields of study or special interest	Individualized, writing

Other information   Goddard has been a pioneer in nontraditional progressive education for more than 60 years. Students design an individualized B.A. or M.A. program in virtually any field based on a faculty-approved learning contract. Or they can follow a predesigned track in business and organizational leadership, education, feminist studies, literature and writing, natural and physical sciences, psychology and counseling, social and cultural studies, or visual and performing arts. An M.F.A. in writing is also available.

The first seven days of each semester are spent in residency, where the work of the coming semester is planned. Students may choose to do the majority of their coursework off campus if they maintain contact by mail every three weeks. Both bachelor's and master's programs require a minimum enrollment: two semesters for the bachelor's, three for the master's.

Students design their own course of study, which may involve research projects, reading assignments, various types of creative projects, a practicum and/or internship and, in the master's programs, a thesis or other major final project. The exact format is tailored to each student's individual needs. At the end of a planned course of study, the student and mentor meet to translate the student's accomplishments into course equivalents and to assign credits.

Credit is available for examinations and prior learning, although life-experience credit is only awarded at the undergraduate level. Students are expected to devote a minimum of 26 hours per week to their studies.

Foreign students are welcome.

Golden Gate University

Many online master's programs (and a bachelor's in public administration) delivered entirely over the Internet.

536 Mission Street
San Francisco, CA 94105

Web site	cybercampus.ggu.edu
Email	cybercampus@ggu.edu
Telephone	(415) 369 5250 • (888) 874 2923
Fax	(415) 227 4502
Year established	1901
Residency	None
Cost	High average
Degree level	Bachelor's, Master's
Fields of study or special interest	Accounting, business administration, healthcare administration, finance, financial planning, marketing, public administration, taxation, telecommunications management
Other information	Golden Gate University's CyberCampus delivers a number of degree programs entirely over the Internet. Courses are taught on a more or less open-ended (asynchronous) basis through study modules and interactive conferences.

Online master's degree programs are available in the above fields. Each program generally involves two to four years of part-time study.

The Bachelor of Public Administration (BPA) completion program is designed for students who have already completed two years (56 semester hours) of undergraduate coursework through another institution (traditionally or otherwise); the remaining two years are completed through GGU.

Undergraduate certificates are available in finance, financial planning, and technology management. Graduate certificates are available in accounting, arts administration, finance, financial planning, healthcare administration, information systems, marketing, and taxation. Each certificate involves four to six courses (12 to 18 semester hours) and takes an average of 18 months to complete.

Governors State University

Bachelor of Arts tailored to the individual interests of students, earned entirely through distance-learning methods.

BOG Program
University Park, IL 60466

Web site	www.govst.edu/bog
Email	gsubog@govst.edu
Telephone	(708) 534 4092 • (800) 478 8478
Fax	(708) 534 1645
Year established	1969
Ownership status	Nonprofit, state
Residency	None
Cost	Low average
Degree level	Bachelor's
Fields of study or special interest	Individualized major

Other information Governors State offers a B.A. in individualized studies through a nontraditional program designed to allow working adults with family and other responsibilities the chance to complete their degree requirements off campus. No majors are offered by the program.

A maximum of 105 of the required 120 credits can be transferred into the prorgam from regionally accredited institutions; up to 80 of these may be lower-level credits. Those credits may come from prior schooling, correspondence courses, life-experience learning (including but not limited to military and job-related training), and ACT, CLEP, and DANTES exams. The university stresses that skills and knowledge acquired by nonacademic means can be evaluated for academic credit.

The time to complete this degree depends on the amount of prior credit.

The credits earned at GSU must be completed with a final grade of C or higher. GSU offers over 50 media-based courses in a broad range of fields.

Harvard University

Over 600 correspondence and online courses in 50 fields of study can be applied towards Harvard Extension's liberal arts programs.

Division of Continuing Education
51 Brattle Street
Cambridge, MA 02138

Web site	extension.dce.harvard.edu
Email	ext@hudce.harvard.edu
Telephone	(617) 495 4024
Fax	(617) 495 0500
Year established	1636
Ownership status	Nonprofit, independent
Residency	Variable
Cost	Moderately high
Degree level	Associate's, Bachelor's, Master's
Fields of study or special interest	Information technology, liberal studies (with 19 specializations)
Other information	Harvard Extension, the continuing education program of one of the most prestigious universities in the United States, now offers associate's, bachelor's, and master's programs that can be completed largely through correspondence and online study; a growing number of certificate programs are also available.

The Associate in Arts, Bachelor of Liberal Arts, and Master of Liberal Arts in liberal studies is available with concentrations in the following fields: anthropology and archaeology, biology, Celtic languages and literatures, classical civilizations, dramatic arts, English and American literature and language, foreign literature and culture in translation, French language and literature, government, history, history of art and architecture, history of science, literature and creative writing, psychology, religion, Russian and East European studies, Spanish language, studio arts and film, and women's studies. The master's concludes with a thesis.

The Master of Liberal Arts in information technology, the most Internet-based of Harvard's programs, requires ten courses and a capstone software project.

Graduate certificates are available in administration and management, applied sciences, museum studies, public health, publishing and communications, and technologies of education.

The number of courses that must be taken on campus in Cambridge varies by program. While it doesn't appear possible to complete an entire degree program through distance learning just yet, online offerings are numerous and growing.

Henley Management College

Largely nonresident graduate degrees in business administration and project management, geared to experienced managers, from a respected British school.

Greenlands
Henley-on-Thames
Oxfordshire RG9 3AU
United Kingdom

Web site	www.henleymc.ac.uk
Email	enquiries@henleymc.ac.uk
Telephone	+44 (1491) 571 454
Fax	+44 (1491) 571 635
Year established	1945
Ownership status	Nonprofit, independent
Residency	Periodic weekend residencies
Cost	Variable
Degree level	Master's, Doctorates
Fields of study or special interest	Business administration, project management

Other information   Henley bills itself as the oldest independent management college in Europe. It has about 7,000 distance-learning MBA students in some 80 countries.

The MBA program is delivered through a range of methods, including printed correspondence texts and courses prepared by and for the institution, interactive online workshops (using Lotus Notes), and local tutorial support (offered at many locations in the U.K. and abroad). The program's stated objective is "to help students to develop their management skills and self-awareness to enable them to gain an in-depth knowledge of how organizations operate and how they can function most effectively to achieve their goals." Three years of relevant managerial experience is required for admission to the course of study. Generally, a residential weekend is required every six months; international students may group their residencies into week-long blocks. The program takes three years to complete, and requires a substantial master's dissertation (thesis of about 15,000 words). Specializations in project management and telecommunications are available.

In recent years, Henley has also added a DBA that can be completed in a low-residency mode. Students must attend an annual residential study week at one of the school's centers in the U.K., France, or Singapore.

Heriot-Watt University

International MBA from a respected British university entirely through home study and proctored examinations—no entrance exams or bachelor's degree required for admission. Also offers a bachelor's in management and a diploma in malting and brewing.

FTKnowledge, Inc.
Student Services
2 World Trade Center, Suite 1700
New York, NY 10048

Web site	www.hwmba.edu
Email	info@hwmba.edu
Telephone	(212) 390 5030 • (800) 622 9661
Fax	(212) 344 3469
Year established	1821
Ownership status	Nonprofit, state
Residency	None
Cost	Average to high average
Degree level	Bachelor's, Master's
Fields of study or special interest	Business administration, malting and brewing, management
Other information	Heriot-Watt offers the only internationally recognized MBA program that explicitly does not require a bachelor's degree and can be done entirely by home study and proctored examinations. With more than 8,000 students in over 120 countries (including more than 4,000 students in the U.S. and Canada), it is by far the largest MBA program in the world. The only requirement for earning the degree is passing nine rigorous three-hour examinations, one for each of the required nine courses (marketing, economics, accounting, finance, strategic planning, etc.) The exams are given four times per year on hundreds of college campuses worldwide (some 100 in the U.S. and Canada).

Students buy the courses one or more at a time, as they are ready for them. The courses consist of looseleaf textbooks (average 500 pages) written by prominent professors specifically for this program. Courses are not interactive and there are no papers to write, quizzes, or other assignments, and no thesis or capstone project. Each course averages about 160 hours of study time. The entire MBA can technically be completed in a year, although 18 to 36 months is more common.

A bachelor's in management, available through a similar examination-based model, is also available, as is a postgraduate diploma in malting and brewery. For more information on the malting and brewery program, contact Heriot-Watt directly at Heriot-Watt University, Edinburgh EH14 4AS, Scotland (*www.hw.ac.uk*).

Heriot-Watt University has a 350-acre campus in Edinburgh, Scotland, with more than 10,000 on-campus students pursuing bachelor's, master's, and doctorates in many scientific, technical, and business fields.

Indiana University

Two flexible bachelor's programs and four master's programs entirely by distance learning.

School of Continuing Studies
Owen Hall 001
Bloomington, IN 47405

Web site	scs.indiana.edu
Email	scs@indiana.edu
Telephone	(812) 855 8995 • (800) 334 1011
Fax	(812) 855 8997
Year established	1912
Ownership status	Nonprofit, state
Residency	None
Cost	Average
Degree level	Bachelor's, Master's
Fields of study or special interest	Adult education, general studies, labor studies, language and literacy education, nursing, therapeutic recreation
Other information	Indiana University offers the Bachelor of General Studies entirely through nonresidential study. This is an interdisciplinary program in which students study several fields of knowledge, including the humanities, social studies, natural sciences, and behavioral sciences. It is possible to specialize in one field as a concentration within the general studies major. The average student takes four to six years to complete this degree, but it can be done more quickly if the student has substantial prior credit. Of the 120 semester units required for the degree, 90 can be transfer units. The remaining 30 must be earned through Indiana University, usually online or by correspondence. One quarter of the units earned must be upper division (junior or senior level). Transfer credit is awarded for prior schooling, including correspondence courses, military and other noncollegiate training, a range of proficiency exams, and life-experience learning. Indiana offers a course that assists students in developing a life-experience portfolio. Persons over 21 years of age without a high school diploma (or equivalent) may be admitted provided that they can show a "fair prospect of success." A B.S. in labor studies is also available.
	Master's programs are available in adult education, language and literacy education, nursing (B.S. in nursing required), and therapeutic recreation.

ISIM University

Master's degrees in business administration (MBA), information management, and information technology, earned entirely over the Internet.

501 South Cherry Street
Room 350 – Admissions Office
Denver, CO 80246

Web site	www.isimu.edu
Email	admissions@isimu.edu
Telephone	(303) 333 4224 • (800) 441 4746
Fax	(303) 336 1144
Year established	1987
Ownership status	Proprietary
Residency	None
Cost	Average
Degree level	Master's
Fields of study or special interest	Business administration, information management, information technology

Other information This school offers an MBA and M.S.'s in information management and information technology. Education takes place via ISIM's "electronic campus"—instructor-guided learning that uses the school's interactive virtual classroom, accessible through the Internet.

ISIM has won numerous awards from the United States Distance Learning Association (USDLA) for their graduate degree courses.

ISIM requires the following for admission into their programs: a bachelor's degree from an accredited or good state-approved institution, a resumé demonstrating professional accomplishments, a goals statement, transcripts indicating undergraduate and/or postgraduate work, three letters of recommendation, and a $75 application fee.

A maximum of 15 credits out of a total of 36 can be earned through a combination of transfer credits, credit by examination, or prior experience. A capstone project is required of every student. The average student takes two years to complete an ISIM master's program. No financial aid is available. Foreign students are welcome.

ISIM University's accreditation comes from the Distance Education and Training Council (DETC). ISIM, formerly known as the International School of Information Management, is a division of Cardean University, a subsidiary of UNext.com (a large education corporation).

Jones International University

Nonresidential bachelor's and master's programs from the first virtual university to gain U.S. regional accreditation.

9697 East Mineral Avenue
Englewood, CO 80112

Web site	www.international.edu
Email	info@international.edu
Telephone	(303) 784 8045 • (800) 811 5663
Fax	(303) 784 8547
Year established	1995
Ownership status	Proprietary
Residency	None
Cost	High average
Degree level	Bachelor's, Master's
Fields of study or special interest	Business administration, business communication
Other information	In 1999, Jones International University became the first completely "virtual" (online) university to be accredited by one of the six U.S. regional accrediting agencies. There is no traditional campus. All discussions, interactions, lectures, and assignments are conducted over the Internet. No face-to-face, telephone, fax, or "snail mail" interaction is necessary.

Jones offers an online MBA, as well as online B.A. and M.A. degrees in business communication. Certificates are also available in global communication, Internet-based education, leadership and communication skills, new communication technologies, and public relations and marketing.

Jones was formerly known as International University, which in turn was originally International University College.

Judson College

Nonresidential bachelor's degrees in a dozen different fields from a venerable Southern women's college.

302 Bibb Street
Marion, AL 36756

Web site	www.judson.edu
Email	adultstudies@future.judson.edu
Telephone	(334) 683 5169 • (800) 447 9472
Fax	(334) 683 5147
Year established	1838
Ownership status	Nonprofit, church
Residency	None
Cost	Average
Degree level	Bachelor's
Fields of study or special interest	Business administration, criminal justice, elementary education, English, history, management information systems, music, music education, psychology, religious education, secondary education
Other information	This Baptist women's college offers entirely nonresident bachelor's degrees to women age 22 and older. Students may choose a major in one of the fields listed above; alternately, an individualized track allows the student (with faculty approval) to major in any field she chooses. Individualized study programs are based on learning contracts between the student and the school. The learning contract details the learning to be accomplished and how that learning will be accomplished.

Of the 128 hours required for the bachelor's degree, 32 hours must be completed through Judson (residentially, nonresidentially, or through faculty-designed proficiency examinations). Up to 96 hours of credit may be awarded for work done at other schools, ACE military recommendations, prior life-experience learning, and standard equivalency examinations (CLEP and College Board AP exams).

Full-time students with prior credits can finish in two to three years; part-time students generally take longer. Student services include academic advising and assistance with state and federal financial aid procedures.

Foreign students are not eligible for this program.

Kansas State University

Totally nonresident bachelor's and master's programs from a large state university.

13 College Court
Manhattan, KS 66506

Web site	www.dce.ksu.edu
Email	info@dce.ksu.edu
Telephone	(785) 532 5686 • (800) 622 2578
Fax	(785) 532 5637
Year established	1863
Ownership status	Nonprofit, state
Residency	None for most programs; short for some master's programs (see below)
Cost	Average
Degree level	Bachelor's, Master's
Fields of study or special interest	Agribusiness, animal sciences and industry, business, chemical engineering, civil engineering, electrical engineering, engineering management, family financial planning, food science and industry, industrial/organizational psychology, interdisciplinary social science, software engineering

Other information

Kansas State offers four bachelor's-degree completion programs: the B.S. in interdisciplinary social science, the B.S. in animal sciences and industry, the B.S. in food science and industry, and the B.S. in business. Applicants to the social science, food science, or animal science programs must already have earned at least 60 semester hours from an accredited institution that can be applied towards the degree. Applicants to the business degree program must have earned at least 45 hours of general credit courses, and must possess a 2.5 GPA. Assessment of prior learning is available after acceptance into the program. Credit is awarded for military experience and a wide range of equivalency examinations. Students must earn at least 30 KSU credits after acceptance into the program. Courses are delivered by videotape, audiocassette, print, CD-ROM, and the Internet. Foreign students are admitted provided that they live in the U.S., though they must provide evidence of English fluency.

The Master in Agribusiness (MAB) takes place largely over the Internet, with two 1-week residential sessions required each year. The M.S. in industrial and organizational psychology involves Internet coursework, two 2-week summer residencies, and a guided capstone practicum. The M.S. in family financial planning, approved by the Certified Financial Planner (CFP) Board of Standards, can be completed entirely online; the program generally takes about three years of part-time study. The master's programs in engineering-related fields—engineering management, software engineering, chemical engineering, and civil engineering—can be completed entirely nonresidentially through a mix of online classes and videocourses.

For Kansas residents only, an online bachelor's completion program in early childhood education is also available.

Laurentian University

Canada's largest bilingual distance-education provider offers nonresidential bachelor's degrees, an M.A. in humanities, and certificate programs in a variety of fields.

Centre for Continuing Education
935 Ramsey Lake Road
Sudbury, Ontario P3E 2C6
Canada

Web site	www.laurentian.ca
Email	cce_l@nickel.laurentian.ca
Telephone	+1 (705) 673 6569
Fax	+1 (705) 675 4897
Year established	1913
Ownership status	Nonprofit
Residency	None
Cost	Average to high average
Degree level	Bachelor's, Master's
Fields of study or special interest	Family life studies and human sexuality, gerontology, liberal science, Native studies, nursing, psychology, religious studies, social work (Native human services), sociology, women's studies
Other information	Established in 1913 as a Jesuit institution (later adopted by an interdenominational coalition), this bilingual English-French university offers entire bachelor's degree programs, bachelor's completion programs, and certificates entirely through online study and correspondence. In addition to its English-French support, Laurentian maintains a commitment to become a "trilingual" institution through special courses designed for speakers of First Nation languages.

B.A. programs are available in gerontology, Native studies, psychology, religious studies, sociology, and women's studies. Bachelor's completion programs are available in social work (with emphasis in Native human services), nursing (for registered nurses), and liberal science. Certificate programs are available in family life and sexuality and in gerontology.

The Laurentian M.A. in humanities is conducted via two-way audio and/or video technology, and may soon be available entirely via the Internet.

U.S. and Canadian residents are eligible for Laurentian's distance-learning programs, and residents of other countries may be accepted on a case-by-case basis.

Murdoch University

This large Australian university offers nonresidential bachelor's and master's programs to students worldwide.

External Studies Unit
90 South Street
Murdoch, WA 6150
Australia

Web site	www.murdoch.edu.au
Email	p_martin@cleo.murdoch.edu.au
Telephone	+61 (8) 9360 2498
Year established	1973
Ownership status	Nonprofit, state
Residency	Short or no residency
Cost	Low average
Degree level	Bachelor's, Master's
Fields of study or special interest	See below

Other information Murdoch University offers many bachelor's and master's programs through a mix of correspondence and online classes. Some (most notably engineering and health programs) generally require short on-campus workshop sessions, but these may sometimes be negotiated.

B.A. programs are available in Aboriginal and Islander studies, Asian studies, communication studies, education, English and comparative literature, general studies, history, philosophy, politics and international relations, theology, and women's studies. B.S. programs are available in applied computational physics, chemistry, computer science, education, environmental science, general studies, mathematics and statistics, mineral science (emphasis in extractive metallurgy), and sustainable development. A B.Ed. is available with emphasis in primary or secondary education. Bachelor's programs of various other denominations are available in applied science, computer studies, development studies, ecological public health, ecologically sustainable development, economics, education studies (with optional emphasis in teaching languages other than English), engineering, environmental impact assessment, environmental science, policy studies (specializing in city, public, or science and technology policy), professional studies, renewable energy technology, social research and evaluation, sociology, software engineering, telecommunications management, and theology (Th.B.).

Master's programs are available in Asian studies, city policy, development studies, ecological public health, ecologically sustainable development, education (M.Ed.) with emphasis in primary or secondary education, environmental science, renewable energy technology, science and technology policy, software engineering (M.Eng.), telecommunications management, and veterinary studies (emphasis in small animal medicine).

A number of certificate and diploma programs are also available in the fields listed above.

Murray State University

Bachelor of Independent Studies with one day of residency, and a master's for registered nurses through satellite programs.

P.O. Box 9
Murray, KY 42071

Web site	www.mursuky.edu
Email	marla.poyner@murraystate.edu
Telephone	(270) 762 5322 • (800) 669 7654
Year established	1922
Ownership status	Nonprofit, state
Residency	Minimum of one day for bachelor's program
Cost	Low average
Degree level	Bachelor's, Master's
Fields of study or special interest	Independent studies, nursing

Other information Murray State offers a Bachelor of Independent Studies through a range of methods including online study, correspondence, television, contract learning courses, and traditional classes. Some evening and weekend classes are also available. All distance-learning students must attend a day-long seminar, held on Saturdays in April, August, and December. Admission to the program is based on satisfactory completion of the seminar. All students must earn credit in basic skills, humanities, science, social sciences, and electives, and complete a senior thesis. The school feels that it is best suited to adults who are already established in their field.

Students must take 32 of the 128 required semester hours through Murray State. Credit is awarded for military and other prior learning (Murray State charges a relatively low fee for portfolio assessment), as well as CLEP, College Board, and DANTES exams. In addition, departmental challenge exams are available in some fields; if the exam is passed, credit is awarded.

Murray State also offers an MSN for registered nurses who already have a B.S. in nursing. Courses are delivered by remote television to three sites within a 100-mile radius of the campus.

Financial aid, academic advising, and job placement assistance are offered. Students living outside of the United States are not admitted.

Naropa University

Low-residency master's programs in contemplative education and transpersonal studies, a certificate in ecopsychology, and a variety of online graduate-level courses in creative writing from an established university with a strong progressive history.

2130 Arapahoe Avenue
Boulder, CO 80302

Web site	www.ecampus.naropa.edu
Email	admissions@naropa.edu
Telephone	(303) 444 0202
Fax	(303) 444 0410
Ownership status	Nonprofit, independent
Residency	10–14 day annual summer residency
Cost	High average
Degree level	Master's
Fields of study or special interest	Contemplative education, ecopsychology, transpersonal studies
Other information	Beginning fall 2001, Naropa University offers the M.A. in contemplative education and the M.A. in transpersonal studies through a low-residency format. Students complete coursework through online study and attend a yearly two-week summer residency in Boulder. Each program can be completed in about three years of serious part-time study.

A certificate in ecopsychology is also available through online study. Although at the present time students are still required to complete a few intensive classes on campus, it is expected that all required courses for this program will eventually be available online.

Naropa has announced that it is taking distance education very seriously. A vast number of graduate-level courses are available online (including some introductory classes on the Tibetan language), and it seems likely that more degree and certificate programs will become available over the next several years.

We have heard rumors that Naropa's Jack Kerouac School of Disembodied Poetics may eventually adapt its M.F.A. program to a low-residency format, and judging by the number of courses in this field now available online it looks as though a substantial portion of the program can already be completed off campus. Contact the school for details.

National Technological University

Nonresidential master's programs in many technology-related and management-related fields, earned entirely through online study or televised courses.

700 Centre Avenue
Fort Collins, CO 80526

Web site	www.ntu.edu
Email	admissions@mail.ntu.edu
Telephone	(970) 495 6400 • (800) 582 9976
Fax	(970) 484 0668
Year established	1984
Ownership status	Nonprofit, independent
Residency	None
Degree level	Master's
Cost	High average
Fields of study or special interest	Business administration, chemical engineering, computer engineering, computer science, electrical engineering, engineering management, environmental systems management, individualized major, information systems, international business, management of technology, manufacturing systems engineering, materials science and engineering, mechanical engineering, optical science, project management, software engineering, systems engineering
Other information	NTU offers a wide range of graduate courses and noncredit courses in technological subjects, transmitted by satellite digital compressed video from 46 university campuses (in locations from Alaska to Florida) to corporate, government, community, and university worksites. Working professionals and technical managers may take the classes, often in "real time" (as they are being taught on the campuses), with telephone, fax, and email links to the classrooms. NTU offers master's programs using this approach in all of the fields listed above.

Furthermore, it is now possible to complete an M.S. in computer engineering, computer science, software engineering, or systems engineering entirely through online study without relying on the telecourse network.

No credit is awarded for any prior learning, traditional or nontraditional. Geared toward working professionals and managers, all studies are conducted on a part-time basis. The degree is awarded after completion of 30 to 45 credit hours depending on the program of study; this generally takes about three years.

Foreign students are admitted.

New Jersey Institute of Technology

Bachelor's and master's programs in IT fields entirely through distance learning.

Office of Distance Learning
University Heights, NJ 07102

Web site	www.njit.edu
Email	dl@njit.edu
Telephone	(973) 596 3177 • (800) 624 9850
Fax	(973) 596 3203
Year established	1881
Ownership status	Nonprofit, state
Residency	None
Cost	High
Degree level	Bachelor's, Master's
Fields of study or special interest	Computer science, engineering management, information systems
Other information	New Jersey Institute of Technology offers bachelor's programs in computer science and information systems, as well as master's programs in computer science, engineering management, and information systems. Study takes place through a variety of media including online conferencing, videocassette-based study, telephone, and fax. Students must have Internet access. Distance students study on the same schedule as on-campus students. Examinations can be administered in remote locations through an approved proctor.
	New Jersey Institute of Technology also offers graduate certificate programs that can be applied directly to the appropriate master's degree upon completion. Most of these programs (including computer networking, e-commerce, object-oriented design, practice of technical communications, project management, and telecommunications networking) can be taken in part or wholly by distance learning.
	A noncredit webmaster certification program is also available, and can be completed entirely through online study.

Northwood University

Bachelor's in management with several concentrations, with only two 3-day seminars required on campus.

University College
4000 Whiting Drive
Midland, MI 48640

Web site	www.northwood.edu
Email	uc@northwood.edu
Telephone	(517) 837 4411 • (800) 445 5873
Fax	(517) 837 4600
Year established	1959
Ownership status	Nonprofit, independent
Residency	Six days total
Cost	Average
Degree level	Bachelor's
Fields of study or special interest	Management (automotive management, computer science, marketing)

Other information Northwood University is a private, not-for-profit, professional school of management. Through its University College, it offers a B.S. in management that can be completed entirely by distance learning. Targeted to students 25 years of age and older, the college tailors the program to suit individual student needs. Pre-approved specializations are available in automotive management, computer science, and marketing.

The school has campuses and outreach centers in Midland, MI; Cedar Hills (Dallas), TX; and West Palm Beach, FL. Additional outreach centers are located in Carlsbad, NM; Indianapolis, IN; Chicago, IL; Lansing, MI; Fort Worth, TX; Louisville, KY; Detroit, MI; New Orleans, LA; Flint, MI; Selfridge ANG Base, MI; and Tampa, FL.

Students who cannot attend class at any of the outreach centers may complete coursework through correspondence or online study. Two 3-day seminars on campus are required, and students must complete an oral/written comprehensive examination.

Norwich University

Mentor-based degrees from one of the oldest nontraditional programs in North America.

Vermont College
College Street
Montpelier, VT 05602

Web site	www.norwich.edu/vermontcollege
Email	vcadmis@norwich.edu
Telephone	(802) 828 8500 • (800) 336 6794
Fax	(802) 828 8855
Year established	1834
Ownership status	Nonprofit, independent
Residency	Short residency
Cost	High average
Degree level	Bachelor's, Master's
Fields of study or special interest	Art therapy, education (individualized specialization), individualized major, visual arts, writing, writing for children

Other information Vermont College of Norwich University offers several of the oldest external degree programs in North America for adult learners. Based on the mentor system used at Oxford and other European universities, students work one-on-one with a faculty member to design a program of study to meet their unique learning needs and professional goals.

The adult degree program (B.A.), begun in 1963, features nine-day residencies at the beginning of each six-month semester, or one weekend residency each month, alternating with home study. Another undergraduate option—the New College B.A.—is a one-on-one mentored program with one 1-week and two 2-week residencies each year.

The individualized graduate program, started in 1969, offers self-designed studies in the humanities, arts, education, and social sciences (including psychology and counseling). Regional meetings with program faculty are held quarterly or monthly; students who prefer not to attend regional meetings may choose an online option wherein the student must attend an initial five-day colloquium, but may complete the rest of the program entirely nonresidentially. Students work with two advisors: a core faculty member who is responsible for a geographical region of the country and a field advisor who is a local expert in the student's field of study.

The M.A. in art therapy is a 15-month program that includes summer residencies in Vermont. M.F.A. programs in music performance, writing, writing for children, and visual arts are also available. The program in music performance involves short, intensive summer and winter residency sessions alternating with six-month nonresident study projects; the M.F.A. programs in writing and visual arts are offered through off-campus arrangements with nine-day residencies required twice per year.

Finally, there's a program designed for "traditional age" students that combines brief on-campus stays with off-campus travel, internships, and relevant jobs. Each student is given a notebook computer, and she stays in touch with a faculty member and other students via the Internet.

Nova Southeastern University

Nontraditional bachelor's, master's, and doctorates in a wide range of fields, designed for working adults.

3301 College Avenue
Fort Lauderdale, FL 33314

Web site	www.nova.edu
Email	cwis@nova.edu
Telephone	(954) 262 8500 • (800) 541 6682
Year established	1964
Ownership status	Nonprofit, independent
Residency	Varies by program
Cost	High average
Degree level	Bachelor's, Master's, Doctorates
Fields of study or special interest	See below
Other information	Class schedules, research requirements, and residency requirements vary by program; in general, required research activities emphasize direct application to the workplace. Classes are taught by Nova Southeastern University full-time faculty, and part-time faculty from institutions around the country.

At the bachelor's level, B.S. completion programs, consisting of online study supplemented with intensive seminars, are available in professional studies and education (with emphasis in early childhood education, elementary education, exceptional education, middle school science, or secondary education).

At the master's level, most programs require some residency in the form of cluster groups; others (most notably those offered through the School of Computer and Information Sciences) can be completed entirely through online study. Programs are as follows: Master of Accounting, MBA (with emphasis in finance, management information systems, or marketing), Master of Medical Science, and M.S. degrees in child and youth studies, computer information systems, computer science, computing technology in education, curriculum instruction and technology, dispute resolution, educational media, education with emphasis in teaching in learning, instructional technology and distance education, management and administration of educational programs, management information systems, and social studies education.

Nova Southeastern University also offers some of the more nontraditional doctoral programs ever to achieve regional accreditation. The typical student attends one group meeting each month (generally two or three days in duration), plus two 1-week residential sessions, and from three to six practicums, which emphasize direct application of research to the workplace. Total time: about three and a half years. A major part of instruction in these programs is through teleconferencing and Web-based study. Residential work is available in 23 states. Nova will consider offering the program anywhere in the continental United States where a cluster of 20–25 students can be formed. Ed.D. programs are available in computing technology in education and educational leadership. Ph.D. programs are available in child and youth studies, computer information systems, computer sciences, computing technology in education, dispute resolution, information science, information systems, instructional technology and distance education, occupational therapy, and physical therapy. The degrees of Doctor of Occupational Therapy and Doctor of Physical Therapy are also available.

Formerly Nova University, they merged with Southeastern Medical School (hence the name change).

Ohio University

A quite inexpensive Bachelor of Specialized Studies entirely through home study.

External Student Program
301 Tupper Hall
Athens, OH 45701

Web site   www.cats.ohiou.edu

Email   external.student@ohiou.edu

Telephone   (740) 593 2150 • (800) 444 2420

Fax   (740) 593 0452

Year established   1804

Ownership status   Nonprofit, state

Residency   None

Cost index   Low average

Degree level   Bachelor's, Master's

Fields of study or special interest   Specialized studies, business administration

Other information   This extremely flexible self-paced program leads to a Bachelor of Specialized Studies (B.S.S.) that can easily be earned entirely through nonresidential study. Students define their own subject areas and design their own interdisciplinary degrees.

Credit towards the degree can come from portfolio assessment of military and other noncollegiate learning experiences, correspondence courses, independent study projects, and CLEP exams. For many correspondence courses, you can take the examination only; if you pass, a grade is given for the course. These exams can be administered anywhere in the world but must be supervised by an Ohio University–approved proctor. A maximum of 144 quarter hours can be transferred into the program from prior schooling or the above sources; 48 credits must be completed after enrolling at Ohio.

The External Student Program provides an advising service, including some career counseling, and also acts as a liaison in dealing with other university offices.

The university also offers a college program for the incarcerated at unusually low cost.

Foreign students are admitted but must be fluent in English in order to successfully complete coursework.

An MBA is also available through a mix of extension coursework and week-long intensive sessions on campus.

Open University

Nonresident degrees at all levels from one of the largest nontraditional programs in the world.

Walton Hall
Milton Keynes MK7 6AA
United Kingdom

Web site	www.open.ac.uk
Email	ces-gen@open.ac.uk
Telephone	+44 (1908) 274 066
Fax	+44 (1908) 653 744
Year established	1969
Ownership status	Nonprofit, state
Residency	None
Cost	Low average
Degree level	Bachelor's, Master's, Doctorates, Law
Fields of study or special interest	Arts, business, computing, education, health and social welfare, languages, law, mathematics, social science, technology

Other information   Established in 1969, the Open University is now one of the largest distance education institutions in the world. There are currently 200,000 undergraduate students registered, as well as some 9,000 higher degree students. Similar ventures around the globe now model themselves on this highly successful educational experiment.

As at other British universities, the earning of credit is based entirely on a combination of achieving a specified level of continuous assessment and passing the course examination. Open University students study in their own homes and on their own schedules, using correspondence texts, audio- and videocassettes, and sometimes online supplementary material. Study can lead to a degree, certificate, or diploma.

Some courses have week-long summer schools or weekend residential schools, and some require that the applicant be a resident of the UK or other European country.

The Open University has recently established an autonomous branch in the U.S., the United States Open University, which has (as of press time) achieved candidacy status for regional accreditation. Degrees offered through this initiative include both bachelor's degrees (in business administration, computing, English, European studies, humanities, information technology, international studies, liberal arts, and social sciences) and master's degrees (an MBA and an M.S. in computing). For more information on the United States Open University, visit its Web site at *www.open.edu* or call toll-free: (800) 232 7705.

Open University and Open College

Associate's, bachelor's, and certificate programs available worldwide through British Columbia's Open Learning Agency.

Open Learning Agency
4355 Mathissi Place
Burnaby, BC V5G 4S8
Canada

Web site	www.ola.bc.ca
Email	olainfo@ola.bc.ca
Telephone	+1 (604) 431 3000 • (800) 663 1663
Fax	+1 (604) 431 3333
Year established	1978
Ownership status	Nonprofit
Residency	None
Cost	Average
Degree level	Associate's, Bachelor's
Fields of study or special interest	See below

Other information Canada's Open Learning Agency offers a number of associate's, bachelor's, certificate, and diploma programs to students worldwide, and additional programs for Canadian residents. Coursework is delivered via online instruction, computer conferencing, videocassettes, televised classes, printed materials, telephone, and video. Degrees are offered through the Open Learning Agency's Open University, while certificates and diplomas are offered through its Open College.

Bachelor's degrees are available worldwide in the following fields: business administration (with optional emphasis in public sector management through a program offered in cooperation with the University of Victoria), chemical science, earth science, engineering science, English, general science, general studies, history, life science, mathematics, psychology, physical science, and sociology.

Additional bachelor's degrees are available to Canadian residents: fine arts, health science (emphasis physiotherapy, psychiatric nursing, or respiratory nursing), and music (emphasis jazz or performance).

Certificate programs are available in business skills, computer programming, database administration, general studies, home support attendant training, information technology management, management studies, network specialist training, nurse refresher training, office skills, practical nurse refresher training, solution developer training (IT-oriented), and workplace leadership foundations. Diploma programs are available in general studies and management studies.

Formerly British Columbia Open University.

Prescott College

Low-residency bachelor's and master's programs in many fields through individualized, mentored study.

220 Grove Avenue
Prescott, AZ 86301

Web site	www.prescott.edu
Email	admissions@prescott.edu
Telephone	(520) 778 2090 • (800) 628 6364
Fax	(613) 533 6805
Year established	1966
Ownership status	Nonprofit, independent
Residency	Occasional weekends
Cost	High average
Degree level	Bachelor's, Master's
Fields of study or special interest	Adventure education, counseling and psychology, education, environmental studies, human services, humanities, liberal arts, management

Other information   Prescott's external undergraduate program offers a student-centered, independent-study format, using instructors from the student's home community. Students normally take two courses every three months, meeting weekly with local mentors wherever they live (Prescott helps locate them). Students must come to the college for a three-day weekend orientation at the beginning of their program, and for an additional liberal arts seminar, also held over a three-day weekend. The B.A. is available in counseling, human services, liberal arts, management, and teacher education.

Entering students normally have at least 30 semester hours (or 45 quarter hours) of prior college work. Credit for life experience can be awarded through the writing of a life-experience portfolio; credit can also be earned through CLEP exams.

Student-directed master's programs are offered in adventure education, counseling and psychology, education, environmental studies, and humanities. Two weekend residencies are required each term.

The school's Center for Indian Bilingual Teacher Education serves the needs of Native American students. Foreign students are accepted under some circumstances.

Queens University

Bachelor of Arts in quite a few fields through a major Canadian university, based entirely on correspondence and online study.

99 University Avenue
Kingston, ON K7L 3N6
Canada

Web site	www.queensu.ca/pts
Email	cds@post.queensu.ca
Telephone	+1 (613) 533 2471
Fax	+1 (613) 533 6805
Year established	1841
Ownership status	Nonprofit, state
Residency	None
Cost	Low average
Degree level	Bachelor's
Fields of study or special interest	German, history, political studies, psychology; other majors available on a rotating basis (see below)

Other information Queens University is one of the most respected Canadian universities. The school offers students in Canada and other countries a B.A. through distance education with a concentration in German, history, political studies, or psychology. Curricula for these programs consist of 15 courses that can be completed entirely through correspondence or via online study. Students submit assignments for grading throughout the course of the class and then take final examinations under supervision at various centers worldwide.

In the past, it has been possible to complete programs in English and women's studies entirely through correspondence or online study; available majors rotate periodically based on the number of courses available in a specific field. Required coursework for other concentrations not listed here might be fulfilled through residential study and/or transfer credit from Queens-approved courses taken through other universities. Contact the school for details.

Regent University

Master's and doctoral programs through online study and short residencies, plus the first ABA-accredited distance-learning law program of any kind.

Distance Education Program
1000 Regent University Drive
Virginia Beach, VA 23464-9800

Web site	www.regent.edu
Email	admissions@regent.edu
Telephone	(757) 226 4127 • (800) 373 5504
Fax	(757) 424 7051
Year established	1977
Ownership status	Nonprofit, independent
Residency	Short or no residency
Cost	High average
Degree level	Master's, Doctorates, Law
Fields of study or special interest	Business administration, communication, computer-mediated communication, education, educational leadership and Christian schools, international tax law, journalism, management, organizational leadership, political management, public administration, public policy

Other information   Founded by the Rev. Pat Robertson as CBN (Christian Broadcasting Network) University in 1977, Regent University offers an array of low-residency graduate programs conducted almost entirely through online study. The university integrates traditional Judeo-Christian ethical principles in the teaching of each course. Student support services available to nontraditional students include academic advising, career counseling, financial aid, tutoring, and job placement assistance.

Regent School of Business offers an MBA and M.A. in management largely through online study, with a two-and-a-half-day residency required at the beginning of each term.

Regent's School of Government offers M.S. programs in public policy, political management, and public administration, conducted largely online and supplemented by annual two-week residencies.

M.A. programs in communication studies (with optional emphasis on computer-mediated communication), journalism, and organizational leadership can be completed entirely through online study with no required annual residency sessions. M.A. programs in biblical studies and practical theology begin with a nine-day colloquium, and the remaining work takes place online.

M.Ed. programs are also available in Christian school administration and educational leadership; students complete requirements online during the school year, then attend Regent for annual summer residency sessions.

The Regent University School of Law offers an LL.M. in international taxation that can be completed mostly through online study; this is, to our knowledge, the first low-residency degree of any kind to be offered through a law school accredited by the American Bar Association (ABA).

Ph.D. programs in communication and organizational leadership are conducted largely online, supplemented by annual two- to four-week summer residencies.

Regis University

This Jesuit school offers several bachelor's and master's programs entirely through online study, including an M.S. in computer information systems that was designed in consultation with Sun Microsystems.

3333 Regis Boulevard
Denver, CO 80221

Web site www.regis.edu

Email regisadm@regis.edu

Telephone (303) 458 4900

Year established 1877

Ownership status Nonprofit, church

Residency None

Cost High average

Degree level Bachelor's, Master's

Fields of study or special interest Business administration, computer information systems, insurance, nonprofit management

Other information Regis University's School for Professional Studies is a nationally acclaimed adult learning program serving over 11,000 students. The Regis MBA, probably the most well known of its distance-learning programs, can be completed entirely online.

The Regis B.S. completion program in business management (with emphasis in insurance) is designed for students who have already completed a substantial amount of college work; all degree requirements can be completed through online study.

The M.S. in computer information systems, designed in consultation with Sun Microsystems, addresses cutting-edge issues relevant to the IT industry. Students may choose to specialize in databases, networking, or object-oriented technologies. The program is completed entirely through online study.

The Master of Nonprofit Management is tailored specifically to those who work for, within, or on behalf of nonprofit organizations. The program may be completed by online study or, if the student prefers, through video-based coursework.

Rensselaer Polytechnic Institute

Master's and certificate programs in many business, engineering, and technology fields, available online and through video-based study.

Professional and Distance Education
CII Suite 4011
110 8th Street
Troy, NY 12180-3590

Web site	www.rsvp.rpi.edu
Email	rsvp@rpi.edu
Telephone	(518) 276 7787
Fax	(518) 276 8026
Year established	1824
Ownership status	Nonprofit, independent
Residency	None
Cost	High average
Degree level	Master's
Fields of study or special interest	Business, engineering, technology
Other information	Rensselaer Polytechnic Institute offers a number of degree programs and certificates by distance learning through the RSVP program. Students may complete degree requirements online or through videocourses on an individual basis, or through two-way streaming video at corporate sites.

Master's degrees are available in business administration (MBA), computer science, computer and systems engineering, electrical engineering (emphasis microelectronics), electric power engineering, management of technology, manufacturing systems engineering, microelectronics manufacturing engineering, industrial and management engineering (emphasis quality engineering or service systems), information technology, management, mechanical engineering, and technical communication. Each master's program involves three to five years of part-time study.

Graduate level certificate programs are available in bioinformatics, computer graphics and data visualization, computer networks, computer science, database systems design, electric power engineering, graphical user interfaces, human-computer interaction, management and technology, manufacturing systems engineering, mechanical engineering, microelectronics manufacturing engineering, microelectronics technology and design, quality and reliability, service systems, software engineering, and technical program management for commercial business. Each certificate program involves four courses; an average student can complete such a program in two years of part-time study.

Rochester Institute of Technology

Nonresident bachelor's, master's, and certificate programs in professional, technical, and health-related fields from a 172-year-old school.

91 Lomb Memorial Drive
Rochester, NY 14623-5603

Web site	distancelearning.rit.edu
Email	online@rit.edu
Telephone	(716) 475 5089 • (800) 225 5748
Fax	(716) 475 5077
Year established	1829
Ownership status	Nonprofit, independent
Residency	None or short
Cost	High average
Degree level	Bachelor's, Master's
Fields of study or special interest	See below

Other information The Rochester Institute of Technology offers over 30 bachelor's, master's, and certificate programs through online study. Two degree programs among the many described below require short laboratory residencies, but the rest can be completed with no residency at all.

The B.S. in applied arts and sciences is designed primarily for students who already hold an associate's degree or the equivalent number of credits. Credit can be awarded for military and other noncollegiate training, and for a number of standardized proficiency examinations. Students choose a specialization from the following list: applied computing, digital imaging and publishing, disaster and emergency management, e-business, environmental management and technology, health systems administration, management, manufacturing management technology, mechanical technology, organizational change, quality management, safety and health technology, structural design, technical communication, or telecommunications.

Other B.S. programs are available in electrical and mechanical engineering technology (requires some short on-campus laboratory residencies), environmental management and technology, safety technology, and telecommunications engineering technology.

M.S. programs are available in applied statistics, cross-disciplinary professional studies (individualized program), environmental health and safety management (requires short on-campus laboratory sessions), health systems administration, imaging science, information technology, microelectronics manufacturing engineering, and software development and management. Up to 12 semester hours may be transferred into an RIT graduate program.

Undergraduate and graduate certificates are available in many of the same fields.

Applications for admission can be processed online. Financial aid is available at the graduate level; standard state and federal programs are open to undergraduates, as well as a number of payment options.

International students are welcome, although demonstrated proficiency in English (minimum TOEFL score of 550) is required.

Saint Joseph's College

Bachelor's and master's degrees in a range of fields through a program requiring only two weeks on campus.

278 White's Bridge Road
Standish, ME 04084-5263

Web site	www.sjcme.edu
Email	admiss@sjcme.edu
Telephone	(800) 752 4723
Year established	1912
Ownership status	Nonprofit, church
Residency	Two weeks
Cost	Average
Degree level	Bachelor's, Master's
Fields of study or special interest	Business, criminal justice, education, health care, health service administration, liberal studies, nursing, pastoral studies
Other information	St. Joseph's offers the following programs: B.S.'s in business, education, health care, and nursing; B.A.'s in criminal justice and liberal studies; a Master of Health Service Administration (M.H.S.A.); an M.A. in pastoral studies; and M.S.'s in education (with emphasis in lifelong teaching and learning) and nursing.

All programs are offered through faculty-directed independent study. Students must attend a two-week summer residency at some point during their course of study. The average undergraduate degree takes two to five years, and the average graduate program takes three to five. The average St. Joseph's undergraduate distance-education student is in his or her forties.

Foreign students are welcome in both graduate and undergraduate programs, provided they can show proof of English-language proficiency as evidenced by TOEFL scores.

Saint Mary-of-the-Woods College

For women only, low-residency bachelor's degrees in 24 fields; students of both sexes are eligible for SMWC's innovative master's programs in art therapy, earth literacy, music therapy, and pastoral theology.

Saint Mary-of-the-Woods, IN 47876

Web site	www.smwc.edu
Email	adm-smwc@smwc.edu
Telephone	(812) 535 5106 • (800) 926 7692
Year established	1840
Ownership status	Nonprofit, church
Residency	Short residencies
Cost	Low average
Degree level	Bachelor's, Master's
Fields of study or special interest	See below

Other information   Saint Mary-of-the-Woods offers bachelor's degrees for women, with majors available in the following fields: accounting, business administration, computer information systems, early childhood studies, elementary education, English, gerontology, human resource management, human services, humanities, journalism, K-3 education, K-12 education, marketing, mathematics, paralegal studies, philosophy, psychology, science, secondary education (emphasis in English or social studies), special education (emphasis in learning disabilities or mild mental handicaps), and theology. Education majors must live within 200 miles of the campus.

The undergraduate must attend a two-and-a-half-day seminar at the beginning of the program, and a half-day seminar at the start of each semester. All other work is done by independent study; faculty guidance is provided via mail, email, and phone. Course assignments are usually submitted online or by mail.

Prior learning credit is awarded to those with college-level knowledge acquired by means other than classroom instruction. This knowledge is evaluated through proficiency examinations and portfolio assessment. Up to 95 of the 125 semester hours required for the bachelor's degree may be transferred in, but least one half of courses in the student's major must be taken through the college.

Students of both sexes are eligible for M.A. programs in art therapy, earth literacy, music therapy, and pastoral theology. Students must attend an on-campus workshop at the beginning of each semester. A limited number of transfer credit is accepted for these programs, as assessed on a student-by-student basis.

Salve Regina University

Bachelor's and master's degrees almost entirely by distance learning, with only five days required on campus.

100 Ochre Point Avenue
Newport, RI 02840-4192

Web site	www.salve.edu
Email	sruadmis@salve.edu
Telephone	(401) 847 6650 • (800) 637 0002
Fax	(401) 341 2938
Year established	1934
Ownership status	Nonprofit, independent
Residency	Five days
Cost	High
Degree level	Bachelor's, Master's
Fields of study or special interest	Business, human development, international relations, liberal studies, management, nursing

Other information

Salve Regina University offers bachelor's degrees in business, liberal studies, and nursing, and master's degrees in business administration (MBA), human development, international relations, and management. Certificates are available in correctional administration, management, and information systems science.

All students must attend an intensive five-day session in early June at some point during the program. All work must be completed within five years of enrollment, but most students take less time to finish.

Instruction is by online classes, correspondence courses, and guided independent study, supported by regular mail, email, and telephone contact with faculty. There is no thesis, but all students must complete a brief "exit review" paper that details what they have achieved in the program.

The bachelor's is a degree completion program: an entering student must have at least 45 accredited credits already under his belt. Students then complete at least fifteen 4-credit courses through Salve Regina for a total of 120 required credits.

At the master's level, graduates of U.S. military colleges may transfer in a maximum of 18 earned credits towards a degree; CPCUs may transfer 12 earned credits towards the management degree. Other students may transfer up to 6 of the 36 required credits into the program from prior collegiate schooling or ACE military recommendations.

Salve Regina boasts students from almost a dozen countries; all foreign students must take the TOEFL and submit a statement of finances.

Saybrook Graduate School

Master's and doctoral degrees in human science, organizational systems inquiry, and psychology through distance learning, with two weeks per year in San Francisco.

450 Pacific, 3rd Floor
San Francisco, CA 94133

Web site	www.saybrook.edu
Email	saybrook@saybrook.edu
Telephone	(415) 433 9200 • (800) 825 4480
Fax	(415) 433 9271
Year established	1971
Ownership status	Nonprofit, independent
Residency	Short yearly residencies
Cost	High
Degree level	Master's, Doctorates
Fields of study or special interest	Human science, organizational systems inquiry, psychology
Other information	Founded in 1971, Saybrook is an accredited graduate school and research center designed to focus on the study of psychology and human science with a distinctive emphasis on humanistic values. Saybrook offers its academic programs through a distance-learning format that allows midcareer professionals and others who may have difficulty attending classes in traditional settings to pursue their careers while earning a master's or doctoral degree.

Students are mentored through a rigorous program of disciplined, independent academic study. Relationships with faculty tend to be highly personalized and interactive.

M.A. and Ph.D. programs are available in human science, organizational systems inquiry, and psychology. Students must attend two residential conferences in the San Francisco Bay Area each academic year.

Students may begin the program in September or March. A financial aid application must be completed at least three months before the proposed enrollment date if a student wishes to receive aid.

Skidmore College

Its University Without Walls program, founded in 1971, offers individualized bachelor's and master's degrees almost entirely by home study.

University Without Walls
815 North Broadway
Saratoga Springs, NY 12866

Web site	www.skidmore.edu
Email	uww@skidmore.edu
Telephone	(518) 580 5450
Fax	(518) 580 5449
Year established	1911
Ownership status	Nonprofit, independent
Residency	Three days for the bachelor's; eight days for the master's
Cost	Low average
Degree level	Bachelor's, Master's
Fields of study or special interest	Individualized major, liberal studies

Other information
Skidmore is one of the pioneers of the nontraditional movement, having offered a University Without Walls program since 1971. It is possible to earn its B.A. or B.S. with a total of three days on campus: one for an admissions interview, a second for advising and planning, and a third to present a degree plan to a faculty committee. In addition to fulfilling all other requirements in the degree plan, each student completes a final project demonstrating competence in his or her field.

The B.A. and B.S. are based on a student-defined, faculty-approved plan of study. Pre-approved majors are available in American studies, anthropology, art history, arts management, Asian studies, biology, business, chemistry, classics, communications, computer science, dance, economics, English, environmental studies, French, geology, German, government, history, human behavior, Latin American studies, mathematics, music, organizational behavior, philosophy, physics, political science, psychology, religion, sociology, Spanish, studio art, theater, and women's studies.

In 1992, Skidmore launched a Master of Arts in liberal studies (M.A.L.S.), modeled on its highly successful undergraduate program. It is possible to earn an M.A.L.S. degree with a total of eight days on campus: one day for an admission interview, six days for an entrance seminar, and one day to present an academic plan to a faculty committee. Coursework consists of the 3-credit entrance seminar, 24 credit hours of integrative study, and a 3-credit written final project/thesis. Students work with two faculty advisors to develop a highly individualized course of study that may draw on many local resources and life experiences.

Southwestern Adventist University

Bachelor's degrees in 20 different fields, with only six days required on campus.

Adult Degree Program
Keene, TX 76059

Web site	www.swau.edu
Email	admissions@swau.edu
Telephone	(817) 556 4705 • (800) 433 2240
Fax	(817) 556 4742
Year established	1893
Ownership status	Nonprofit, church
Residency	Six days at the beginning of the program
Cost	Average
Degree level	Bachelor's
Fields of study or special interest	Accounting, broadcasting, business administration, computer information systems, computer science, corporate communication, criminal justice, elementary education, English, history, international affairs, journalism, management, mathematics, office administration, office technology, psychology, religion, secondary education, social science

Other information

Southwestern Adventist offers bachelor's degrees in the above fields through its Adult Degree Program (ADP).

Students must attend a six-day admissions seminar (in March, June, or October); following this seminar, virtually all of the degree work can be completed at a distance through independent study. Coursework options may include Web-based classes, audio- and videocassettes, phone and mail instruction, independent study projects, study guides, and supervised fieldwork.

Credit can be transferred from prior approved schooling and is also awarded for proficiency exams (CLEP, DANTES, and other approved examination standards), as well as for military or other nonacademic learning. A maximum of 96 of the 128 semester hours required for this degree may come from these sources.

ADP students pay 20 percent less than on-campus students do. The average ADP student takes four to seven years to complete the program. Student services available include help with federal financial aid programs, academic counseling, and career advice.

Foreign students are welcome; those from non-English-speaking countries must score at least 550 on the TOEFL.

Although this school is operated by the Seventh-Day Adventist Church, it is open to all qualified applicants. Applicants must be at least 22 years old, and preference is given to those who have at least some college experience.

Stanford University

An online master's in electrical engineering from one of the most prominent research universities in the United States.

Stanford Center for Professional Development
496 Lomita Mall, Durand Building, Room 401
Stanford, CA 94305-4036

Web site	stanford-online.stanford.edu
Email	sitn-registration@stanford.edu
Telephone	(650) 725 3000
Fax	(650) 725 2868
Year established	1885
Ownership status	Nonprofit, independent
Residency	None
Cost	High average
Degree level	Master's
Fields of study or special interest	Electrical engineering with emphasis on telecommunications, for individuals; computer science, for corporate subscribers
Other information	In the fall of 1998, Stanford became the first major U.S. research university to offer a master's degree entirely through Internet study: an M.S. in electrical engineering with emphasis in telecommunications. A variety of non-degree graduate courses can also be completed online and transferred into a participating degree program at another school.

The program involves 15 courses (45 semester hours) in fields such as analog integrated circuit design, Fourier optics, wireless communications, computer systems, fiber optics, digital filtering, VLSI, and logic design. The program takes approximately three to five years to complete through part-time study.

An M.S. in computer science is also available to corporate and government subscribers through on-site delivery methods such as two-way video, supplemented where appropriate by Stanford's many available online courses in the field.

Stephens College

Bachelor's and master's degrees in a number of fields, with six to seven days required on campus.

Columbia, MO 65215

Web site	www.stephens.edu
Email	sce@wc.stephens.edu
Telephone	(573) 876 7125 • (800) 388 7579
Fax	(573) 876 7248
Year established	1833
Ownership status	Nonprofit, independent
Residency	Six to seven days
Cost	High average
Degree level	Bachelor's, Master's
Fields of study or special interest	Business administration, education, English, health information administration, law/philosophy/rhetoric, psychology

Other information

Stephens offers bachelor's in the above fields, or students may choose to design an individualized program with faculty approval. Dual majors are also available. Students with a bachelor's degree may work toward a certificate in health information management or early childhood and elementary education. The curriculum emphasizes issues of particular concern to women and minorities.

Stephens also offers the MBA as an Internet-based program.

All students are required to attend and satisfactorily pass (grade of C or better) an on-campus introductory course, held on a seven-day or double-weekend (three weeks apart) format.

Degree requirements can be met through independent study and Internet courses working individually with Stephens College faculty. For those within driving distance of campus, weekend courses may supplement independent study. Students communicate with instructors by mail, telephone, and, when possible, email. Students may also earn credits through approved courses taken locally, standardized exams (CLEP, DANTES, College Board AP tests, and departmental exams), and portfolio assessment for military and other prior college-level learning gained outside the classroom. Thirty-six semester hours of credit must be taken with Stephens College faculty.

Open to women and men 23 years of age and older. Foreign students able to attend the on-campus introductory course may be accepted, provided that they can demonstrate a TOEFL score of 550 or better.

Syracuse University

Associate's, bachelor's, and master's degrees in a number of fields, with as little as three weeks per year on campus.

Independent Study Degree Programs
700 University Avenue
Syracuse, NY 13244-2530

Web site	www.yesu.syr.edu
Email	suisdp@uc.syr.edu
Telephone	(315) 443 3480 • (800) 442 0501
Fax	(315) 443 4174
Year established	1870
Ownership status	Nonprofit, independent
Residency	Short
Cost	High
Degree level	Associate's, Bachelor's, Master's
Fields of study or special interest	Advertising design, business administration, communications management, engineering management, information resources management, liberal studies, library science, nursing, social science, telecommunications and network management
Other information	The Independent Study Degree Program of this well-known university offers an A.A. and B.A. in liberal studies; an M.A. in advertising design or illustration; an MBA; a Master of Library Science; a Master of Social Science; and M.S.'s in communications management, engineering management, information resources management, nursing, and telecommunications and network management. All require a short residency on campus. During the home study phase, students communicate with professors by mail, fax, email, Internet, or telephone.

The master's degrees are designed for completion in two or three years. For the bachelor's degree, a minimum of 30 credits must be earned through Syracuse. No standardized tests are required for the B.A. in liberal studies, the Master of Social Science, or the M.A. in illustration or advertising design. The GMAT is required for the MBA; the GRE is required for the M.L.S. and the M.S. programs. The M.A. degrees and the communications management degree require a portfolio review.

Foreign students are admitted to all programs, provided they have a satisfactory TOEFL score.

Texas Tech University

A nonresidential bachelor's in general studies and several nonresidential master's degrees in technical fields.

Outreach and Extended Studies
6901 Quaker Avenue
Lubbock, TX 79413

Web site	www.ttu.edu
Email	distlearn@ttu.edu
Telephone	(806) 742 7200 • (800) 692 6877
Fax	(806) 742 7222
Year established	1923
Ownership status	Nonprofit, state
Residency	None
Cost	Average
Degree level	Bachelor's, Master's
Fields of study or special interest	Engineering (five fields), general studies, technical communication
Other information	Texas Tech University offers six distance-learning programs designed primarily for adult learners.

The Bachelor of General Studies (B.G.S.) is a nontraditional program offered through the Department of Continuing Education (*www.dce.ttu.edu*) and designed primarily for students who have earned 30 semester hours or more of credit at another institution (though TTU does offer the necessary courses to fulfill this basic requirement). Students choose three "concentration areas," each involving six courses (or 18 semester hours of credit), from the following list: behavioral sciences, communication, English, general business, history, humanities and fine arts, psychology, and restaurant/hotel/institution management. Course requirements can be fulfilled through a variety of nontraditional means including online study, correspondence coursework, and credit by examination.

The online M.A. in technical communication offered through the Department of English (*english.ttu.edu*) involves 12 courses (36 semester hours of coursework); a thesis is optional, and may be taken in lieu of two courses. Nonthesis students must pass a comprehensive written examination. The Web site stresses that the online M.A. is patterned after the on-campus M.A., and requirements for the two degrees are identical.

The College of Engineering's distance-learning initiative (*aln.coe.ttu.edu*) offers four master's programs nonresidentially: the general Master of Engineering (M.Eng.) and M.S. programs in petroleum engineering, software engineering, and systems and engineering management. Lectures are delivered via CD, videocassette, or Internet streaming video; all other interaction occurs over the Internet.

Thomas Edison State College

Associate's and bachelor's degrees in 118 fields entirely through distance learning, and an M.S. in management that requires only a brief residency.

101 West State Street
Trenton, NJ 08608-1176

Web site	www.tesc.edu
Email	admissions@tesc.edu
Telephone	(609) 292 6565 • (888) 442 8372
Fax	(609) 984 8447
Year established	1972
Ownership status	Nonprofit, state
Residency	None for bachelor's, brief for master's
Cost	Low for bachelor's; average for master's
Degree level	Associate's, Bachelor's, Master's
Fields of study or special interest	Accounting, administrative office management, administration of justice, advertising management, air traffic control, anthropology, architectural design, art, aviation flight technology, aviation maintenance technology, banking, biomedical electronics, biology, chemistry, child development services, civil and construction engineering technology, civil engineering technology, clinical laboratory science, communications, community services, computer information systems, computer science, computer science technology, construction, dietetic sciences, dental assisting sciences, dental hygiene, economics, electrical technology, electronic engineering technology, emergency disaster management, engineering graphics, English, environmental sciences, environmental studies, finance, fire protection science, foreign language, forestry, general management, gerontology, health and nutrition counseling, health professions education, health services, health services administration, health services education, health services management, history, horticulture, hospital health care administration, hotel/motel/restaurant management, human resource management, humanities, imaging science, insurance, international business, journalism, labor studies, laboratory animal science, legal services, liberal studies, logistics, manufacturing engineering technology, marine engineering technology, marketing, mathematics, mechanical engineering technology, medical imaging, mental health and rehabilitative services, music, natural sciences and mathematics, nondestructive testing technology, nuclear engineering technology, nuclear medicine technology, nursing, operations management, organizational management, perfusion technology, philosophy, photography, physics, political science, procurement, psychology, public administration, purchasing and materials management, radiation protection, radiation therapy, radiologic technology, real estate, recreation services, religion, respiratory care, respiratory care sciences (advanced), retailing management, small business management and entrepreneurship, social sciences & history, social services, social services administration, social services for special populations, sociology, surveying, theater arts, transportation and distribution management
Other information	This long-recognized leader in nontraditional education offers associate's and bachelor's degrees in all of the above fields; no residency is required. A low-residency M.S. in management is also available, and an M.A. in professional studies is under development.

Unlimited credit can be earned through portfolio assessment; Thomas Edison's own exams in dozens of subjects; guided study (distance-learning courses using texts and videocassettes); the "On-Line Computer Classroom" (many courses available through Edison's innovative CALL system: Computer Assisted Lifelong Learning); equivalency exams; military, business, and industry courses and training programs; telecourses (centered on, for example, PBS's *The Civil War*, etc.); licenses and certificates; and transfer credit from accredited colleges. Unique academic advising available to enrolled students on an 800 number. Foreign students are welcome, with certain restrictions.

Touro University International

As a branch campus of New York's Touro College, TUI offers the first 100% online Ph.D. programs to achieve U.S. regional accreditation.

10542 Calle Lee, Suite 102
Los Alamitos, CA 90720

Web site	www.tourouniversity.edu
Email	info@tourou.edu
Telephone	(714) 816 0366
Fax	(714) 816 0367
Year established	1998
Ownership status	Nonprofit, independent
Residency	None
Cost	High
Degree level	Bachelor's, Master's, Doctorates
Fields of study or special interest	Business administration, health sciences
Other information	In 1971, prominent sociologist, Orthodox rabbi, and civil rights activist Bernard Lander founded Touro College, where he still serves as president. Touro College is a midsized college of fewer than 10,000 students located in New York; branch campuses have been established in China, Israel, and Russia.

In 1998, Touro College established Touro University International in California as its virtual branch campus, offering totally online degrees. When TUI was formally included under Touro College's Middle States Association accreditation, it became the first regionally accredited school of any kind to offer Ph.D. programs 100 percent online with absolutely no required on-campus residency. We also note that TUI is probably the first "university" to offer degrees as a branch campus of a "college," rather than vice-versa.

The Ph.D. programs are in business administration and health science. Bachelor's and master's are also available in these fields. The B.S. completion program in health science is available with specialization in ophthalmic science or physician assistant training. Students pursuing the B.S. should have already completed 56 hours of coursework through a regionally accredited or equivalent university. The master's degree takes a minimum of one year to complete; the Ph.D. takes a minimum of two.

Troy State University Montgomery

Associate's and bachelor's degrees in a range of fields, with only one day required on campus.

P.O. Drawer 4419
Montgomery, AL 36103-4419

Web site	www.tsum.edu
Email	edp@tsum.edu
Telephone	(334) 241 9553 • (800) 355 8786
Fax	(334) 241 5465
Year established	1965
Ownership status	Nonprofit, state
Residency	Very short residency
Cost	Low average
Degree level	Associate's, Bachelor's
Fields of study or special interest	Business, child care, English, history, political science, psychology, social science
Other information	TSUM offers associate's and bachelor's in the above fields. Degrees are earned through a combination of learning contracts, television courses, transfer credit from other regionally accredited colleges and universities, equivalency exams, and assessment of prior learning. Learning-contract courses are also available online.

Upon request, the school will provide guidelines for exam preparation and presentation of prior learning. Other student services include academic and career counseling, tutoring, and job placement assistance.

Study in the program is almost wholly external. Students who live within the state of Alabama must attend a half-day orientation at the beginning of their study, and all students must come to campus for one day near the end of their degree program to present and defend a senior project.

Union Institute

Individualized bachelor's and doctorates through guided independent study, with short seminar residencies; a Ph.D. in professional psychology is also available.

440 East McMillan Street
Cincinnati, OH 45206-1925

Web site	www.tui.edu
Email	admission@tui.edu
Telephone	(513) 861 6400 • (800) 486 3116
Fax	(513) 861 0779
Year established	1964
Ownership status	Nonprofit, independent
Residency	Short; varies by program
Cost	High
Degree level	Bachelor's, Doctorates
Fields of study or special interest	Individualized, professional psychology
Other information	The Union Institute originated in 1964 as a consortium of liberal arts colleges. In 1969, the consortium became known as The Union for Experimenting Colleges and Universities (UECU), and began functioning as a degree-granting institution. It was responsible for the development and implementation of alternative educational systems, including the University Without Walls program that is still in operation at many universities. The consortium later dissolved, but the organization remained, eventually known as The Union Institute. Another name change is in the cards, but details were not available at press time.

The college's Center for Distance Learning offers bachelor's degree programs to individuals throughout the United States, using telecommunication and computer technology in its educational delivery systems. Students participate in a four-day residential seminar each term, held in a number of locations across the country. Students may received credit for prior learning, transcripted and otherwise. The typical student has had some prior college (the average age for students in this program is 38) and completes the program after five semesters of full-time enrollment. Part-time enrollment is also an option. Each program culminates with a senior project based on writing and research.

The Graduate College offers interdisciplinary study and research programs leading to the Ph.D. Students choose their doctoral committee members: two from the Union Institute's faculty as well as two adjunct (external) faculty advisors. As is consistent with the Institute's policy of self-directed education, the student chairs the doctoral committee. Each doctoral program culminates in a Project Demonstrating Excellence (PDE), a significant capstone project. The PDE may take the form of a traditional dissertation, but may also be a creative work or social action project. Students must attend a 10-day entry colloquium (held at Union's established sites) and the student's choice of three 5-day seminars (held monthly at various locations worldwide). The program is not based on credit hours; a minimum of 24 months full-time enrollment is required for graduation, and the typical program is completed in 36 months. International students are accepted.

University of Alabama

Bachelor's in interdisciplinary studies, with only three days of residency.

Tuscaloosa, AL 35487-0001

Web site	bama.ua.edu/~exd
Email	info@exd.ccs.ua.edu
Telephone	(205) 348 3019
Year established	1831
Ownership status	Nonprofit, state
Residency	Three days at beginning of program
Cost	Low average to average
Degree level	Bachelor's
Fields of study or special interest	Interdisciplinary studies with seven specializations; see below

Other information   The University of Alabama External Degree Program awards a B.A. or B.S. in interdisciplinary studies almost entirely through nonresidential independent study. The only residency requirement is an on-campus degree-planning seminar that takes three days at the start of the program. The fields of study for the B.A. are communication, humanities, human services, and social sciences. Fields of study for the B.S. are administrative sciences, applied sciences, and natural sciences. These fields cover a wide range of individualized interdisciplinary programs, allowing students to focus on a particular field of interest.

A minimum of 128 semester hours is required for graduation. Up to 96 hours can be transferred in; at least 32 hours of work must be completed after admission. This can be through out-of-class contract learning, correspondence courses, television courses, weekend college, prior-learning evaluation, or on-campus courses at the university. Credit is awarded for military and other noncollegiate PONSI-approved training, CLEP, DANTES, and departmental challenge exams. A 12-semester-hour senior project is required of all students. Academic advising and planning can be done by telephone.

Foreign students are not admitted.

University of Bradford

Research M.Phil. and Ph.D. programs in 26 fields, with as little as two weeks per year of residency.

Student Registry, Postgraduate
Richmond Road
Bradford BD7 1DP
United Kingdom

Web site	www.brad.ac.uk
Email	pg-admissions@bradford.ac.uk
Telephone	+44 (1274) 233 042
Fax	+44 (1274) 235 810
Year established	1957
Ownership status	Nonprofit, state
Residency	Variable
Cost	Average to high average
Degree level	Master's, Doctorates
Fields of study or special interest	See below

Other information The University of Bradford offers research-based M.Phil. and Ph.D. programs to students worldwide, and its policies express a willingness to work with qualified international students who wish to undertake a low-residency format. Residency varies from program to program, depending on a variety of factors including the student's "home base" facilities; access to necessary resources and, where applicable, appropriate academic or industry research supervision; the specific degree being sought; the field; the dissertation topic; the student's ability to conduct self-directed research; and other extenuating circumstances, including (one might expect) the openness of individual faculty members to negotiating long-distance research arrangements.

It's worth noting, and noting again, that successful applications for nonresidential research arrangements at schools such as Bradford must almost always begin with a solid idea for a research topic. Bradford does not offer a special catalog and application form for "distance learning" doctorates. Students who undertake a nonresidential British research doctorate are seldom described as pursuing distance-learning doctorates; they're just pursuing traditional credentials in cases where all of the work happens to be done off campus.

That said, Bradford offers research programs in an exceptionally broad range of fields, including applied social sciences, archaeological sciences, biomedical sciences, cancer research, chemical engineering, chemistry, civil and environmental engineering, computing, cybernetics, development and project planning, education, electronic and electrical engineering, electronic imaging and media communications, environmental science, European studies, gender and women's studies, health studies, industrial technology, interdisciplinary human studies, management, mathematics, mechanical and medical engineering, modern languages, optometry, peace studies, pharmacy, polymer engineering, and social and economic studies. Research Ph.D. programs generally take four to six years to complete through part-time study, while research M.Phil. programs can generally be completed part-time in two to three years. British research programs involve no courses; each qualified student immediately pursues her thesis topic without formal doctoral-level coursework.

University of Idaho

Master's degrees in 12 fields almost entirely through home study; some majors require two days on campus at the end of the program.

Engineering Outreach Program
P.O. Box 441014
Moscow, ID 83844-1014

Web site	www.uidaho.edu/evo
Email	outreach@uidaho.edu
Telephone	(800) 824 2889
Year established	1889
Ownership status	Nonprofit, state
Residency	None or brief, depending on program
Cost	Average
Degree level	Master's
Fields of study or special interest	Computer science, engineering (ten fields), teaching mathematics
Other information	Idaho's Engineering Outreach Program allows students to earn graduate degrees almost entirely through distance learning. Programs include an M.A.T. (Master of Arts in Teaching) in the teaching of mathematics; M.S.'s in computer science, electrical engineering, and human factors psychology; and M.Eng. programs in biological and agricultural engineering, civil engineering, computer engineering, electrical engineering, engineering management, geological engineering, mechanical engineering, metallurgical engineering, and mining engineering.

Engineering Outreach students are expected to complete all course requirements during the semester in which the course is offered. Courses are taught by on-campus faculty and simultaneously videotaped in specially equipped studio classrooms. Videotapes, plus all related class handouts, are sent by mail to the student. Students and instructors maintain contact using the toll-free number, by fax, and through email and interactive video conferencing. Examinations are sent to an examination proctor recommended by the student and approved by Engineering Outreach. The proctor is responsible for supervising the examination process and returning the exam to Engineering Outreach. At the end of the program, students may need to travel to the Idaho campus for two days, either to present a thesis (M.S. programs) or take a comprehensive examination (M.Eng. programs).

Each program has distinct entrance requirements. No credit is awarded for equivalency exams or noncollegiate learning of any kind. Up to 12 of the 30 to 36 credits required for the degree can be transferred in from an accredited college or university. International students are accepted; those whose native language is not English must present a minimum TOEFL score of 550.

University of Illinois at Urbana-Champaign

Master's programs in a variety of fields over the Internet, from one of the most respected public universities in the United States.

Urbana, IL 61801

Web site	www.uiuc.edu
Email	graduate@admissions.uiuc.edu
Telephone	(217) 333 1000
Fax	(217) 333 9758
Year established	1867
Ownership status	Nonprofit, state
Residency	None
Cost	High average
Degree level	Master's
Fields of study or special interest	Computer science, education, engineering, information science
Other information	The University of Illinois at Urbana-Champaign offers a variety of master's programs online.

The Master of Computer Science (M.C.S.) is a professional degree designed for practicing IT industry specialists. Students are required to take nine courses at a rate of one or two per semester, and can finish the program in three to five years. No thesis or final project is required.

The M.Ed. is available in curriculum, technology, and education reform or in vocational and technical education (with specialization in human resource education). Each program requires eight online courses and can be completed in about three years.

M.S. programs are available in electrical engineering and in library and information science.

Professional development sequences are available in community college teaching, financial engineering and risk management, French translation studies, and math education. Each sequence involves six graduate-level courses, which may be taken online; a sequence can be completed in two years.

University of Iowa

Interdisciplinary Bachelor of Liberal Studies entirely through home study.

Division of Continuing Education
116 International Center
Iowa City, IA 52242-1802

Web site	www.uiowa.edu
Email	credit-programs@uiowa.edu
Telephone	(319) 335 2575 • (800) 272 6430
Fax	(319) 335 2740
Year established	1847
Ownership status	Nonprofit, state
Residency	None
Cost	High average
Degree level	Bachelor's
Fields of study or special interest	Liberal studies

Other information Iowa offers an interdisciplinary Bachelor of Liberal Studies through what is essentially a degree completion program. Applicants must have already completed at least 62 credits elsewhere or hold an associate's degree. An additional 30 credits may be transferred into the program; 32 more must be taken from the University of Iowa itself. All of the work can, however, be done nonresidentially.

The degree does not have a major in the traditional sense; rather, students concentrate in three of five broad subject areas: communication and arts, humanities, natural science and math, professional fields, and social sciences. Credit is awarded for ACE military or vocational training recommendations, as well as CLEP, DANTES, and College Board AP exams. No credit is given for life experience.

Within the program, distance-learning options include courses taken through other schools (either on a local campus or by correspondence), Iowa's own correspondence courses, and Iowa Communications Network (interactive television) courses that allow classes to be held at remote sites throughout Iowa. Iowa offers more than 160 distance-learning courses, and all requirements for the B.L.S. can be fulfilled through this method.

Foreign students are not admitted, but Americans living overseas may enroll.

In addition, readers may be interested in LionHawk, the Pennsylvania State University and University of Iowa Joint External Degree Program, which allows students to earn an Extended Letters, Arts, and Sciences Associate Degree (E.L.A.S.) from Penn State, then transfer directly to the University of Iowa where they would pursue the B.L.S. degree. Students who earn the E.L.A.S. degree through Penn State are guaranteed admission to Iowa's B.L.S. program.

University of Kent at Canterbury

M.Phil., LL.M., and Ph.D. programs in 65 fields through external research arrangements, with six weeks or less on campus each year.

The Registry
Canterbury, Kent CT2 7NZ
United Kingdom

Web site	www.ukc.ac.uk
Email	graduate-office@ukc.ac.uk
Telephone	+44 (1227) 824 040
Fax	+44 (1227) 452 196
Year established	1965
Ownership status	Nonprofit, state
Residency	Variable
Cost	Average to high average
Degree level	Master's, Doctorates, Law
Fields of study or special interest	See below
Other information	The University of Kent at Canterbury offers research-based LL.M., M.Phil., and Ph.D. programs to students worldwide. Each student works through an approved university in her area. Students pursuing the LL.M. program must generally hold the J.D. (LL.B.) or equivalent, students pursuing the M.Phil. should hold at least a good bachelor's, and students pursuing the Ph.D. should have a master's and significant documented research work (a master's thesis, published work, or other equivalent material). Students generally spend six weeks per year on campus.

The LL.M. is available in general law, feminist law, and sociolegal studies. M.Phil. and Ph.D. programs are available in the following fields: accounting, actuarial science, American studies, applied language studies in computing, applied linguistics, applied mathematics, biochemistry, biodiversity management, biotechnology, cartoons and caricature, chemistry, classical archaeology, classical studies, communication and image studies, comparative literary studies, computer science, drama, economics, electronic engineering, English, environmental anthropology, environmental law and conservation, environmental social science, European studies, film studies, forensic psychology, German, health psychology, history, history and cultural studies of science, history and theory of art, industrial relations, international conflict analysis, international relations, Italian, law and philosophy, learning disability, management, management science, medicine and health sciences, medieval and Tudor studies, mental health, microbiology, operations research, personal social services, philosophy, physics, politics and government, postcolonial studies, psychology, psychotherapy, pure mathematics, social anthropology, social policy, social psychology, social work, sociology, Spanish, statistics, theology and religious studies, urban studies, and women's studies.

British research Ph.D. programs involve no courses; a student, once accepted, immediately pursues her thesis topic without formal doctoral-level coursework.

University of Leicester

Nonresidential master's degrees in 19 fields from an 80-year-old British school.

University Road
Leicester LE1 7RH
United Kingdom

Web site	www.leicester.ac.uk
Email	higherdegrees@le.ac.uk
Telephone	+44 (116) 252 2298
Fax	+44 (116) 252 2200
Year established	1921
Ownership status	Nonprofit, state
Residency	None
Cost	Average
Degree level	Master's
Fields of study or special interest	See below

Other information Leicester offers master's degrees in 19 fields through correspondence and online study; each program consists of four to six modules and a capstone dissertation (master's thesis).

Of particular interest to U.S. students might be the M.S. in training and human resource management, offered through Leicester's Centre for Labour Market Studies. The Centre has made a special outreach to the North American and Asian Pacific market, with specially prepared course materials and regular faculty visits for optional meetings with students. Although Leicester is a royally chartered university in its own right, the Centre for Labour Market Studies has achieved additional voluntary accreditation through the Distance Education and Training Council (DETC) in the U.S.

Other master's programs are offered in applied linguistics, archaeology, business administration (MBA), criminal justice, European Union law, finance, forensic and legal psychology, human resources, law and employment relations, marketing, mass communications, museum studies, organizational development, primary education, public order studies, risk and crisis management, security and crime risk management, and sport sociology.

People without an accredited bachelor's degree who possess certain professional qualifications and several years of practical experience may be considered for some programs.

University of London

Nonresident bachelor's, master's, and law degrees in a variety of fields from the school that invented the whole concept of external study.

The External Programme
Senate House, Malet Street
London WC1E 7HU
United Kingdom

Web site	www.lon.ac.uk/external
Email	enquiries@external.ac.uk
Telephone	+44 (20) 7862 8360
Fax	+44 (20) 7862 8358
Year established	1836
Ownership status	Nonprofit, state
Degree level	Bachelor's, Master's, Doctorates, Law
Fields of study or special interest	See below

Other information

The University of London was the first in the world to offer its degree through external study, and with more than 26,000 students registered, it is still one of the most popular.

The University offers B.A. degrees in English, French, geography, German, Italian, Jewish history, philosophy, and Spanish and Latin American studies. Dual language degrees (German and Italian, French and German, Spanish and French, and so forth) are also available. B.S. degrees are available in accounting and finance, banking and finance, computing and information systems, computing and statistics, economics (with optional emphasis in geography, sociology, or politics and international relations), information systems and management, law and management, management, mathematics and computing, and mathematics and statistics. Also available are the Bachelor of Laws (LL.B.) and Bachelor of Divinity (B.D.).

Master's degrees are available in agricultural development, agricultural economics, applied environmental economics, business administration (MBA), clinical dentistry (for practicing dentists), community dental practice, dental public health, dental radiology, developmental finance, distance education, drug and alcohol policy and intervention, environment and development, environmental management, epidemiology, financial economics, financial management, food industry management and marketing, geography, health systems management, infectious diseases, law (LL.M.), livestock health and production, managing rural change, materials science and engineering, occupational psychology, organizational behavior, public policy and management, and sustainable agriculture and rural development.

Self-paced programs can be completed in three to eight years for undergraduate programs, two to five years for master's programs. Assessment is mainly by examination. The university provides subject guides and past examination papers along with an academic handbook and resource guide, but students are responsible for organizing their own program of study. Several independent correspondence schools offer noncredit, nondegree preparation courses for London's exams.

University of Maryland

The University of Maryland's University College offers 15 bachelor's programs, 18 master's programs, and dozens of certificate programs entirely through online study.

University College
3501 University Boulevard East
Adelphi, MD 20783

Web site	www.umuc.edu
Email	umucinfo@umuc.edu
Telephone	(301) 985 7000 • (800) 888 8682
Fax	(301) 454 0399
Year established	1856
Ownership status	Nonprofit, state
Residency	None
Cost	Average
Degree level	Bachelor's, Master's
Fields of study or special interest	See below

Other information   University College, the continuing education campus of the University of Maryland system, offers bachelor's and master's degrees entirely through online study with no required on-campus residency.

Bachelor's degrees are available in accounting, behavioral and social sciences, business and management, communication studies, computer and information science, computer studies, English, environmental management, fire science, history, humanities, information systems management, management studies, paralegal studies, and psychology.

Online master's degrees are available in biotechnology studies, business administration (MBA), computer systems management (with four specializations), distance education, education, electronic commerce, environmental management, information technology, international management (with three specializations), management (with nine specializations), software engineering, teaching, technology management (with three specializations), and telecommunications management.

Undergraduate certificates are available in the areas of business and management, computing and technology, and workplace Spanish. Graduate certificates are available in distance education, general management, information technology systems, international management, and technology and environmental management.

University of Melbourne

Off-campus research M.Phil. and Ph.D. programs in 155 fields from one of Australia's most highly regarded universities.

Victoria 3010
Australia

Web site	www.unimelb.edu.au/research
Email	j.gilbert@sgs.unimelb.edu.au
Telephone	+61 (3) 8344 8670
Year established	1989
Ownership status	Nonprofit, state
Residency	Special
Cost	Average to high average
Degree level	Master's, Doctorates
Fields of study or special interest	See below

Other information   The University of Melbourne offers research-based M.Phil. and Ph.D. programs to students worldwide through remote campus arrangements; each student must find a suitable nearby university or medical school research facility and a suitable supervisor in the relevant field of study. The Ph.D. requires at least one year of supervised full-time research (or two years of supervised part-time research) at this remote facility; it generally takes four to six years to complete an Australian Ph.D. program, and the dissertation can run to about 100,000 words. The list of colleges approved as remote facilities is large and growing. Students who do not live near an approved site may petition to have a nearby site added to the list of approved schools.

Common sense would logically dictate one's success rate in negotiating such a program; for example, a petition to study doctoral-level electronic engineering at a small four-year liberal arts college would probably not be feasible, while a petition to study for a Ph.D. in Japanese under an established scholar in the field at a major state university would probably be accepted with no serious controversy at all.

The following list of possible fields is by no means complete; we simply don't have the space to list them all: accounting, agribusiness, American studies, anatomy, ancient and medieval studies, anthropology, applied linguistics, Arabic studies, archaeology, architecture, art history, Asian studies, atmospheric science, audiology, behavioral science, biochemistry, biology, business, chemistry, Chinese, civil engineering, classical studies, computer education, computer science, construction management, creative arts, creative writing, criminology, cultural studies, dance, dental science, drama, earth sciences, econometrics, economics, education, engineering, English, environmental studies, film and television, forestry, French, geology, genetics, geography, German, health and physical education, Hebrew, history, information systems, Islamic studies, Latin, law, linguistics, management, marketing, mathematics and statistics, media arts, meteorology, music, nursing, pharmacology, philosophy, photography, physical therapy, physics, Polish, political science, Portuguese, print making, project management, psychology, public health, rural health, Russian, Semitic languages, Slavic studies, sociology, software engineering, Spanish, Thai, theater studies, urban planning, veterinary science, women's studies, and zoology.

University of New England

Degrees at all levels in an impressive array of fields, from Australia's oldest distance-education provider.

Armidale
New South Wales 2351
Australia

Web site	www.une.edu.au
Email	ipo@metz.une.edu.au
Telephone	+61 (2) 6773 3333
Fax	+61 (2) 6773 3122
Year established	1938
Ownership status	Nonprofit, state
Residency	None for most programs; variable for research doctorates
Cost	Low average
Degree level	Bachelor's, Master's, Doctorates, Law
Fields of study or special interest	See below

Other information   The University of New England is Australia's oldest distance-education provider and has thousands of students enrolled in external programs. Learning takes place via printed correspondence texts, audio- and videotapes, radio and television broadcasts, and the Internet.

Bachelor's degrees are available in aboriginal studies, agriculture, ancient history, archaeology, Asian societies, Asian studies, biomedical science, biosystematics, Chinese, classical studies, commerce, communication studies, composition, computer science, ecology, economic history, economics, engineering technology (audio or electronics), English, environmental science, ethnomusicology, European cultures, financial administration, French, general science, geography and planning, German, Greek, history, horticultural science, Indonesian, international relations, Italian, Japanese, Latin, law (LL.B.), linguistics, mathematics, modern Greek, molecular biology, musicology, natural resources, paleoanthropology, philosophy, political science, psychology, rural science, social science, sociology, studies in religion, technology, theater studies, urban and regional planning, and women's and gender studies.

Master's degrees are available in American studies, ancient history, archaeological heritage, Asian societies, Asian studies, biology, business administration (MBA) with eight concentrations, Chinese, classics, communication studies, computer science, computer studies, defense studies, development studies, economic studies with six concentrations, education, English, ethnomusicology, European cultures, French, German, geography and planning, Greek, history, Indonesian, international relations, Islamic studies, Italian, Japanese, Latin, law (LL.M.), linguistics, mathematics, molecular and cellular biology, musicology, philosophy, peace studies, political science, public policy, sociology, statistics, studies in religion, theater studies, women's and gender studies, and zoology.

Research M.Phil. and Ph.D. programs are available in a variety of specializations, including arts, biological sciences, business, classics, communication, computer science, cultures, economics, education, engineering, English, health, history, human and environmental studies, languages, law, linguistics, mathematics, music, physical sciences, professional studies, religion, and theater.

University of Northern Iowa

Bachelor's and master's programs in a broad range of fields, with little or no required residency.

1227 West 27th Street
Cedar Falls, IA 50614

Web site	www.uni.edu
Email	contined@uni.edu
Telephone	(319) 273 2121 • (800) 772 1746
Year established	1847
Ownership status	Nonprofit, state
Residency	Usually none
Cost	Average
Degree level	Bachelor's, Master's
Fields of study or special interest	Education (many specializations), English, industrial technology, liberal studies, library science, public relations
Other information	Northern Iowa offers bachelor's completion programs in liberal studies, elementary education, and industrial technology. The liberal studies degree is interdisciplinary; students concentrate in three of five broad subject areas: communication and arts, humanities, professional fields, science and math, and social sciences.

Credit is earned primarily through guided correspondence study courses, but other options include on-campus evening and weekend courses, televised courses, off-campus course sites throughout Iowa, courses from other regionally accredited four-year colleges (both on-campus and correspondence), and online courses. To qualify for admission, a student must live in the United States and have completed 62 transferable units or have an associate's degree.

M.A. programs are offered in communication education, education (specializing in educational leadership, elementary reading and language arts, middle school education, or special education), educational technology, English, industrial technology, library science, middle school mathematics, or public relations. An M.Mus. in music education is also available.

University of Oklahoma

Bachelor's and master's degrees in liberal studies, with a negotiable amount of time on campus.

College of Liberal Studies
1700 Asp Avenue, Suite 226
Norman, OK 73072-6400

Web site	www.ou.edu/cls
Email	cls@ou.edu
Telephone	(405) 325 1061 • (800) 522 4389
Fax	(405) 325 7132
Year established	1890
Ownership status	Nonprofit, state
Residency	Two to four weeks
Cost	Low average
Degree level	Bachelor's, Master's
Fields of study or special interest	Liberal studies

Other information   Oklahoma offers the Bachelor and Master of Liberal Studies through directed independent study.

Bachelor's students begin the program by attending an introductory seminar held over two consecutive weekends, and then continue by completing independent study assignments and attending two to four 10-day seminars on campus, depending on the number of credit hours they transfer into the program. There are no majors; students work in three general areas: humanities, natural sciences, and mathematics. Some of the on-campus residencies may be waived based on prior study. Credit is available for ACE-evaluated training programs and military recommendations, as well as equivalency examinations.

Master's students are allowed to self-design a degree program incorporating interdisciplinary perspectives or may choose from the following career-oriented program tracks: administrative leadership, health and human services, interdisciplinary education, or museum emphasis. M.L.S. students complete the program by attending a total of three 10-day seminars on campus and by finishing several directed independent reading assignments. It may be possible to negotiate alternatives for some of these residency requirements. The college does not allow transfer credit hours in the master's program.

University of Phoenix

Bachelor's and master's degrees entirely through online study, from the largest private university in the U.S.

4615 East Elwood Street
Phoenix, AZ 85072

Web site	www.phoenix.edu
Phone	(480) 966 9577 • (800) 742 4742
Fax	(480) 829 9030
Year established	1976
Ownership status	Proprietary
Residency	None for bachelor's and master's; brief residencies for doctorate
Cost	High
Degree level	Bachelor's, Master's, Doctorates
Fields of study or special interest	Business (see fields below), education, information technology, nursing
Other information	The University of Phoenix established its online campus in 1989. The following programs are currently available entirely over the Internet: bachelor's degrees in business (specializing in accounting, administration, information systems, management, or marketing), e-business, information technology, and nursing; and master's degrees in business administration (specializing in accounting, e-business, global management, or technology), computer information systems, education, nursing, and organizational management. A low-residency Doctor of Management (D.M.) in organizational leadership is also available.

All of the degrees are designed for midcareer professionals. Students get their assignments, have group discussions, and ask questions of their professors online, from wherever they and their computers happen to be. Each class meeting is spread out over an entire week, allowing busy students to complete their work at the most convenient time for them. Software instruction and technical orientation are provided once a student enrolls.

The University of Phoenix also offers bachelor's and master's programs in business through evening and weekend study at 52 locations throughout the country.

University of Sarasota

Bachelor's, master's, specialist, and doctoral degrees in a range of fields focusing primarily on business, education, and psychology.

5250 17th Street
Sarasota, FL 34235

Web site	www.sarasota.edu
Telephone	(941) 379 0404 • (800) 331 5995
Fax	(941) 379 9464
Year established	1969
Ownership status	Proprietary
Residency	Eight weeks
Cost	High average
Degree level	Bachelor's, Master's, Doctorates
Fields of study or special interest	See below

Other information The University of Sarasota offers a B.S. in business administration and organizational management; M.A.'s in counseling psychology, education, guidance counseling, and mental health counseling; an MBA specializing in finance, health care administration, human resources, international business, international trade, or marketing; Ed.S.'s in curriculum and instruction, educational leadership, and school counseling; a DBA specializing in accounting, information systems, international business, management, or marketing; and Ed.D.'s in counseling psychology, curriculum and instruction, educational leadership, and pastoral community counseling.

For all of these programs, eight weeks of intensive coursework are required at one of Sarasota's three campuses (Sarasota, FL; Tampa, FL; or Orange, CA); these intensive courses are divided into one-week blocks offered during traditional winter, summer, and spring break periods. The university's programs consist of seminars, supervised individual research, and writing. The average student takes two to four years to earn a degree. Many of the students are teachers, school administrators, professors, university administrators, and professionals in the behavioral sciences.

Master's candidates must write a thesis or complete a directed independent study project; doctoral students must write a dissertation.

International students are welcome; a TOEFL score of 550 is required for doctoral and Ed.S. candidates, and a score of 500 is required for master's candidates.

Note: We heard reports that the University of Sarasota may change its name to Argosy University (the school is owned by the Argosy Education Group), but the matter was still not settled when we went to press.

University of South Africa

Nonresidential bachelor's, master's, doctoral, and law degrees in many fields from one of the largest distance-education universities in the English-speaking world.

P.O. Box 392
Unisa 0003
South Africa

Web site	www.unisa.ac.za
Email	study-info@alpha.unisa.ac.za
Telephone	+27 (12) 429 3111
Fax	+27 (12) 429 3221
Year established	1873
Ownership status	Nonprofit, state
Residency	None
Cost	Low
Degree level	Bachelor's, Master's, Doctorates, Law
Fields of study or special interest	See below
Other information	UNISA offers a vast number of courses, degrees, and diplomas at all levels, and nearly all of them are available entirely through distance learning (usually via guided research or correspondence, though UNISA has recently begun to offer online courses as well). Examinations may be taken at South African embassies and consulates worldwide. At one time, UNISA offered the least expensive nonresidential credentials in the world; this was due to the fact that until recently, UNISA subsidized students worldwide. This practice is being phased out at press time, though UNISA's unsubsidized rates are still extremely low by U.S. standards.

Bachelor's degrees are available in the following fields: accounting, African languages (with nine specializations), African politics, Afrikaans, ancient history, anthropology, applied mathematics, Arabic, art history, astronomy, auditing, biblical studies (B.A. or Th.B.), business management, chemistry, church history (Th.B.), classics, commerce, communication, computer science, criminology, development administration, economics, education, educational management, English, French, gender studies, geography, German, gifted child education, Greek, guidance and counseling, history, industrial psychology, information science, information systems, international politics, Islamic studies, Italian, Judaica, Latin, law (LL.B.), linguistics, mathematics, missiology (Th.B.), modern Hebrew, musicology, New Testament (Th.B.), Old Testament (Th.B.), operations research, penology, philosophy, physics, police science, politics, Portuguese, practical theology (Th.B.), preprimary education, primary education, psychology, public administration, quantitative management, religious studies, Romance languages, Russian, secondary education, Semitic languages, social science (with five specializations), Spanish, statistics, systematic theology (Th.B.), theological ethics (Th.B.), theory of literature, and transport economics.

Master's degrees are available in nearly all of the above fields, as well as the following: ancient languages and cultures, archaeology, banking law (LL.M.), business leadership, Christian spirituality (Th.M.), clinical psychology, commercial law, comparative education (M.Ed.), corporate law (LL.M.), counseling psychology, criminal law and criminal procedure, didactics, educational management, environmental education, history of education, insurance law (LL.M.), intellectual property law (LL.M.), international communication, international economic law (LL.M.), labor law (LL.M.), mathematics education, mental health, natural science education, nursing science (with five specializations), pastoral therapy (Th.M.), philosophy of education, philosophy of law (LL.M.), psychology of education, socio-education, sociolinguistics, urban ministry (Th.M.), and visual arts (M.V.A.).

Doctorates are available in virtually all of the fields listed above, and awarded as follows: the D.Litt. and D.Phil. for degrees in the arts; the Ph.D. for degrees awarded in the natural and social sciences; the Ed.D. for degrees awarded in education; the Th.D. for degrees awarded in theology; and the LL.D. for degrees awarded in law. As is true in the case of British programs, South African doctoral programs are based entirely around the student's dissertation research and do not involve preparatory courses as such (although students are frequently assigned preliminary reading lists upon undertaking a doctoral program).

U.S. students interested in UNISA should contact UNISA's U.S. agent, the American International Higher Education Corporation (AIHEC), by telephone at (512) 343 2031, by fax at (512) 343 8644, by email at *jcraparo@aihec.com*, or on the Web at *www.aihec.com*.

University of South Australia

Nonresidential degrees at all levels through correspondence, online coursework, and guided research.

G.P.O. Box 2471
Adelaide, SA 5001
Australia

Web site	www.unisa.edu.au
Email	international.office@unisa.edu.au
Telephone	+61 (8) 8302 0114
Fax	+61 (8) 8302 0233
Year established	1991
Ownership status	Nonprofit, state
Residency	None for most programs; variable for research doctorates
Cost	Average to high average
Degree level	Bachelor's, Master's, Doctorates
Fields of study or special interest	Focuses largely on business and education; see below
Other information	The University of South Australia has made its distance-learning programs available to students worldwide through a variety of nontraditional learning methods.

Bachelor's degrees are available in accountancy, business administration (BBA), business banking and finance, communication and media management, computer and information science, early childhood studies (B.Ed.), nursing (for licensed or registered nurses), and pharmacy; master's degrees are available in business administration (MBA), manufacturing management, project management, and social science (with a specialization in counseling).

At the doctoral level, students can complete a DBA or Ed.D. through a mix of correspondence coursework and guided research. External research Ph.D.'s are also available in business and management and in education (with specializations in art education, curriculum leadership, distance education, early childhood studies, religious education, and women in education).

University of Southern Queensland

Many, many online and correspondence-based bachelor's, master's, and doctoral programs through this Australian "University of the Year."

International Office
Toowoomba Qld
Queensland 4350
Australia

Web site	www.usqonline.com.au or www.usq.edu.au
Email	international@usq.edu.au
Phone	+61 (74) 631 2362
Fax	+61 (74) 636 2211
Year established	1967
Ownership status	Nonprofit, state
Residency	None
Cost	Average
Degree level	Bachelor's, Master's, Doctorates
Fields of study or special interest	See below
Other information	Voted joint "University of the Year 2000-2001" (alongside the prestigious University of Wollongong) by the Australian Good Universities Guide, the University of Southern Queensland is generally regarded as one of the most energetic universities in Australia when it comes to global online education. Although most programs still require some correspondence coursework, many programs can now be completed entirely by online study.

Bachelor's programs are available in accounting, administrative management, anthropology, applied economics and resource management, applied finance, applied mathematics, Asian studies, banking, business administration (BBA), communication and media studies, computer software development, computing, education, engineering (with ten specializations), engineering technology (with five specializations), English literature, finance, further education and training, general studies, geographic information systems, human resource management practices, Indonesian language, information technology (with six specializations), information technology management, international relations, journalism, logistics and operations management, marketing, mathematics, nursing, psychological studies, psychology, public relations, statistics, strategic human resource management, and surveying. Double majors are generally also available.

Master's programs are available in accounting, applied finance, applied linguistics, arts management, business administration (MBA), business information technology, business law, commercial law, e-business, editing and publishing, education (with twelve specializations, including children's literature), educational technology, engineering (with six specializations), engineering technology (with six specializations), environmental management, finance, geomatics, health communication systems, human resource management, information systems, information technology, international business, leadership, management, marketing, midwifery, nursing, occupational health and safety, occupational health and safety nursing, online education, open and distance learning, professional accounting, professional communication, project management, and rural and remote health.

At the doctoral level, students may choose the Doctor of Business Administration (DBA) or the Ed.D. in professional leadership. It may also be possible to negotiate a research M.Phil. or Ph.D. on a case-by-case basis.

University of Texas

Several online master's degrees (including an MBA) from one of the largest state-funded university systems in the United States.

Office of Information Technology and Distance Education
201 West Seventh Street
Austin, TX 78701

Web site	www.telecampus.utsystem.edu
Email	telecampus@utsystem.edu
Phone	(512) 499 4207 • (888) 786 9832
Year established	1973
Ownership status	Nonprofit, state
Residency	None
Cost	Average for in-state students; high average for out-of-state students
Degree level	Master's
Fields of study or special interest	Business administration, computer science, educational technology, electrical engineering, kinesiology, reading
Other information	The University of Texas Telecampus pools the distance-learning offerings of the 15-campus University of Texas system. Work is completed through the Telecampus, and the relevant specific branch of the University of Texas awards the degree.

The UT Telecampus Online MBA in general business administration involves 48 semester hours of coursework and takes two to six years to complete. Each student must apply to a "home campus" at the beginning of the program (Arlington, Brownsville, Dallas, El Paso, Pan American, Permian Basin, San Antonio, or Tyler). Instruction takes place through the UT Telecampus, and the home campus awards the degree. Entrance requirements and curricula may vary depending on the home campus chosen.

The online M.Ed. in educational technology is awarded by the University of Texas at Brownsville. The program involves 36 semester hours of coursework and generally takes two to three years to complete. Thesis and non-thesis tracks are available. Up to one third of the program may consist of approved elective coursework, allowing wide berth for student-defined specialization.

Other master's degrees offered through online study are the M.Ed. in health and kinesiology (awarded by Tyler), the M.Ed. in reading with emphasis in ESL (Arlington), the M.S. in computer science (Arlington and Dallas), the M.S. in computer science and engineering (Arlington), the M.S. in electrical engineering (Arlington and Dallas), and the M.S. in kinesiology (El Paso, Permian Basin, and Pan American). Online graduate-level certificates are available in ESL (Arlington) and telecommunications (Arlington and Dallas).

University of Wales—Lampeter

Nonresidential correspondence-based master's degrees and research-based doctorates from an 179-year-old Welsh university.

Ceredigion, Wales SA48 7ED
United Kingdom

Web site	www.lamp.ac.uk
Email	pg-office@lampeter.ac.uk
Telephone	+44 (1570) 424 748
Fax	+44 (1570) 422 840
Year established	1822
Ownership status	Nonprofit, state
Residency	None for taught master's programs; variable for research programs
Cost	Low average to average
Degree level	Master's, Doctorates
Fields of study or special interest	Most are related to history, philosophy, and/or religion; see below
Other information	Lampeter offers a number of correspondence-based master's programs in some highly specialized humanities-oriented fields.

The M.A. in death and immortality is a good example of Lampeter's unique programs. Students study such topics as the Self in Indian thought, Christian concepts of death, bereavement counseling, reincarnation, life-death ethical issues, and death in popular culture. The program involves an extensive reading list. Similar M.A. programs are available in death studies (focusing more on anthropology and history than philosophy and religion) and ethics of life and death (focusing pretty much exclusively on medical ethics, the ethics of war, capital punishment, and so forth).

Other correspondence-based M.A. programs are available in British Empire and Commonwealth studies, Celtic Christianity, feminist theology, religion/politics/international relations (addressing religion's influence on war and international politics), religious experience, study of religion, and visual representations of history. A Th.M. in church history is also available.

Research-based M.Phil. and Ph.D. programs are available in anthropology, archaeology, classics, English, geography, history, Islamic studies, philosophy, religious studies, and theology. Residency is negotiated on a case-by-case basis.

University of Waterloo

Nonresidential bachelor's degrees in a number of fields for people in Canada and the United States, and a nonresidential master's degree in technology management available to students worldwide.

Web site	dce.uwaterloo.ca
Email	distance@admmail.uwaterloo.ca
Telephone	+1 (519) 888 4050
Fax	+1 (519) 746 6393
Year established	1957
Ownership status	Nonprofit, state
Residency	None
Cost	Low for Canadians; average to high average for non-Canadians
Degree level	Bachelor's, Master's
Fields of study or special interest	See below
Other information	The University of Waterloo's bachelor's degrees, which can be earned entirely through distance education, include a non-major B.A. or B.S.; a B.A. with a major in Canadian studies, classical studies, economics, English, environmental studies, French, geography, history, medieval studies, philosophy, psychology, religious studies, social development studies, or sociology; and a Bachelor of Environmental Studies in geography.

The undergraduate distance courses are normally available to people residing in Canada and the United States. Others may be eligible to enroll in some undergraduate distance courses if they can meet criteria related to communication and assignment due dates and if they are willing to assume extra charges related to the delivery of materials and proctoring of examinations. Non-Canadians pay three times as much tuition for undergraduate courses as Canadian citizens.

Upon approval and evaluation, credit may be given for prior academic experience, but none for experiential learning.

UW's undergraduate distance-learning courses are offered on a time schedule in which papers and exams must be done by specific times within one of three terms available each academic year. Both online and correspondence-based classes are available.

The Master of Applied Science in management of technology is designed for engineers and scientists who need to deal with technology management in their jobs. This part-time program is available to students worldwide, and may be completed through a mix of online and correspondence courses.

University of Wisconsin—Superior

An individualized Bachelor of Science degree completed through off-campus study assignments with occasional student-faculty meetings.

Extended Degree Program
Erlanson 105
P.O. Box 2000
Superior, WI 54880

Web site	edp.uwsuper.edu
Email	extdegree@uwsuperior.edu
Telephone	(715) 394 8487
Fax	(715) 394 8139
Year established	1893
Ownership status	Nonprofit, state
Residency	Negotiable
Cost	Average
Degree level	Bachelor's
Fields of study or special interest	Individualized
Other information	In Superior's Extended Degree Program (EDP), the student can design a B.S. program in any field of academic or professional interest, provided that the faculty is willing and able to accommodate the intended program of study. The student earns credit by following pre-designed study plans or by negotiating new learning contracts for faculty review. Work is organized around negotiable meetings between the student and faculty member; during these meetings the student and faculty member review prior work and plan the next phase of independent study.

A considerable amount of credit is available for prior learning through transfer credit, credit by examination, and life-experience assessment. |

Upper Iowa University

Associate's, bachelor's, and master's degrees in business-related and other fields entirely through home study.

P.O. Box 1861
Fayette, IA 52142

Web site	www.uiu.edu
Email	extdegree@uiu.edu
Telephone	(319) 425 5252 • (888) 877 3742
Fax	(319) 425 5353
Year established	1857
Ownership status	Nonprofit, independent
Residency	None
Cost	High average
Degree level	Associate's, Bachelor's, Master's
Fields of study or special interest	Accounting, business, business leadership, human resource management, human services, management, marketing, public administration, social science
Other information	Upper Iowa's External Degree program offers the opportunity to earn a B.S. in accounting, business, human resource management, human services, management, marketing, public administration, or social science. An A.A. with a liberal arts or general business concentration is also available. The program is based on directed independent study. Frequent interaction with the faculty by phone, mail, or email is encouraged. Enrollment is open to anyone, and applicants with a high school diploma or G.E.D. are almost always admitted. Students are admitted throughout the year and can enroll in courses at any time. Optional one-week summer sessions are offered on the Fayette campus, allowing students to complete up to 6 semester hours of credit in a small amount of time. Credits may be awarded for previous college work (including online or correspondence courses from other institutions), job and military training, other noncollegiate educational experiences, life experience, and equivalency exams. Up to 90 of the 120 semester credits required for the degree can be transferred into the program. Students must complete a minimum of 30 semester hours with Upper Iowa University.

UIU also offers an online Master of Arts in business leadership with three areas of emphasis: human resource management, organizational development, and quality management.

International students are admitted, and those interested should contact the school for application details.

Walden University

Master's and doctorates in many fields by guided independent study.

155 Fifth Avenue South
Minneapolis, MN 55401

Web site	www.waldenu.edu
Email	info@waldenu.edu
Telephone	(612) 338 7224 • (800) 925 3368
Fax	(612) 338 5092
Year established	1970
Ownership status	Independent
Residency	No residency for master's programs; some residency for doctorates
Cost	High average
Degree level	Master's, Doctorates
Fields of study or special interest	Applied management and decision sciences, education, educational technology, health services, human services, psychology

Other information Walden is a pioneer in offering graduate-level education by distance learning. Its degrees are earned through a combination of independent study, intensive weekend sessions held regionally (optional except for doctoral students), personal interaction with faculty, and a summer session held at Indiana University (also optional except for doctoral students). Indiana and Walden collaborate to give students online access to the Indiana University library and reference services.

Online master's degrees are available in educational technology and psychology, and typically take 18 months to complete.

The doctoral programs in applied management and decision sciences, education, health services, human services, and psychology allow students to complete an individualized study plan within a curriculum developed by Walden faculty. In the final phase of doctoral study, students design and carry out a research project written up as a dissertation, which must be orally defended. Most students complete their doctorate within three years of enrolling, but each student determines his or her own pace.

Walden students are mostly midcareer professionals. They engage in self-directed research in consultation with the faculty mentors and by interacting with other students, both during residential periods and by use of the Internet.

Walden is a pioneer in offering graduate-level education by distance learning.

Washington State University

Bachelor's and master's programs available to students everywhere by distance learning.

Extended Degree Programs
Van Doren Hall 204
P.O. Box 645220
Pullman, WA 99164-5220

Web site	www.eus.wsu.edu/edp
Email	edp@wsu.edu
Telephone	(509) 335 3557 • (800) 222 4978
Fax	(509) 335 4850
Year established	1890
Ownership status	Nonprofit, state
Residency	None (except for Pharm.D.)
Cost	Average
Degree level	Bachelor's, Master's, Doctorates
Fields of study or special interest	Agriculture, business administration, criminal justice, education, engineering management, human development, manufacturing engineering, pharmacy, social sciences
Other information	Washington State University's office of Extended Degree Programs (EDP) currently offers five degrees to students nationally and internationally. Courses are delivered through a variety of distance-learning technologies, primarily Internet and videotape delivery.

The B.A. in social sciences is a broad-based, interdisciplinary liberal arts degree. Working with an academic advisor, each student develops a program of study that best meets his or her educational goals. The B.A. in business administration leads students through a broad range of business disciplines. The B.A. in criminal justice offers a policy-focused curriculum based on a 24-credit major and 24 credits of electives in psychology and sociology. The B.A. in human development involves a supervised internship in the student's local community setting. The B.S. in agriculture is offered by the Tri-State Agricultural Distance Delivery Alliance (TADDA), a cooperative distance delivery program developed jointly with the University of Idaho and Oregon State University.

Applicants to WSU's bachelor's programs must have already completed at least 27 semester credits of coursework. Credit may be awarded by examination. Instruction takes place through a mix of online, correspondence, and video-based courses. The university offers more than 150 distance courses.

An M.S. in agriculture is also available.

Washington residents are also eligible for the following low-residency programs: a B.A. in education (with teaching certificate), a B.S. in manufacturing engineering, a Master of Engineering Management, and a Doctor of Pharmacy.

Foreign students are admitted if they can provide a working email address.

Western Illinois University

An individualized, student-centered B.A. with no required on-campus residency.

Non-Traditional Programs
5 Horrabin Hall
1 University Circle
Macomb, IL 61455

Web site	www.wiu.edu/users/mintp
Email	np-bot@wiu.edu
Telephone	(309) 298 1929
Fax	(309) 298 2226
Year established	1899
Ownership status	Nonprofit, state
Residency	None
Cost	Low average
Degree level	Bachelor's
Fields of study or special interest	Individualized major

Other information   Western Illinois University offers The Board of Trustees Bachelor of Arts through a nontraditional program designed to allow working adults with family and other responsibilities the chance to complete their degree requirements off campus. No major need be declared.

Of the 120 credits required for the B.A., at least 15 must be earned through WIU. Remaining credit can be awarded based on prior schooling at other regionally accredited colleges or universities, military and job-related training, examination (including CLEP, DANTES, and ECE), departmental exams, and other documentation of college-level learning. The university stresses that skills and knowledge acquired by nonacademic means can be evaluated for academic credit. Western Illinois provides a helpful guide to the preparation of a prior-learning portfolio.

Students who did not graduate from an Illinois high school must pass an exam on the United States and Illinois state constitutions or take an equivalent course in political science. All students must pass a university writing exam.

The time to complete the B.A. depends on the amount of transferable prior credit and the level of academic activity after admission.

The total cost of the program depends on the number and type of courses taken.

Students from other countries may be admitted, but should have a U.S. address to which materials may be sent.

Appendix A

Law Degrees

There are two ways to become a lawyer in the United States without going to a traditional law school. One way is to earn a law degree from a correspondence law school whose graduates can take the Bar exam. The other is to qualify for the Bar exam through apprenticeship study, the way Abraham Lincoln, four or five other U.S. presidents, and thousands of others have done. (Study by firelight is not required.)

Law degrees by mail

Many states used to permit people who studied law by correspondence study to sit for their Bar exams. Now only California has this policy. Earning a law degree by correspondence requires either three or four years of study, but only the four-year programs qualify for taking the California Bar. The four-year degree is earned by studying at home for 864 hours a year (an average of about 2½ hours a day) for four years. There are no shortcuts; you must take the full four calendar years, even if you have time for more study. At the end of the first year, correspondence students must take the First Year Law Students' Qualifying Exam, known as the "Baby Bar," which the California Bar requires as an indication of whether a student is being well trained. Only about 20 percent of students pass the Baby Bar at any given sitting. After completing the Baby Bar, there are three more years of study, followed by the regular Bar exam, the same one taken by students at Stanford, Berkeley, and all the state's traditional law schools.

None of California's correspondence law schools is approved by the American Bar Association, but they are accredited by the California Bar, thus qualifying students to take the regular Bar exam. Pass rates for individual schools vary widely, ranging from zero to over 75 percent (Oak Brook College).

The following is a list of all the Bar-exam-qualifying correspondence law schools:

Abraham Lincoln University
3000 South Robertson Blvd., Suite 420
Los Angeles, CA 90034
Phone: (310) 204 0222
Fax: (310) 204 7025
Email: info@alulaw.com
Web site: www.alulaw.com

**British-American University
School of Law**
2026 Summer Wind
Santa Ana, CA 92704
Phone: (714) 850 1027 •
   (888) 264 3261
Fax: (714) 850 4621
Email: info@lawprogram.com
Web site: www.british-american.edu

Concord University School of Law
1133 Westwood Blvd., Suite 2000
Los Angeles, CA 90024
Phone: (310) 824 6980 •
   (800) 439 4794
Fax: (888) 564 6745
Email: info@concordlawschool.com
Web site: www.concord.kaplan.edu

Newport University School of Law
20101 S.W. Birch Street, Suite 120
Newport Beach, CA 92660
Phone: (949) 757 1155 •
   (800) 345 3272
Fax: (949) 757 1156
Email: info@newport.edu
Web site: www.newport.edu

Northwestern California University School of Law
1750 Howe Ave., Suite 535
Sacramento, CA 95825
Phone: (916) 922 9303
Fax: (916) 922 0418
Email: nculaw@aol.com
Web site: www.nwculaw.edu

Oak Brook College of Law and Government Policy
P. O. Box 26870
Fresno, CA 93729
(559) 650 7755 • (888) 335 3425
Fax: (559) 650 7750
Email: info@obcl.edu
Web site: www.obcl.edu

Saratoga University
780 Blairwood Court
San Jose, CA 95120
Phone: (408) 927 6760 •
   (800) 870 4246
Email: mhn@saratogau.edu
Web site: www.saratogau.edu

Southern California University for Professional Studies
1840 East 17th Street
Santa Ana, CA 92705-8605
Phone: (714) 480 0800 •
   (800) 477 2254
Fax: (714) 480 0834
Email: enroll@scups.edu
Web site: www.scups.edu

University of Honolulu School of Law
1031 McHenry Ave., Suite #13
Modesto, CA 95350
Phone: (209) 523 4064
Fax: (209) 522 3312
Email: uhlaw@thevision.net
Web site: www.thevision.net/uhlaw

William Howard Taft University
201 East Sandpointe Ave., #400
Santa Ana, CA 92707-5703
Phone: (714) 850 4800 •
   (800) 882 4555
Fax: (714) 708 2082
Email: admissions@taftu.edu
Web site: www.taftu.edu

The apprenticeship approach

There are still a few states left where it is possible to qualify for the Bar exam by studying law privately under the supervision of either a lawyer or a judge. Though it's not easy to set up an apprenticeship program on one's own, it can be, and has been, done.

All of the states where apprenticeship is possible—Alaska, California, Maine, New York, Vermont, Virginia, Washington, and Wyoming—require evidence of four continuous years of law study. Some of those—Alaska, Maine, New York, and Wyoming—require that one of those years be at an ABA-approved law school. California also requires one year at a law school, but it doesn't have to be ABA-approved. (These are general guidelines; be sure to contact the individual state's Bar for specific requirements.)

For those aspiring to become a lawyer by apprenticeship, one noteworthy resource is the Law School Apprenticeship Program (2565 I-Rd., Grand Junction, CO 81501; (800) 529 9383; *www.lawprogram.com*), operated by Roger Agajanian, who also runs the British-American University School of Law (see listing above). Its library of over 200 video lectures (available over the Web, on CD-ROM, or on tape) is designed to supplement the study of apprentice law students.

The parlay approach

Some of the California correspondence law schools have written about a "parlay" approach, in which their graduates would go on to do a Master of Law (LL.M.) degree—a higher degree than the J.D.!—at an ABA-accredited law school. Following this one-year residential program, the claim is made that the student would be permitted to take the Bar in most states of the United States. While the idea is creative, no one has yet actually done it, and we would urge exercising of caution before becoming involved in such a parlay approach.

Appendix B

For More Information on Schools in This Book

If you have questions about one of the schools described in this book, don't hesitate to write to us. We'll do our best to help. These are the ground rules:

What to do before writing to us

1. Point your Web browser to *www.degree.net/updates/mailandinternet*. At this site we will post updates and corrections to the school listings in this book.
2. Do your own homework. Check first with your local library, the relevant state education department, or the Better Business Bureau, as well as, of course, searching on the Internet. Any major search engine should locate a school's Web site. There is, for instance, a complete university list in the "universities" section of *www.yahoo.com*.
3. Schools do move, and the post office will only forward mail for a short while. If a letter comes back as "undeliverable," call directory assistance ("information") in the school's city and see if a number is listed. They can give you a new street address as well.
4. Schools do change phone numbers, and the telephone company will only notify you of the new number for a short while. If you can't reach a school by phone, write to it, or try directory assistance to see if there has been a change.

Writing to us

If you cannot reach a school by phone or mail or on the Internet, if you have new information you think we should know, or if you have questions or problems, then please write and let us know. We may be able to help.

- Enclose a self-addressed, stamped envelope. If you are outside the United States, enclose two international postal reply coupons, available at your post office.
- If you want extensive advice or opinions on your personal situation, you will need to use the Degree Consulting Service that John established (although he no longer runs it). This service is described in Appendix D.
- Don't get too annoyed if we don't respond promptly. We do our best, but we get overwhelmed sometimes, and we travel a lot.
- Please don't telephone.
- Write to us at:

  Bears' Guide
  P.O. Box 7123
  Berkeley, CA 94707 USA

- Or email us at *johnandmariah@degree.net*.

Again, do let us know of any mistakes or outdated information you find in this book; we will post corrections at *www.degree.net/updates/mailandinternet*.

Appendix C

For Information on Schools Not in This Book

There are four reasons why a school in which you might be interested is not described in this book:

1. It might be relevant, but we chose not to designate it one of the best schools.

2. It is not relevant for this book since it does not offer degrees entirely or mostly by distance learning.

3. It's new and we hadn't heard about it before this book went to press. (If so, write and tell us about it.)

4. It does not have recognized accreditation.

If you have questions about a school that is not described in this book, here is what we suggest, in the following order:

1. Check *Bears' Guide to Earning Degrees by Distance Learning*, which is a complete source for all distance-learning programs, and is published by Ten Speed Press. In it we list over 2,500 schools that offer degrees by home study—good, bad, and otherwise. For more information, write to the address below, or visit our Web site at *www.degree.net*.

2. Look it up in one of the standard school directories that you can find in any public library or bookstore: Lovejoy's, Barron's, Peterson's, Patterson's, ARCO, and half a dozen others. These books describe virtually every traditional college and university in the United States and Canada.

3. Ask for the help of a reference librarian. Your tax dollars pay their salaries.

4. If you know the location of the school, even just the state, check with the relevant state education agency.

If none of the above approaches produce any useful information, then write to us and we will do what we can to help.

- Enclose a self-addressed, stamped envelope.

- If you want extensive advice or opinions on your personal situation, you will need to use the Degree Consulting Service described in Appendix D.

- Don't get too annoyed if we don't respond promptly. We do our best, but we get overwhelmed sometimes, and we travel a lot.

- Please don't telephone.

- Write to us at:

  Bears' Guide
  P.O. Box 7123
  Berkeley, CA 94707

- Or email us at *johnandmariah@degree.net*.

Appendix D

For Personal Advice on Your Own Situation

If you would like advice and recommendations on your own specific situation, a personal counseling service offers this information, by mail only. John started this service in 1977 at the request of many readers. While he still remains a consultant, since 1981 the actual consulting and personal evaluations have been done by two colleagues of his, who are leading experts in the field of nontraditional education.

For a modest consulting fee, these things are done:

1. You will get a long personal letter evaluating your situation, recommending the best degree programs for you (including part-time programs in your area, if relevant) and estimating how long it will take and what it will cost you to complete your degree(s).

2. You will get answers to any specific questions you may have with regard to programs you may now be considering, institutions you have already dealt with, or other relevant matters.

3. You will get detailed, up-to-the-minute information on institutions and degree programs, equivalency exams, sources of the correspondence courses you may need, career opportunities, resumé writing, sources of financial aid, and other topics in the form of extensive prepared notes.

4. You will be entitled to telephone the service for a full year for unlimited follow-up counseling, to keep updated on new programs and other changes, and to otherwise use the service as your personal information resource.

If you are interested in this personal counseling, please write or call and you will be sent descriptive literature and a counseling questionnaire, without cost or obligation.

If, once you have these materials, you do want counseling, simply fill out the questionnaire and return it, with a letter and resumé if you like, along with the fee. Your personal reply and counseling materials will be airmailed to you as quickly as possible.

For free information about this service, write, telephone, or email:

Degree Consulting Services

P.O. Box 3533
Santa Rosa, CA 95402
Phone: (707) 539 6466
Fax: (707) 538 3577
Email: degrees@sonic.net.
Web site: www.degreeconsult.com

Appendix E

Higher Education Agencies

The following agencies license, regulate, or are otherwise concerned with higher education in their state, province, or country. If you have any concerns about the legality of an institution, or its right to award degrees, these are the places to ask. This information changes on almost a daily basis. If you discover errors or changes, please let us know at *johnandmariah@degree.net*. Thank you.

United States: State Agencies

Alabama
Commission on Higher Education
100 North Union St.
Montgomery, AL 36130
Phone: (334) 242 1998
Fax: (334) 242 0268
Web site: www.ache.state.al.us

Alaska
Alaska Commission on
    Postsecondary Education
3030 Vintage Boulevard
Juneau, AK 99801
Phone: (907) 465 2962
Fax: (907) 465 5316
Web site: www.state.ak.us/acpe

Arizona
Arizona Commission for
    Postsecondary Education
2020 North Central Ave.,Suite 275
Phoenix, AZ 85004
Phone: (602) 229 2591
Fax: (602) 229 2599
Web site: www.acpe.asu.edu

Arkansas
Arkansas Department of Higher
    Education
114 East Capitol Ave.
Little Rock, AR 72201
Phone: (501) 371 2000
Fax: (501) 371 2003

California
Bureau for Private, Postsecondary
    and Vocational Education
1027 10th St., 4th Floor
Sacramento,CA 95814
Phone: (916) 445 3427
Fax: (916) 323 6571
Web site: www.dca.ca.gov/bppve

Colorado
Colorado Commission on Higher
    Education
1300 Broadway, 2nd Floor
Denver, CO 80203
Phone: (303) 866 2723
Fax: (303) 860 9750

Connecticut
Board of Governors for Higher
    Education
61 Woodland St.
Hartford, CT 06105
Phone: (860) 947 1801
Fax: (860) 947 1310
Web site: ctdhe.commnet.edu

Delaware
Delaware Higher Education
    Commission
Carvel State Office Building
820 North French St.
Wilmington, DE 19801
Phone: (302) 577 3240
Fax: (302) 577 6765
Web site: www.doe.state.de.us

District of Columbia
Office of Postsecondary Education
    Research and Assistance
2100 Martin Luther King, Jr. Ave.
    SE
Suite 401
Washington, DC 20020
Phone: (202) 727 3688
Fax: (202) 727 2739

Florida
Florida Postsecondary Education
    Planning Commission
Turlington Building
Tallahassee, FL 32399
Phone: (904) 488 7894
Fax: (904) 922 5388

Georgia
Board of Regents
270 Washington St. SW
Atlanta, GA 30334
Phone: (404) 656 2202
Fax: (404) 657 6979
Web site: www.usg.edu

Hawaii
State Postsecondary Education
    Commission
2444 Dole St., Room 209
Honolulu, HI 96822
Phone: (808) 956 8207
Fax: (808) 956 5286

Idaho
Idaho Board of Education
P.O. Box 83720
Boise, ID 83720-0027
Phone: (208) 334 2270
Fax: (208) 334 2632
Web site: www.sde.state.id.us/Dept

Illinois
Board of Higher Education
431 East Adams, 2nd Floor
Springfield, IL 62701
Phone: (217) 782 2551
Fax: (217) 782 8548
Web site: www.ibhe.state.il.us

Indiana
Indiana Commission for Higher
    Education
101 West Ohio St., Suite 550
Indianapolis, IN 46204
Phone: (317) 464 4400
Fax: (317) 464 4410
Web site: www.che.state.in.us

Iowa
Board of Regents
100 Court Ave., Suite 203
Des Moines, IA 50319
Phone: (515) 281 3934
Fax: (515) 281 6420
Web site: www2.state.ia.us/regents

Kansas
Kansas Board of Regents
700 S.W. Harrison, Suite 1410
Topeka, KS 66603
Phone: (913) 296 3421
Fax: (913) 296 0983
Web site: www.kansasregents.org

Kentucky
Kentucky Council on Postsecondary
    Education
1024 Capital Center Dr., Suite 320
Frankfort, KY 40601
Phone: (502) 573 1555
Fax: (502) 573 1535
Web site: www.cpe.state.ky.us

Louisiana
Board of Regents
150 Third St., Suite 129
Baton Rouge, LA 70801
Phone: (504) 342 4253
Fax: (504) 342 9318
Web site: www.regents.state.la.us

Maine
Department of Education Office of
    Higher Education
23 State House Station
Augusta, ME 04333
Phone: (207) 287 5323
Fax: (207) 287 1344
Web site: janus.state.me.us/education

Maryland
Maryland Higher Education
    Commission
16 Francis St.
Annapolis, MD 21401
Phone: (410) 974 2971
Fax: (410) 974 3513
Web site: www.mhec.state.md.us

Massachusetts
Massachusetts Board of Higher
    Education
1 Ashburton Place, Room 1401
Boston, MA 02108
Phone: (617) 727 7785
Fax: (617) 727 6397
Web site: www.mass.edu

Michigan
Michigan Department of Career
    Development
Office of Postsecondary Services
P.O. Box 30714
Lansing, MI 48909
Phone: (517) 373 3820
Fax: (517) 373 2759
Web site: www.state.mi.us/career

Minnesota
Minnesota Higher Education
  Services Office
1450 Energy Park Dr., Suite 350
St. Paul, MN 55108
Phone: (651) 642 0502
Fax: (651) 642 0672
Web site: www.mheso.state.mn.us

Mississippi
Board of Trustees of State
  Institutions of Higher Learning
3825 Ridgewood Road
Jackson, MS 39211
Phone: (601) 982 6623
Fax: (601) 987 4172
Web site: www.ihl.state.ms.us

Missouri
Coordinating Board for Higher
  Education
3515 Amazonas Dr.
Jefferson City, MO 65109
Phone: (573) 751 2361
Fax: (573) 751 6635
Web site: www.mocbhe.gov

Montana
Office of the Commissioner of
  Higher Education
Montana University System
2500 Broadway
Helena, MT 59620
Phone: (406) 444 6570
Fax: (406) 444 1469
Web site: www.montana.edu/
  wwwoche

Nebraska
Coordinating Commission for
  Postsecondary Education
P.O. Box 95005
Lincoln, NE 68509
Phone: (402) 471 2847
Fax: (402) 471 2886
Web site: www.ccpe.state.ne.us

Nevada
University and Community College
  System of Nevada
2601 Enterprise Road
Reno, NV 89512
Phone: (775) 784 4905
Fax: (775) 784 1127
Web site: www.nevada.edu

New Hampshire
New Hampshire Postsecondary
  Education Commission
2 Industrial Park Dr.
Concord, NH 03301
Phone: (603) 271 2555
Fax: (603) 271 2696
Web site: www.state.nh.us/
  postsecondary

New Jersey
Commission on Higher Education
20 West State St.
P.O. Box 542
Trenton, NJ 08625
Phone: (609) 292 4310
Fax: (609) 292 7225
Web site: www.state.nj.us/
  highereducation

New Mexico
Commission on Higher Education
1068 Cerrillos Road
Santa Fe, NM 87501
Phone: (505) 827 7383
Fax: (505) 827 7392
Web site: www.nmche.org

New York
New York State Education
  Department
89 Washington Ave.
Albany, NY 12234
Phone: (518) 474 5844
Fax: (518) 473 4909
Web site: www.nysed.gov

North Carolina
Commission on Higher Education
  Facilities
UNC General Administration
910 Raleigh Rd., P.O. Box 2688
Chapel Hill, NC 27515
Phone: (919) 962 4611
Fax: (919) 962 0008

North Dakota
North Dakota University System
10th Floor, State Capitol
600 East Boulevard Ave., Dept. 215
Bismarck, ND 58505
Phone: (701) 328 2960
Fax: (701) 328 2961
Web site: www.ndus.nodak.edu

Ohio
Ohio Board of Regents
30 East Broad St., 36th Floor
Columbus, OH 43266
Phone: (614) 466 6000
Fax: (614) 466 5866
Web site: www.bor.state.oh.us

Oklahoma
Oklahoma State Regents for Higher
    Education
500 Education Building
State Capitol Complex
Oklahoma City, OK 73105
Phone: (405) 524 9100
Fax: (405) 524 9230
Web site: www.okhighered.org

Oregon
Governor's Office of Education and
    Workforce Policy
Office of Degree Authorization
255 Capitol St. NE, Suite 126
Salem, OR 97310
Phone: (503) 378 3921
Fax: (503) 378 4789
Web site: www.ode.state.or.us

Pennsylvania
Pennsylvania Department of
    Education
Postsecondary and Higher Education
333 Market St., 12th Floor
Harrisburg, PA 17126
Phone: (717) 787 5041
Fax: (717) 783 0583
Web site: www.pde.psu.edu

Puerto Rico
Puerto Rico Council on Higher
    Education
P.O. Box 19900
San Juan, PR 00910
Phone: (787) 724 7100
Fax: (787) 725 1275

Rhode Island
Office of Higher Education
301 Promenade Street
Providence, RI 02908
Phone: (401) 222 6560
Fax: (401) 222 6111
Web site: www.uri.edu/ribog

South Carolina
South Carolina Commission on
    Higher Education
1333 Main St., Suite 200
Columbia, SC 29201
Phone: (803) 737 2260
Fax: (803) 737 2297
Web site: www.che400.state.sc.us

South Dakota
South Dakota Board of Regents
306 E. Capital Ave.
Pierre, SD 57501
Phone: (605) 773 3455
Fax: (605) 773 5320
Web site: www.ris.sdbor.edu

Tennessee
Tennessee Higher Education
    Commission
Parkway Towers, Suite 1900
404 James Robertson Pkwy.
Nashville, TN 37243
Phone: (615) 741 3605
Fax: (615) 741 6230
Web site: www.state.tn.us/thec

Texas
Texas Higher Education
    Coordinating Board
P.O. Box 12788
Austin, TX 78711
Phone: (512) 427 6101
Fax: (512) 483 6127
Web site: www.thecb.state.tx.us

Utah
Utah State Board of Regents
3 Triad Center, Suite 550
Salt Lake City, UT 84180
Phone: (801) 321 7101
Fax: (801) 321 7199
Web site: www.utahsbr.edu

Vermont
State Department of Education
Career and Lifelong Learning
120 State St.
Montpelier, VT 05620
Phone: (802) 828 3147
Fax: (802) 828 3140
Web site: www.cit.state.vt.us/educ

Virginia
State Council of Higher Education
    for Virginia
James Monroe Building, 9th Floor
101 N. 14th St.
Richmond, VA 23219
Phone: (804) 225 2600
Fax: (804) 371 7911
Web site: www.schev.edu

Washington
Higher Education Coordinating
    Board
917 Lakeridge Way
P.O. Box 43430
Olympia, WA 98504
Phone: (360) 753 7800
Fax: (360) 753 7808
Web site: www.hecb.wa.gov

West Virginia
West Virginia Higher Education
    Policy Commission
1018 Kanawha Blvd., East, Suite 700
Charleston, WV 25301
Phone: (304) 558 2101
Fax: (304) 558 5719
Web site: www.hepc.wvnet.edu

Wisconsin
Higher Educational Aids Board
131 W. Wilson St., Room 902
Madison, WI 53703
Phone: (608) 267 2206
Fax: (608) 267 2808
Web site: heab.state.wi.us

Wyoming
Wyoming Community College
    Commission
2020 Carey Ave., 8th Floor
Cheyenne, WY 82002
Phone: (307) 777 7763
Fax: (307) 777 6567
Web site: commission.wcc.edu

Canada

Alberta
Alberta Learning
7th Floor, Commerce Place
10155-102 St.
Edmonton, Alberta T5J IX4
Phone: +1 (780) 427 7219
Fax: +1 (780) 422 1263

British Columbia
Private Postsecondary Education
    Commission
960 Quayside Dr., Suite 405
New Westminster, BC V3M 6G2
Phone: +1 (604) 660 4400
Fax: +1 (604) 660 3312

Manitoba
Department of Education and
    Training
2nd floor, 800 Portage Ave.
Winnipeg, Manitoba R3C 0N4
Phone: +1 (204) 945 2211
Fax: +1 (204) 945 8692
Web site: www.gov.mb.ca/educate

New Brunswick
Department of Training and
    Employment Development
P.O. Box 6000
470 York St.
Frederickton, NB E3B 5H1
Phone: +1 (506) 453 2597
Fax: +1 (506) 453 3038

Newfoundland
Newfoundland and Labrador
    Council on Higher Education
3rd Floor, West Block,
    Confederation Building
P.O. Box 8700
St. John's, Newfoundland A1B 4J6
Phone: +1 (709) 729 2083
Fax: +1 (709) 729 3669
Web site: www.gov.nf.ca/edu

Nova Scotia
Department of Education
P.O. Box 578
2021 Brunswick St., Ste. 402
Halifax, NS B3J 2S9
Phone: +1 (902) 424 5168
Fax: +1 (902) 424 0511
Web site: www.ednet.ns.ca

Ontario
Ministry of Education
14th Floor, Mowat Block
900 Bay St.
Toronto, ON M7A 1L2
Phone: +1 (416) 325 2929
Fax: +1 (416) 325 2934
Web site: www.edu.gov.on.ca

Prince Edward Island
Department of Education
Second Fl., Sullivan Building
16 Fitzroy Street, P.O. Box 2000
Charlottetown, PEI C1A 7N8
Phone: +1 (902) 368 4600
Fax: +1 (902) 368 4663
Web site: www.gov.pe.ca

Quebec
Ministere de l'Education
1035, rue De La Chevrotière
Édifice Marie-Guyart, 28e étage
Québec G1R 5A5
Phone: +1 (418) 643 7095
Web site: www.meq.gouv.qc.ca

Saskatchewan
Saskatchewan Education
2220 College Ave.
Regina, SK S4P 3V7
Phone: +1 (306) 787 6030
Fax: +1 (306) 787 7392
Web site: www.sasked.gov.sk.ca

Agencies Outside the U.S. and Canada

Australia
Department of Education, Training,
   and Youth Affairs
Sydney
Phone: +61 (2) 9298 7200
Web site: www.deet.gov.a

Belgium
Ministry of National Education
Centre Arts Lux, 4th & 5th Floors
58 Ave. des Arts, BP5
1040 Brussels
Phone: +32 (2) 512 66 60

Brazil
Ministry of Education and Culture
Esplanada dos Ministerios, Bloco L
74.047 Brasilia, DF
Phone: +55 (61) 214 8432

Bulgaria
Ministry of Education and Science
Blvd. A, Stamboliski 18
Sofia 1000

Cuba
Ministry of Higher Education
Calle 23y F, Vedado
Havana

Denmark
The Danish Ministry of Education
Frederiksholms Kanal 21
DK-1220 Copenhagen
Phone: +45 3392 5000
Fax: +45 3392 5547
Web site: www.uvm.dk/eng

Egypt
Ministry of Education
12 El Falaki Street, Cairo
Phone: +20 (2) 516 9744
Fax: +20 (2) 516 9560

Finland
Ministry of Education
P.O. Box 293
FIN-00171 Helsinki
Phone: +358 (9) 1341 71
Fax: +358 (9) 135 9335
Web site: www.minedu.fi

France
Ministry of National Education
110 Rue de Grenelle
75700 Paris
Phone: +33 (1) 45 50 10 10

Germany
Ministry of Education and Science
Heinemannstr. 2
5300 Bonn 2

Greece
Ministry of Education and Science
Odo Mihalakopoulou 80, Athens
Phone: +30 (1) 21 3230461

Hungary
Ministry of Education
Szalay u. 10-14
1055 Budapest
Phone: +36 (1) 302 0600
Fax: +36 (1) 302 3002
Web site: www.om.hu

India
Department of Education
Ministry of Human Resource
    Development
Government of India
Shastri Bhawan, New Delhi-110001
Phone: +91 (11) 3387342
Fax: +91 (11) 3381355
Web site: education.nic.in

Indonesia
Ministry of National Education
Jalan Jenderal Sudirman
Senayan, Jakarta Pusat
Web site: www.pdk.go.id

Ireland
Department of Education and
    Science
Marlborough St.
Dublin 1
Phone: +353 (1) 8734700 ext.2162
Fax: +353 (1) 8786712
Web site: www.irlgov.ie/educ

Israel
Council for Higher Education
P.O. Box 4037
Jerusalem 91040
Phone: +972 (2) 5679911
Fax: +972 (2) 5660625
Web site: www.israel-mfa.gov.il

Italy
Ministry of Public Education
Viale Trastevere 76/A
00153 Rome
Phone: +39 (6) 58 49 1
Web site: www.istruzione.it

Japan
Ministry of Education, Science,
    Sports and Culture
Web site: www.monbu.go.jp

Mexico
Secretaria de Education Publica
Web site: www.sep.gob.mx

Netherlands
Ministry of Education, Culture and
    Science
Department of Foreign Information
P.O.B. 25000
2700 LZ Zoetermeer
Phone: +31 (79) 3232323
Fax: +31 (79) 3232320
Web site: www.minocw.nl

New Zealand
Ministry of Eduation
National Office
45-47 Pipitea St., P.O. Box 1666
Thorndon, Wellington
Phone: +64 (4) 473 5544
Fax: +64 (4) 499 1327

Norway
Ministry of Education, Research and
    Church Affairs
Akersgt. 44, P.O. Box 8119 Dep.
0032 Oslo
Phone: +47 (22) 24 77 01
Fax: +47 (22) 24 27 33
Web site: odin.dep.no/kuf/engelsk

Philippines
Department of Education, Culture
    and Sports
DECS Complex, Meralco Avenue
Pasig City
Phone: +63 (2) 633 7228
Fax: +63 (2) 632 0805
Web site: www.decs.gov.ph

Portugal
Ministry of Education
Av. 5 de Outubro 107
Lisbon
Phone: +351 (1) 21 793 16 03
Fax: +351 (1) 21 796 41 19
Web site: www.min-edu.pt

South Africa
Department of Education
Private Bag X895
Pretoria 0001
Phone: +27 (12) 312 5911
Fax: +27 (12) 325 6260
Web site: education.pwv.gov.za

South Korea
Ministry of Education
77, Sejong-ro, Chongro-ku
Seoul 110-760
Phone: +82 (2) 739 3345
Fax: +82 (2) 723 7691
Web site: www.moe.go.kr/english

Spain
Ministry of Education and Culture
Web site: www.mec.es

Sweden
Ministry of Education and Cultural
    Affairs
Mynttorget 1
Stockholm 103 33
Phone: +46 (8) 736 10 00

Turkey
Ministry of Education, Youth, and
    Sports
Milli Egitum, Genclik ve Spor
Bakanligi, Anakara

United Kingdom
Department of Education and
    Science
Elizabeth House, York Rd.
London SEI 7PH
Phone: +44 (171) 928 9222

Appendix F

State Laws in Transition

Laws are rarely carved in stone—both the laws themselves and their interpretations can change. This is certainly true in the areas of school recognition and degree acceptance. Often, the laws are quite imprecise. For instance, a school-licensing law may say, "The State Department of Education shall establish standards and procedures for licensing degree-granting schools, and implement them by [such and such a date]." It is then up to the appropriate state officials to make the policies. And even then, laws are always subject to challenge by people who don't like them (or are arrested for violation of them).

Many nontraditional schools and most unaccredited schools have addresses in one of eight U.S. states: Alabama, California, Florida, Hawaii, Iowa, Louisiana, South Dakota, and Wyoming. The situation in these states changes with some regularity due to new laws, new interpretations, or both. And it is not uncommon for any given school to move (or, more likely, simply to change its mailing address) from one place to another, as the laws change. California used to be the haven for many nonwonderful schools. When California laws got tougher, many schools moved to Arizona, then to Louisiana, then to Hawaii (which had more than 200 "universities" in 2000, all but a few run from mailbox services), and now to places like Alabama, South Dakota and Wyoming, where the laws are not very restrictive.

Alabama

For many years, Alabama has had a school licensing law. It doesn't have much power. There is no evaluation; no visit by the state is required. The "campus" can be a post office box or secretarial service. Indeed, some Alabama universities are, in fact, run from Louisiana, Rhode Island, California, and other locations. The situation has been, for years, complicated by the fact that four universities operated by Dr. Lloyd Clayton from Birmingham (Chadwick, American Institute of Computer Science, and two health and nutrition schools) did not even have the most minimal state license, yet they clearly operated with the knowledge and, it seemed, permission of the state. They did not, however, accept students living in the state of Alabama. The schools' position was that not taking Alabama students was simply their policy. It took us nearly five years of writing letters, sending faxes, and making telephone calls before we finally learned the truth. It seems that in the 1980s, the then-attorney general of Alabama issued a ruling that schools that did not do business in the state of Alabama did not need to be licensed by the state.

In 1996, however, this all changed. In response to a request from the Department of Education, the current attorney general ruled that all institutions based in the state *must* be licensed by the state, regardless of their policy for accepting in-state students. Nearly two years later, Chadwick and the others finally got their license to operate, and one of Dr. Clayton's schools, the American Institute of Computer Science, even went on to get recognized accreditation.

But in 2000, the state still does not evaluate the schools that it allows to call themselves "state approved." Some may be quite good; others have a "campus" that is a mailbox rental store. The state doesn't care.

Arizona

Arizona went from being one of the worst states to one of the toughest, following publication of a four-day series called "Diploma Mills: a festering sore on the state of Arizona" in the Phoenix newspaper in the 1980s. But Arizona law does allow new degree-granting universities to be established, as long as it is done on a small scale: fewer than 100 students unless and until the school gains recognized accreditation.

California

Well, at least California is unfailingly interesting. For many years, until the late 1980s, California was the laughingstock of the nation (a mantle subsequently assumed by Louisiana, and then by Hawaii, and now the current holder, South Dakota—with Wyoming and Montana warming up in the bullpen). California authorization required little more than a short disclosure form and evidence of $50,000 in assets. Shady operators were declaring that their homes were their universities, or buying a bundle of obsolete textbooks and declaring that they were worth $100 each. At the time diploma mill operator Ernest Sinclair went to federal prison for mail fraud (selling degrees), his California Pacifica University was still a state-authorized institution.

For a few years, the state had a three-tiered system: authorized (the $50,000 rule) for entire schools, state approved (for specific programs within schools), or accredited. The authorized category was dropped, and approval was extended to entire schools, resulting in the current two-tier system. At that time, dozens of schools closed down, and some of the big ones opened offices in other states: Kennedy-Western in Idaho (later Hawaii and Wyoming), Century in New Mexico, Pacific Western in Louisiana (later Hawaii), Kensington in Hawaii (later Montana), etc.

State approval used to be granted by the Department of Education, through the Council on Private Postsecondary and Vocational Education. In 1997 this agency was abolished and, after much political wrangling, replaced by the Bureau of Private Postsecondary and Vocational Education, which would move from the Department of Education to the Department of Consumer Affairs. And thus it came to pass that California has become the only state in the country, perhaps the only government in the world, in which school licensing and regulation does not take place in the Department of Education.

After a few years of operation, it seems that the Bureau differs little from the Council. They are still underfunded and understaffed, and they still seem unable to deal with the common situation of schools that are run from California but claim their legitimacy from licensing in an easier state: Kennedy-Western (run from California, license from Wyoming), Kensington (California/Montana), Pacific Western (California/Hawaii), Century (California/New Mexico), and so on.

Another confusion in California is that the state senate decreed that holders of approved degrees should be permitted to take relevant state licensing exams, such as those in marriage, family, and child counseling. But the state board of professional licensing refused to go along with this automatic permission, saying that the standards for approval and the standards for certain exams were not at all the same. They now permit degree-holders from some schools, but not others, to take the exams. And almost no other state will accept California-approved degrees for state licensing purposes. Be sure to check on these matters if state licensing is part of your goal.

Florida

Florida is a classic case of what can happen when legislation gets out of hand. A 1988 Florida statute made it a crime to use an unaccredited degree in any way in that state, even if it is from a school approved or licensed in another state. It was a "misdemeanor of the first degree" [*sic*] for a person with, say, a California-approved or a Minnesota-approved degree, to reveal, within the boundaries of Florida, that he or she has that degree.

This rather extraordinary statute was challenged in court, and in 1995, the state supreme court found it to be unconstitutional. However, the judges strongly suggested that if the legislature were to rewrite the law a bit more carefully, it could achieve the same intent and be within the bounds of the constitution. So at the present time, it would appear that holders of legitimate degrees from other states can use them in Florida, but it is clear the situation is far from over. Indeed the legislature is once again considering a strong school licensing law.

Hawaii

For many years, Hawaii had no higher education laws at all. In 1990, a very weak law was enacted, which permitted anyone to start a university and award degrees, with no evaluation or regulation whatsoever, as long as they put a notice somewhere in their literature that they were not accredited. As a result, Hawaii became the world's haven for unaccredited schools, the vast majority terrible, and all but a few with no presence in the state other than a rented mailbox.

In 1999, properly alarmed by Hawaii's deteriorating reputation in higher education, a new law was enacted, requiring that any degree-granting institution with a Hawaii address must actually have at least one employee in Hawaii (what a novel concept!), and also must have at least 25 full-time students resident in the state of Hawaii. It is not yet clear how this law will be either defined or enforced, but some Hawaii schools are claiming they have been given three years to be in compliance.

Iowa

In Iowa, there is a reasonable law, but the way it is enforced (or not enforced) seems to be fostering the growth of unaccredited schools in the state. As we understand it, the law says that schools must have recognized accreditation to operate there, but if a school is involved in the accreditation process, they are given three years, perhaps longer, to "shape up or ship out." The problem is the meaning of "involved in the accreditation process." There are some less-than-wonderful schools operating from mailbox services in Iowa that have actually applied for accreditation from a recognized accrediting agency. But that process can take several years, possibly many years if the school gets an unfavorable evaluation, then puts the accreditation process "on hold" for a year or two or more while they claim to be making certain changes.

Louisiana

For many years, Louisiana has been the victim of what one highly placed state regulator privately calls the "Woody Jenkins law." Jenkins is the prominent Republican politician who is so opposed to the state regulation of almost anything that even though he graduated from law school with highest honors, he has refused to take the Bar exam, believing that the state has no right to require such of lawyers.

Under Jenkins' influence, the legislature required that Louisiana's Board of Regents register any school that filled out a short form, with no evaluation whatsoever. This permitted some completely phony schools to advertise that they were "Appropriately registered with the Board of Regents," or even (improperly) that they were "Recognized by the Board of Regents."

In 1991, Louisiana passed a new law, which gave the Board of Regents power to regulate proprietary (privately owned) schools, although nonprofit schools were still exempt. In 1992, the Board of Regents decided that only proprietary schools with an actual physical presence in the state could be registered. Since dozens of "Louisiana" schools operate either from mail forwarding services or "executive suite" office-rental-by-the-hour establishments, quite a few schools using Louisiana addresses moved their addresses elsewhere, mostly to Iowa, Hawaii, or South Dakota. More than 20 closed down.

Following Jenkins defeat in his try for the U.S. Senate, Louisiana legislators saw their chance, and in 1999 passed a law regulating not-for-profit schools that ostensibly operate from within Louisiana but, in fact, have nothing more than a convenience address and telephone answering service there. It took effect in early 2000 and, like the laws in Arizona and Iowa, requires unaccredited schools to be on an approved accreditation path. Unlike the other states, Louisiana inaugurated clear and specific requirements.

Louisiana unaccredited schools must now be accepted as an accreditation applicant by the Distance Education and Training Council (DETC), a recognized national accreditor. Schools rejected by DETC either lose their Louisiana license or can choose the one loophole in the new law: dropping all but purely religious degrees.

Schools whose applications are accepted by DETC must then pursue accreditation with all deliberate speed. If they get it, they remained licensed; if not, they lose their license to operate (and presumably look toward South Dakota, Montana, Wyoming, or oblivion).

The Louisiana religious loophole is now a tiny one, but it was not always this way. Previously, religious schools were exempt from licensing, but there was no requirement that they offer purely religious degrees. LaSalle University, which operated for years under the religious exemption, used to claim that even their Ph.D.'s in physics, psychology, and political science were religious, because God created everything, including atoms, minds, and lawyers. No matter what you study, they argued, you are studying the work of God. Thankfully, the loophole has been redefined; religious schools can offer only religious degrees: divinity, theology, and so on.

Oregon

Hands down, Oregon has the strictest school laws of any state in the nation. In Oregon, it is *illegal* to use a degree from an institution not accredited by an accrediting agency recognized by the U.S. Department of Education or approved by Oregon's Office of Degree Authorization (ODA). Oregon takes the additional strong step of publishing, at *www.osac.state.or.us/oda*, a list of the most recently reported schools whose degrees are illegal in Oregon.

South Dakota

There are times when we speculate that there must be some secret newsletter circulated among the owners of the dreadful schools of America, in which articles appear analyzing the various states and their tolerance for these kinds of operations. Either that, or just the 'herd' instinct. In any event, as laws and the enforcement thereof showed signs of getting tougher in former havens such as Hawaii, Louisiana, and Iowa, the dreadful schools suddenly began to advertise from addresses in South Dakota, typically in malls and business centers just across the border from some of the larger towns in Iowa. Clearly it had simply never occurred to the good folks who run South Dakota that they needed a bunch of rules on the books to deal with a sudden influx of universities. And so there are virtually none. In the year 2000, one can take out a business license, rent a mailbox in a Mail Boxes Etc. store, hire a telephone answering service, and in little more than 24 hours, this new legal "state-licensed" (i.e. that business license) university can place its first ads in *The Economist* and *USA Today*.

To their credit, the South Dakotans took notice of the situation much more rapidly than most other states have. The newspapers, radio and television stations, and the Better Business Bureau have all been heard from. Can the legislators be far behind?

Wyoming

Wyoming may be the only state that not only does not regulate "religious" schools but also does not question the fact that a school says it is religious. Thus it is the last refuge of that strategy that says, "Let's start a religious school with a nonreligious name, not tell the public that we are religious, and off we go." This has led to some truly dreadful places operating without benefit of any scrutiny or regulation.

Appendix G

Bending the Rules

One of the most common complaints or admonishments we hear from readers goes something like this: "You said thus-and-so, but when I inquired of the school, they told me such-and-such." Often, a school claims that a program we have written about does not exist. Sometimes a student achieves something (such as completing a certain degree entirely by correspondence) that a high official of the school had told us was impossible.

One of the open secrets in the world of higher education is that the rules are constantly being bent. But as with the Emperor's new clothes, no one dares to point and say what is really going on, especially in print.

Unfortunately, we cannot provide many specific examples of bent rules, naming names and all. This is for two good reasons:

1. Many situations where students profit from bent rules would disappear in an instant if anyone dared mention the situation publicly. There is, for instance, a major state university that is forbidden by its charter from granting degrees for correspondence study. But some employees there regularly work out special arrangements for students, who are carried on the books as residential students even though all work is done by mail. Indeed, some graduates have never set foot on campus. If this ever got out, the Board of Trustees, the relevant accrediting agency, and all the other universities in that state would probably have conniptions, and the practice would be suspended at once.

2. These kinds of things can change so rapidly, particularly with new personnel or new policies, that a listing of anomalies and curious practices would probably be obsolete before the ink dried.

Consider a few examples of the sort of thing that is going on in higher education every day, whether or not anyone will admit it (except perhaps behind closed doors or after several drinks):

- A friend of John's at a major university was unable to complete one required course for her doctorate before she had to leave for another state. This university does not offer correspondence courses, but she was able to convince a professor to enroll her in a regular course, which she would just happen never to visit in person.

- A man in graduate school needed to be enrolled in nine units of coursework each semester to keep his employer's tuition-assistance plan going. But his job was too demanding one year, and he was unable to do so. The school enrolled him in nine units of "independent study" for which no work was asked or required, and for which a "pass" grade was given.

- A woman at a large school needed to get a certain number of units before an inflexible time deadline. When it was clear she was not going to make it, a kindly professor turned in grades for her, and told her she could do the actual coursework later on.

- A major state university offers nonresident degrees for people living in that state only. When a reader wrote to John saying that he, living a thousand miles from that state, was able to complete his degree entirely by correspondence, we asked a contact at that school what was going on. "We will take students from anywhere in our correspondence degree program," she told us. "But for God's sake, don't print that in your book, or we'll be deluged with applicants."

- If we are to believe a book by a member of Dr. Bill Cosby's dissertation committee at the University of Massachusetts (*Education's Smoking Gun*, by Reginald Damerell), the only class attendance on Cosby's transcript was one weekend seminar, and the only dissertation committee meeting was a dinner party with spouses at Cosby's house.

- Partway through John's final doctoral oral exam, a key member of his committee had to leave for an emergency. He scrawled a note and passed it to the dean who read it, then crumpled it up and threw it away. The grueling exam continued for several hours more. After it was over and the committee had congratulated him and departed, John retrieved the note from the wastebasket. It read, "Please give John my apologies for having to leave and my congratulations for having passed."

- A man applied to a well-known school that had a rigid requirement that all graduate work (thesis or dissertation) must be begun after enrollment. He started to tell an admissions officer about a major piece of independent research he had completed for his employer. "Stop," he was told. "Don't tell me about that. Otherwise, you wouldn't be able to use it for your master's thesis."

- Mariah was denied admission to the University of California at Berkeley because of some "irregularities" on her high school transcript. (It was a nontraditional high school.) The high school's records had been destroyed in a fire. The former principal checked with the university and discovered that the admissions people would be glad to accept her once the computer said it was okay. He typed up a new transcript saying what the computer wanted said. The computer said okay, and three years later, she graduated Phi Beta Kappa. But how many other applicants accepted the initial "no," not realizing that rules can often be bent?

Please use this information prudently. It will probably do no good to pound on a table and say, "What do you mean, I can't do this? John Bear says that rules don't mean anything, anyway." But when faced with a problem, it can surely do no harm to remember that there do exist many situations in which the rules have turned out to be far less rigid than the printed literature of a school would lead you to believe.

Appendix H

Advice for People in Prison

Note: More than a few readers and users of this book are incarcerated, or are friends and relatives of those who are. We have invited a man who has completed his bachelor's, master's, and Ph.D. (University of South Africa) from prison, and who consults often with inmates and others around the country, to offer his thoughts and recommendations. There is some very useful advice for noninstitutionalized people as well.

Arranging Academic Resources for the Institutionalized

by Douglas G. Dean, Ph.D.

One obstacle for any institutionalized person interested in pursuing a degree is limited resources: lack of available community, faculty, library facilities, phone access, and financial aid. To overcome these problems, it helps to streamline the matriculation process. Time spent in preparation prior to admission can help avoid wasted effort and time in a program, thereby reducing operating expenses and cutting down the number of tuition periods.

A second obstacle is finding ways to ensure that a quality education can be documented. Because courses are generally not prepackaged, it is your responsibility as a student to identify varied learning settings, use a range of learning methods, find and recruit community-based faculty, provide objective means to appraise what has been learned, and, indeed, design the study plan itself.

Finding a flexible degree program

Most well-established degree programs grant credit for a variety of learning experiences. In terms of cost and arrangements required, equivalency examinations and independent study projects are the most expedient. Credit for life-experience learning is another option sometimes offered. If a degree program does not offer at least two of these options, it is unlikely that the program as a whole will be able to accommodate your needs as an institutionalized student.

Writing a competency-based study plan

The traditional method of acquiring credits is to take narrowly focused courses of 2 to 4 credits each. Since the nontraditional student must enlist his or her own instructors, find varied learning methods, and quantify the whole experience, the single-course approach creates much needless duplication of effort.

A better approach is to envision a subject area to be studied for 9 to 12 credits (e.g., statistics), and designate a relevant independent-study project. Identify what topics are germane to the area (e.g., probability theory, descriptive statistics, inferential statistics); the level of comprehension to be achieved (e.g., introductory through intermediate or advanced); how the topic is to be studied (e.g., directed reading, programmed textbooks); and how the competencies acquired are to be demonstrated (e.g., oral examination, proctored examination including problem solving). This way a single independent-study project can take the place of a series of successive courses in a given area (e.g., Statistics 101, 201, 301).

Designing the curriculum

Every accredited degree program has graduation requirements. These requirements broadly define the breadth of subject areas that comprise a liberal arts education and the depth to which they are to be studied. It is the responsibility of the external student not only to identify a curriculum fulfilling these requirements but, in most cases, to design the course content that will comprise each study module.

But how do you know what an area of study consists of before you have studied it? The answer lies in meticulous preparation.

Well in advance of formally applying for an off-campus degree program, obtain course catalogs from several colleges and universities. Look at what these schools consider the core curriculum and what is necessary to fulfill the graduation requirements. With this broad outline in mind, you can begin to form clusters of courses fulfilling each criterion. This approach helps shape the study plan academically.

Next, decide which subjects are of interest within each criterion area. Compare topical areas within each subject as described in the course listings and commonalities will emerge. From there, it is simply a matter of writing to the various instructors for copies of their course syllabuses. These course outlines will provide more detailed information about the subject matter and identify the textbooks currently used at that level of study.

Means of study

Having decided what is to be studied, you must then propose various ways to study it. Equivalency exams (such as CLEP) will enable the student to acquire credits instantly, often in core or required areas of study. This helps reduce overall program costs by eliminating the need for textbooks and tuition fees. More importantly, it helps reduce the number of special learning arrangements that must otherwise be made.

"Testing out" of correspondence courses (taking only the examinations without doing the homework assignments) is another excellent way to acquire credits quickly. This can, however, be an expensive method since full course fees are still assessed. Nonetheless, if you study on your own in advance according to the course syllabus, and if the instructor can then be convinced to waive prerequisite assignments, it can be an efficient and cost-effective method to use.

Independent-study projects should form the balance of any study plan. With the topical areas, learning objectives, and learning materials identified, an independent-study project allows you to remain with the same instructor(s) from an introductory through an intermediate or advanced level of study. This eliminates the need for new arrangements to be made every 2 to 4 credits. An independent-study project can take the form of simple directed reading, tutorial instruction, practicum work, or a combination of these methods, culminating in the final product.

Direct tutorial arrangements, similar to the European don system, commit you to learning under a single instructor until he or she is convinced that you have mastered a given subject at a predetermined level of competency. The tutoring itself may take the form of directed reading from both primary and secondary sources, writing and orally defending assigned topical papers, monitored practica, and/or supervised research projects. The caveat is that the tutor determines when you have satisfied all study requirements, so the study plan should meticulously spell out the breadth and depth of what is to be studied.

You may also be able to use existing classroom courses as a setting in which to have your mastery of a given subject evaluated. Some institutions periodically offer an on-site college or vocational course (e.g., communications skills).

Instead of taking such a course for the standard 2 to 3 credits, you may also be able to arrange for specific communication skills (composition, rhetoric) to be evaluated at a given level of mastery (beginning to advanced). In this single step, you may be able to earn advanced credit and fulfill all the communication skills core requirements for graduation.

Various professions require practitioners to earn continuing-education credits, usually through seminars and/or home study courses. These courses represent the latest knowledge in a given field, come prepackaged with an evaluation test, and are an excellent source of study material. The breadth and depth of specialization offered in such courses is especially useful to students with graduate or postgraduate aspirations.

Independent-study projects require the aid of qualified people to act as community faculty and to oversee personally the progress of the work. Therefore, it is highly advantageous to line up faculty in advance of entering the degree program. It is equally important to have alternates available in the event an instructor is unable, for any reason, to fulfill his or her commitment. It is better to anticipate these needs at the preparatory stage than to be scrambling for a replacement while the tuition clock is running.

Multiple treatments of subject matter

The external student is often without benefit of lecture halls, interactions with other students, or readily available academic counseling services. For the institutionalized student, stopping in to see a faculty member (or sometimes even picking up the phone) for help with a study problem is not an option. This is why alternative methods of study are so valuable.

One approach is to use several textbooks covering the same subject matter. If something does not make sense, there is a different treatment of the subject to turn to.

Programmed textbooks make especially good substitute tutors. A programmed text breaks the subject matter into small segments requiring a response from the reader, with periodic tests to check progress. Such texts are now available in many subject areas, but are particularly useful for the sciences. Titles can be obtained from the *Books in Print* subject guide, or by writing directly to textbook publishers.

Audiovisual materials can, to some extent, make up for the lack of lectures and classes typical of college life. Audiovisual departments at large universities often have a catalog of materials available for rental. These materials frequently take the form of a comprehensive tape series and may address even the most advanced subject matter. When using such materials, it is best to obtain them through the school or social-service department of your institution of residence.

Some large campuses have lecture-note services that employ advanced students to attend class lectures and take copious lecture notes, which are then sold to students. Aside from yielding insights into good notetaking, these published notes are an additional treatment of course content and can indicate what topical areas are given special emphasis. Such notes are especially recommended for new students.

Documenting study

The administrators of a degree program must be convinced that there are acceptable ways to document what has been learned, and what levels of subject mastery have been achieved, without just taking the student's word for it. Community faculty members may be asked to provide written or oral examinations, but it does not hurt to make their jobs easier.

It is highly recommended that each study project be evaluated using a number of means (objective tests, essay exams, oral exams) and documented using a variety of methods (student narrative, faculty narrative, test results, final product, grade equivalent, etc.).

Self-evaluation, not unlike personal logs or journals, provides an excellent primary source from which to glean what you truly know, how you came to know it, and what new questions the acquired knowledge has given rise to. Any future employer or admissions counselor unfamiliar with nontraditional or off-campus degree programs can gain a fuller appreciation of the process through such narratives.

Likewise, a narrative evaluation written by the instructor provides a description of your competencies that ordinary assessment methods are unable to detect or reflect. Nuances of learning style, ability to converse in the field of study, and scholarly integrity are examples of such insights.

Depending on the subject at hand, a final product may take the form of a research monograph, video presentation, musical manuscript, senior thesis, etc.—whatever will best prove and record that you have achieved the target level of competency in that field.

Most professions (accounting, psychology, law, medicine, etc.) require licensing and/or board certification examinations. An industry has built up around this need, providing parallel or actual past examinations to help prepare students. If you agree to take a relevant sample examination under proctored conditions, with cutoff scores negotiated in advance, the community faculty member is relieved of having to design his or her own objective examination for just one student. This approach adds validity to the assessment process and provides a standardized score that has some universal meaning. This is an optional approach but it may be worth the effort.

Recruiting community faculty

Just as it is easier for a student to organize a study plan into blocks of subject areas, a competency-based study plan of this sort makes it easier for a prospective instructor to visualize what is being asked of him or her.

A typical independent-study project defines for the instructor what specific topics are to be studied, what levels of mastery will be expected of the student, what textbooks or other materials will be used, and what is expected of the instructor.

Many traditional academics are unfamiliar with external degree programs. Consequently, they tend to assume that serving as your community faculty member will require greater effort and time on their part than for the average student, who in fact may expect their services in many roles, from academic advisor to tutor. The more you can do up front to define clearly the role and expected duties of the community faculty member, the more successful you will be in enlisting instructors for independent-study projects.

Instructors may sometimes be found on the staff of the institution where you are located. They can also be found through a canvass letter sent to the appropriate department heads at area colleges, universities, and technical schools. The same approach can be used to canvass departments within area businesses, museums, art centers, hospitals, libraries, theaters, zoos, banks, and orchestras, to name but a few possibilities. People are often flattered at being asked, provided it is clear to them exactly what they are getting into.

The more you can operate independently and rely on community faculty for little more than assessment purposes, the more likely it is that you will be successful in recruiting help, and thereby broadening your range of study options.

Revealing your institutionalized status

It is generally proper and appropriate to inform potential schools and potential faculty of one's institutionalized status. (Many institutions now have mailing addresses that do not indicate that they are, in fact, institutions.) Some schools or individuals may be put off by this, but then you would not want to deal with them anyway. Others may be especially motivated to help.

A recommended approach is to first make a general inquiry about the prospective school or program. With this information (which is intended for the general student) in hand, you can better tailor inquiries to specific departments or faculty, addressing your specific needs.

Financing the educational process

Unfortunately, there are virtually no generalizations to be made here whatsoever. Each institution seems to have its own policy with regard to the way finances are handled. Some institutionalized people earn decent wages and have access to the funds. Others have little or no ability to pay their own way. Some institutions permit financial gifts from relatives or friends; others do not. Some schools make special concessions or have some scholarship funds available for institutionalized students; many do not. Contact the financial aid office of the prospective school with any such questions.

Again, start with a general inquiry, as would any student, then ask about the applicability of specific programs to your situation. Often a key element is to find someone on campus, perhaps in the financial aid office or in your degree program, who is willing to do the actual legwork, walking your financial aid paperwork to various administrative offices. A financial aid package is of no use to anyone if it cannot be processed.

In conclusion

Institutionalized students must be highly self-directed and honest enough with themselves to recognize if they are not. Because you live where you work, it takes extra effort to set aside daily study time. You not only have to get in the right frame of mind, but you have to accommodate institution schedules, too. It can mean working with a minimum number of books or tapes to comply with property rules. It can mean study periods that begin at eleven o'clock at night, when the cellhall begins to quiet down. It means long periods of delayed gratification in an environment where pursuing education is often suspect. And it is the greatest feeling in the world when it all comes together.

Appendix I

Glossary of Important Terms

academic year: The period of formal academic instruction, usually from September or October to May or June. Divided into semesters, quarters, or trimesters.

accreditation: Recognition of a school by an independent private organization. Not a governmental function in the United States. There are more than 100 accrediting agencies, some recognized by the Department of Education and/or *CHEA*, some unrecognized, some phony or fraudulent.

ACE: American Council on Education; publishes the *National Guide to Educational Credit for Training Programs* and the *Guide to the Evaluation of Educational Experiences in the Armed Forces.*

ACT: American College Testing program, administrators of aptitude and achievement tests.

adjunct faculty: Part-time faculty members, often at a nontraditional school, often with a full-time teaching job elsewhere. More and more traditional schools are hiring adjunct faculty because they don't have to pay them as much or provide health care and other benefits.

advanced placement: Admission to a school at a higher level than usual as a result of getting credit for prior learning experience or passing advanced-placement exams.

alma mater: The school from which one has graduated, as in "My alma mater is Michigan State University."

alternative: Offering an alternate, or different, means of pursuing learning or degrees or both. Often used interchangeably with *external* or *nontraditional.*

alumni: Graduates of a school, as in "This school has some distinguished alumni." Technically for males only; females are *alumnae*. The singular is *alumnus* (male) or *alumna* (female), although neither of these terms are in common use.

alumni association: A confederation of alumni and alumnae who have joined together to support their alma mater in various ways, generally by donating money.

approved: In California, a level of state recognition of a school generally regarded as one step below *accredited.*

arbitration: A means of settling disputes, as between a student and a school, in which one or more independent arbitrators or judges listen to both sides and make a decision. A means of avoiding a courtroom trial. Many learning contracts have an arbitration clause. See *binding arbitration.*

assistantship: A means of assisting students (usually graduate students) financially by offering them part-time academic employment, usually in the form of a teaching assistantship or a research assistantship.

associate's degree: A degree traditionally awarded by community or junior colleges after two years of residential study or completion of 60 to 64 semester hours.

auditing: Sitting in on a class without earning credit for that class.

authorized: Until recently, a form of state recognition of schools in California. This category was phased out beginning in 1990, and now all schools must be approved or accredited to operate. Many formerly authorized schools are now billing themselves as candidates for approval.

bachelor's degree: Awarded in the United States after four years of full-time residential study (two to five years in other countries) or the earning of 120 to 124 semester units by any means.

binding arbitration: Arbitration in which both parties have agreed in advance that they will abide by the result and take no further legal action.

branch campus: A satellite facility, run by officers of the main campus of a college or university, at another location. Can range from a small office to a full-fledged university center.

campus: The main facility of a college or university, usually comprising buildings, grounds, dormitories, cafeterias and dining halls, sports facilities, etc. The campus of a nontraditional school may consist solely of offices.

chancellor: Often the highest official of a university. Also a new degree title, proposed by some schools to be a higher degree than the doctorate, requiring three to five years of additional study.

CHEA: The Council for Higher Education Accreditation, an agency that recognizes accrediting agencies in the U.S.

CLEP: The College-Level Examination Program, a series of equivalency examinations that can be taken for college credit.

coeducational: Education of men and women on the same campus or in the same program. This is why female students are called coeds.

college: In the United States, an institution offering programs leading to the *associate's* and/or *bachelor's*, and sometimes higher degrees. Often used interchangeably with *university*, although traditionally a university is a collection of colleges. In England and elsewhere, *college* may denote part of a university (Kings College, Cambridge) or a private high school (Eton College).

colloquium: A gathering of scholars to discuss a given topic over a period of a few hours to a few days. ("The university is sponsoring a colloquium on marine biology.")

community college: A two-year traditional school offering programs leading to the associate's degree and, typically, many noncredit courses in arts, crafts, and vocational fields for community members not interested in a degree. Also called *junior college*.

competency: The philosophy and practice of awarding credit or degrees based on learning skills rather than time spent in courses.

correspondence course: A course offered by mail and completed entirely by home study, often with one or two proctored, or supervised, examinations.

course: A specific unit of instruction, such as a course in microeconomics or in abnormal psychology. Residential courses last for one or more semesters or quarters; correspondence courses often have no rigid time requirements.

cramming: Intensive preparation for an examination. Most testing agencies now admit that cramming can improve scores on exams.

credit: A unit used to record courses taken. Each credit typically represents the number of hours spent in class each week. Hence a three-credit or three-unit course would commonly be a class that met three hours each week for one quarter or semester.

curriculum: A program of courses to be taken in pursuit of a degree or other objective.

degree: A title conferred by a school to show that a certain course of study has been completed.

Department of Education: The federal agency concerned with all educational matters in the United States that are not handled by the departments of education in the 50 states. In other countries, similar functions are commonly the province of a ministry of education.

DETC: The Distance Education and Training Council (formerly the National Home Study Council) is the recognized accreditor for schools offering degrees and diplomas largely or entirely through distance learning.

diploma: The certificate that shows that a certain course of study has been completed. Diplomas are awarded for completing degrees or other shorter courses of study.

dissertation: The major research project normally required as part of the work for a doctorate. Dissertations are expected to make a new and creative contribution to the field of study or to demonstrate one's excellence in the field. See also *thesis*.

Doctorate: The highest degree one can earn (but see *chancellor*). Includes Doctor of Philosophy (Ph.D.), Education (Ed.D.), and many other titles.

dormitory: Student living quarters on residential campuses. May include dining halls and classrooms.

early decision: Making an earlier-than-usual decision on whether to admit a student. Offered by some schools primarily as a service either to students applying to several schools or to those who are especially anxious to know the outcome of their application.

ECFMG: The Education Commission for Foreign Medical Graduates, which administers an examination to physicians who have gone to medical school outside the United States and wish to practice in the United States

electives: Courses one does not have to take but may choose to take as part of a degree program.

essay test: An examination in which the student writes narrative sentences as answers to questions instead of the short answers required by a multiple-choice test. Also called a *subjective test*.

equivalency examination: An examination designed to demonstrate knowledge in a subject where the learning was acquired outside a traditional classroom. A person who learned nursing skills while working in a hospital, for instance, could take an equivalency exam to earn credit in, say, obstetrical nursing.

external: Away from the main campus or offices. An external degree may be earned by home study or at locations other than on the school's campus.

fees: Money paid to a school for purposes other than academic tuition. Fees might pay for parking, library services, use of the gymnasium, binding of dissertations, etc.

fellowship: A study grant, usually awarded to a graduate student and usually requiring no work other than the usual academic assignments (as contrasted with an *assistantship*).

financial aid: A catch-all term that includes scholarships, loans, fellowships, assistantships, tuition reductions, etc. Many schools have a financial aid officer, whose job it is to deal with all funding questions and problems.

fraternity: A collegiate social organization, usually all male, often identified by Greek letters, such as Zeta Beta Tau. There are also professional and scholastic fraternities open to men and women, such as Beta Alpha Psi, the national fraternity for students of accounting. See *sorority*.

freshman: The name for the class in its first of four years of traditional study for a bachelor's degree, and its individual members. ("She is a freshman and thus is a member of the freshman class.")

grade-point average: The average score a student has achieved in all his or her classes, weighted by the number of credits or units for each class. Also called G.P.A.

grades: Evaluative scores provided for each course and often for individual examinations or papers written for that course. There are letter grades (usually A, B, C, D, F) and number grades (usually percentages from 0 percent to 100 percent), or sometimes grades on a scale of 0 to 3, 0 to 4, or 0 to 5. Some schools use a pass/fail system with no grades.

graduate: One who has earned a degree from a school. Also, the programs offered beyond the bachelor's level. ("He is a graduate of Yale University and is now doing graduate work at Princeton.")

graduate school: A school or a division of a university offering work at the master's or doctoral degree level.

graduate student: One attending graduate school.

GRE: The Graduate Record Examination, which many traditional schools and a few nontraditional ones require for admission to graduate programs.

honorary doctorate: A nonacademic award given regularly by more than 1000 colleges and universities to honor distinguished scholars, celebrities, and donors of large sums of money. Holders of this award may, and often do, call themselves "Doctor."

honor societies: Organizations for persons with a high grade-point average or other evidence of outstanding performance. There are local societies on some campuses, and several national organizations, the most prestigious of which is called Phi Beta Kappa.

honor system: A system in which students are trusted not to cheat on examinations, and to obey other rules, without proctors or others monitoring their behavior.

junior: The name for the class in its third year of a traditional four-year United States bachelor's degree program, or any member of that class. ("She is a junior this year.")

junior college: See *community college*.

language laboratory: A special room in which students can listen to foreign-language tapes over headphones, allowing many students to be learning different languages at different skill levels at the same time.

learning contract: A formal agreement between a student and a school specifying independent work to be done by the student and the amount of credit the school will award on successful completion of the work.

lecture class: A course in which a faculty member lectures to anywhere from a few dozen to many hundreds of students. Often lecture classes are followed by small-group discussion sessions led by student assistants or junior faculty.

liberal arts: A term with many complex meanings, but generally referring to the nonscientific curriculum of a university: humanities, arts, social sciences, history, and so forth.

liberal education: Commonly taken to be the opposite of a specialized education—one in which students are required to take courses in a wide range of fields, as well as courses in their major.

licensed: Holding a permit to operate. This can range from a difficult-to-obtain state school license to a simple local business license.

life-experience portfolio: A comprehensive presentation listing and describing all learning experiences in a person's life, with appropriate documentation. The basic document used in assigning academic credit for life-experience learning.

LSAT: The Law School Admission Test, required by most U.S. law schools of all applicants.

maintenance costs: The expenses incurred while attending school other than tuition and fees. Includes room and board (food), clothing, laundry, postage, travel, etc.

major: The subject or academic department in which a student takes concentrated coursework leading to a specialty. ("His major is in English literature; she is majoring in chemistry.")

MCAT: The Medical College Admission Test, required of all applicants by most U.S. medical schools.

mentor: Faculty member assigned to supervise independent study work at a nontraditional school; comparable to *adjunct faculty*.

minor: The secondary subject or academic department in which a student takes concentrated coursework. ("She has a major in art and a minor in biology.") Optional at most schools.

multiple-choice test: An examination in which the student chooses the best of several alternative answers provided for each question; also called an *objective test*. ("The capital city of England is (a) London, (b) Ostrogotz-Plakatz, (c) Tokyo, or (d) none of the above.")

multiversity: A university system with two or more separate campuses, each a major university in its own right, such as the University of California or the University of Wisconsin.

narrative transcript: A transcript issued by a nontraditional school in which, instead of simply listing the courses completed and grades received, there is a narrative description of the work done and the school's rationale for awarding credit for that work.

nonresident: (1) A means of instruction in which the student does not need to visit the school; all work is done by correspondence, Internet, telephone, or exchange of audiotapes or videotapes; (2) a person who does not meet residency requirements of a given school and, as a result, often has to pay higher tuition or fees.

nontraditional: Something done in other than the usual or traditional way. In education, refers to learning and degrees completed by methods other than spending many hours in classrooms and lecture halls.

objective test: An examination in which questions requiring a very short answer are posed. It can be multiple choice, true/false, fill-in-the-blank, etc. The questions are related to facts (thus objective) rather than to opinions (which would be subjective).

on the job: In the United States, experience or training gained through employment that may be converted to academic credit. In England, slang for having sex, which either confuses or amuses English people who read about "credit for on-the-job experience."

open admissions: An admission policy in which everyone who applies is admitted, on the theory that those who are unable to do university work will drop out before long.

out-of-state student: One from a state other than that in which the school is located. Because most state colleges and universities have much higher tuition rates for out-of-state students, many people attempt to establish legal residence in the same state as their school.

parallel instruction: A method in which nonresident students do exactly the same work as residential students, during the same general time period, except they do it at home.

pass/fail option: Instead of getting a letter or number grade in a course, the student may elect, at the start of the course, a pass/fail option in which the only grades are either "pass" or "fail." Some schools permit students to elect this option on one or two of their courses each semester.

Phi Beta Kappa: A national honor society that recognizes students with outstanding grades.

plan of study: A detailed description of the program an applicant to a school plans to pursue. Many traditional schools ask for this as part of the admission procedure. The plan of study should be designed to meet the objectives of the *statement of purpose*.

portfolio: See *life-experience portfolio*.

prerequisites: Courses that must be taken before certain other courses may be taken. For instance, a course in algebra is often a prerequisite for a course in geometry.

private school: A school that is privately owned, rather than operated by a governmental department.

proctor: A person who supervises the taking of an examination to be certain there is no cheating and that other rules are followed. Many nontraditional schools permit unproctored examinations.

professional school: School in which one studies for the various professions, including medicine, dentistry, law, nursing, veterinary, optometry, ministry, etc.

PSAT: Preliminary Scholastic Aptitude Test, given annually to high-school juniors.

public school: In the United States, a school operated by the government of a city, county, district, state, or the federal government. In England, a privately owned or run school.

quarter: An academic term at a school on the "quarter system," in which the calendar year is divided into four equal quarters. New courses begin each quarter.

quarter hour: An amount of credit earned for each classroom hour spent in a given course during a given quarter. A course that meets four hours each week for a quarter would probably be worth four quarter hours, or quarter units.

recognized: A term used by some schools to indicate approval from some other organization or governmental body. The term usually does not have a precise meaning, so it may mean different things in different places.

registrar: The official at most colleges and universities who is responsible for maintaining student records and, in many cases, for verifying and validating applications for admission.

rolling admissions: A year-round admission procedure. Many schools only admit students once or twice a year. A school with rolling admissions considers each application at the time it is received. Many nontraditional schools, especially ones with nonresident programs, have rolling admissions.

SAT: Scholastic Aptitude Test, one of the standard tests given to qualify for admission to colleges and universities.

scholarship: A study grant, either in cash or in the form of tuition or fee reduction.

score: Numerical rating of performance on a test. ("His score on the Graduate Record Exam was not so good.")

semester: A school term, generally four to five months. Schools on the semester system usually have two semesters a year, with a shorter summer session.

semester hour: An amount of credit earned in a course representing one classroom hour per week for a semester. A class that meets three days a week for one hour, or one day a week for three hours, would be worth three semester hours, or semester units.

seminar: A form of instruction combining independent research with meetings of small groups of students and a faculty member, generally to report on reading or research the students have done.

senior: The fourth year of study of a four-year U.S. bachelor's degree program, or a member of that class. ("Linnea is a senior this year, and is president of the senior class.")

sophomore: The second year of study in a four-year U.S. bachelor's degree program, or a member of that class.

sorority: A women's social organization, often with its own living quarters on or near a campus. Usually identified with two or three Greek letters, such as Sigma Chi. The male version is called a *fraternity*.

special education: Education of the physically or mentally handicapped, or, often, of the gifted.

special student: A student who is not studying for a degree because he or she either is ineligible or does not wish the degree.

statement of purpose: A detailed description of the career the applicant intends to pursue after graduation. A statement of purpose is often requested as part of the admission procedure at a university.

subject: An area of study or learning covering a single topic, such as the subject of chemistry, or economics, or French literature.

subjective test: An examination in which the answers are in the form of narrative sentences or long or short essays, often expressing opinions rather than reporting facts.

syllabus: A detailed description of a course of study, often including the books to be read, papers to be written, and examinations to be given.

thesis: The major piece of research that is completed by many master's degree candidates. A thesis is expected to show a detailed knowledge of one's field and the ability to do research and integrate knowledge of the field.

TOEFL: Test of English as a Foreign Language, required by many schools of those for whom English is not their native language.

traditional education: Education at a residential school in which the bachelor's degree is completed through four years of classroom study, the master's in one or two years, and the doctorate in three to five years.

transcript: A certified copy of the student's academic record showing courses taken, examinations passed, credits awarded, and grades or scores received.

transfer student: A student who has earned credit in one school and then transfers to another school.

trimester: A term consisting of one-third of an academic year. A school on the trimester system has three equal trimesters each year.

tuition: In the United States, the money charged for formal instruction. In some schools, tuition is the only expense other than postage. In other schools, there may be fees as well as tuition. In England, tuition refers to the instruction or teaching at a school, such as the tuition offered in history.

tuition waiver: A form of financial assistance in which the school charges little or no tuition.

tutor: See *mentor*. A tutor can also be a hired assistant who helps a student prepare for a given class or examination.

undergraduate: Pertaining to the period of study from the end of high school to the earning of a bachelor's degree; also to a person in such a course of study. ("Barry is an undergraduate at Reed College, one of the leading undergraduate schools.")

university: An institution that usually comprises one or more undergraduate colleges, one or more graduate schools, and, often, one or more professional schools.

Appendix J: Subject Index

For years, our readers have been telling us how nice it would be if this book had a complete index to the subjects offered by the many degree programs described. We are delighted that finally, after eight editions, thanks to the excellent work of Tom Head, what lies before you is indeed a comprehensive subject index. For each field of study, we list the offering schools, the degrees offered (B, M, D), and whether or not they are entirely nonresident (NR) or require short residency (SR). To save space, we do not list the page numbers. The schools are easy enough to find, since they are listed in the book alphabetically.

There are three more things to say about subject areas:

1. Many subject areas are so broad ("general studies") or all-inclusive ("social science") that a wide range of things can be done in them.

2. There are "side door" approaches to various fields. If a school offers only "history" and a student wishes to study "technology," it may be possible to do a degree in the "history of technology." The field of education is another commonly used side door.

3. There are a great many courses available by distance learning that do not result in a degree, but which may be applied to another school's degree. For instance, although there is no listing here for botanical sciences, there are individual courses available. A student could, for instance, take courses from any of a dozen universities, and apply those courses to the B.S. degree of schools such as Excelsior College, Thomas Edison State College, and Charter Oak State College. How does one find these courses? See the earlier chapter called "Correspondence Courses."

Accounting
Auburn University (M, SR)
Caldwell College (B, SR)
Capital University (B, SR)
Charles Sturt University (B-M-D, NR)
City University (B, NR)
Deakin University (M, NR)
Edith Cowan University (B-M, NR)
Empire State College (B, NR)
Excelsior College (A-B, NR)
Golden Gate University (M, NR)
Nova Southeastern University (M, SR)
St. Mary-of-the-Woods College (B, SR)
Thomas Edison State College (B, NR)
University of Kent at Canterbury (M-D, SR)
University of London (B, NR)
University of Maryland (B, NR)
University of Melbourne (M-D, NR)
University of New England (M, NR)
University of South Africa (B-M-D, NR)
University of South Australia (B, NR)
University of Southern Queensland (B-M, NR)
Upper Iowa University (B, NR)
See also **Finance**
See also **Taxation**
Acquisition Management and Procurement
Thomas Edison State College (B, NR)
Addiction Counseling and Intervention
Edith Cowan University (B, NR)
University of London (M, NR)

Adult and Continuing Education
Edith Cowan University (M-D, NR)
Indiana University (M, NR)
St. Joseph's College (M, SR)
University of Southern Queensland (B-M, NR)
Adventure Education
Prescott College (M, SR)
Aerospace Engineering
Auburn University (M, SR)
African Languages and Literature
University of South Africa (B-M-D, NR)
See also **Afrikaans Language and Literature**
African Politics
University of South Africa (B-M-D, NR)
Afrikaans Language and Literature
University of South Africa (B-M-D, NR)
Agribusiness
See **Agriculture and Agriculture Management**
Agricultural Engineering
Colorado State University (M, NR)
University of Idaho (M, NR)
University of Southern Queensland (B-M, NR)
Agriculture and Agriculture Management
Charles Sturt University (B-M-D, NR)
Colorado State University (M, NR)
Kansas State University (M, NR)
University of London (M, NR)
Washington State University (B-M, NR)

Agriculture Law
De Montfort University (M, NR)
American Studies
University of Kent at Canterbury
(M-D, SR)
University of Melbourne (M-D, NR)
University of New England (M, NR)
Ancient History
University of Melbourne (M-D, NR)
University of New England (B-M, NR)
University of South Africa (B-M-D, NR)
Ancient Languages and Cultures
University of South Africa (M, NR)
Animal Science
See **Veterinary Science**
Anthropology
Charter Oak State College (B, NR)
Edith Cowan University (B, NR)
Thomas Edison State College (B, NR)
University of Kent at Canterbury
(M-D, SR)
University of Melbourne (M-D, NR)
University of South Africa (B-M-D, NR)
University of Southern Queensland
(B, NR)
University of Wales—Lampeter
(M-D, NR)
Applied and Professional Studies
Antioch University (D, SR)
California State University—Dominguez
Hills (B, NR)
Murdoch University (B, NR)
Nova Southeastern University (B, SR)
Thomas Edison State College (M, NR)
Applied Economics
University of Southern Queensland
(B, NR)
See also **Economics**
Applied Linguistics
Edith Cowan University (M-D, NR)
University of Kent at Canterbury
(M-D, SR)
University of Leicester (M, NR)
University of Melbourne (M-D, NR)
University of Southern Queensland
(M, NR)
See also **Linguistics**
Applied Mathematics
University of Kent at Canterbury
(M-D, SR)
University of South Africa (B-M-D, NR)
University of Southern Queensland
(B, NR)
See also **Mathematics**
Applied Social Studies
See **Social Sciences**
See **Social Work**
See **Sociology**
Aquaculture
Deakin University (M, NR)
Arabic Language and Literature
University of Melbourne (M-D, NR)
University of South Africa (B-M-D, NR)

Archaeology
University of Kent at Canterbury
(M-D, SR)
University of Leicester (M, NR)
University of Melbourne (M-D, NR)
University of New England (B-M, NR)
University of South Africa (M, NR)
University of Wales—Lampeter
(M-D, NR)
Architecture
University of Melbourne (M-D, NR)
See also **Contracting and Building**
Art
Burlington College (B, SR)
Caldwell College (B, SR)
California State University—Dominguez
Hills (M, NR)
De Montfort University (M-D, SR)
Norwich University (M, SR)
Thomas Edison State College (B, NR)
University of Kent at Canterbury
(M-D, SR)
University of Melbourne (M-D, NR)
University of South Africa (B-M-D, NR)
See also **Cartooning**
Art Education
Edith Cowan University (M-D, NR)
Art History
Charter Oak State College (B, NR)
University of Kent at Canterbury
(M-D, SR)
University of Melbourne (M-D, NR)
University of South Africa (B-M-D, NR)
University of Wales—Lampeter (M, NR)
Art Therapy
Norwich University (M, SR)
Asian Studies
Murdoch University (B-M, NR)
University of Melbourne (M-D, NR)
University of New England (B-M, NR)
University of Southern Queensland
(B, NR)
Asthma Education
Charles Sturt University (M, NR)
Astronomy
University of South Africa (B-M-D, NR)
Audiology
Central Michigan University (D, NR)
University of Melbourne (M-D, NR)
Auditing
University of South Africa (B, NR)
Australian Studies
Charles Sturt University (M-D, NR)
University of Melbourne (M-D, NR)

Banking
See **Finance**
Biblical Studies
Regent University (M, SR)
University of South Africa (B-M-D, NR)
Biochemistry
University of Kent at Canterbury
(M-D, SR)
University of Melbourne (M-D, NR)

Bioethics
University of South Africa (M, NR)
University of Wales—Lampeter (M, NR)
Biology
Charter Oak State College (B, NR)
Excelsior College (B, NR)
Thomas Edison State College (B, NR)
University of Melbourne (M-D, NR)
University of New England (B-M-D, NR)
Biophysics
Georgia Institute of Technology (M, NR)
Biotechnology
University of Maryland (M, NR)
British and Commonwealth Studies
University of Wales—Lampeter (M, NR)
Building Services
See **Contracting and Building**
Business and Commerce (General)
Athabasca University (B, NR)
California College for Health Sciences
(B, NR)
Charles Sturt University (B-M-D, NR)
Charter Oak State College (B, NR)
City University (B, NR)
De Montfort University (B, NR)
Eastern Oregon University (B, NR)
Edith Cowan University (B-M-D, NR)
Empire State College (B-M, NR)
Excelsior College (B, NR)
Judson College (B, NR)
Kansas State University (B, NR)
Open University (B-M-D, NR)
St. Joseph's College (B, SR)
Salve Regina University (B, SR)
University of Maryland (B, NR)
University of Melbourne (M-D, NR)
University of New England (B-M, NR)
University of South Africa (B-M-D, NR)
University of South Australia (B, NR)
University of Southern Queensland
(B-M, NR)
Upper Iowa University (B, NR)
See also **Business Administration**
See also **Finance**
See also **Management**
Business Administration (BBA/MBA/DBA)
Athabasca University (M, SR)
Auburn Univeristy (M, SR)
Baker College (B-M, NR)
Bellevue University (M, NR)
California College for Health Sciences
(M, NR)
California State University—Dominguez
Hills (M, NR)
Capella University (M, SR)
Charles Sturt University (M-D, NR)
City University (M, NR)
Colorado State University (M, NR)
Edith Cowan University (M, NR)
Empire State College (M, SR)
Excelsior College (B-M, NR)
Golden Gate University (M, NR)
Henley Management College (M-D, NR)
Heriot-Watt University (M, NR)
ISIM University (M, NR)
Jones International University (M, NR)
National Technological University
(M, NR)

Nova Southeastern University (M, SR)
Regent University (M, SR)
Regis University (M, NR)
Rensselaer Polytechnic Institute (M, NR)
Salve Regina University (M, SR)
Syracuse University (M, SR)
University of Leicester (M, NR)
University of London (M, NR)
University of Maryland (M, NR)
University of New England (M, NR)
University of Phoenix (M, NR)
University of Sarasota (M-D, SR)
University of South Australia
(B-M-D, NR)
University of Southern Queensland
(B-M-D, NR)
University of Texas (M, NR)
Business Administration (Other)
Athabasca University (B, NR)
Caldwell College (B, SR)
Central Michigan University (B-M, NR)
City University (B, NR)
Columbia Union College (B, NR)
Judson College (B, NR)
St. Mary-of-the-Woods College (B, SR)
Southwestern Adventist University (B, SR)
Stephens College (B, SR)
University of Sarasota (B, SR)
University of South Africa (B-M-D, NR)
University of South Australia (D, NR)
University of Southern Queensland
(B, NR)
Washington State University (B, NR)
See also **Business**
See also **Management**
Business Communication
Jones International University (B-M, NR)
See also **Communication**
Business Information Systems
Bellevue University (B, NR)
University of Southern Queensland
(M, NR)
See also **Management Information
Systems**
Business Law
De Montfort University (M, NR)
University of London (B, NR)
University of South Africa (M, NR)
University of Southern Queensland
(M, NR)
Business Management
See also **Business Administration**
See also **Management**

Canadian Studies
University of Waterloo (B, NR)
Cancer Research
See also **Oncology**
Cartooning
University of Kent at Canterbury
(M-D, SR)
Catalan Language and Literature
University of Melbourne (M-D, NR)
Celtic Christianity
University of Wales—Lampeter (M, NR)

B = Bachelor's • M = Master's • D = Doctorate • NR = Nonresident • SR = Short Residency

Chemical Engineering
Auburn University (M, SR)
Excelsior College (B, NR)
Kansas State University (M, NR)
National Technological University
(M, NR)
University of Bradford (M-D, NR)
University of Melbourne (M-D, NR)

Chemistry
Charles Sturt University (B, NR)
Charter Oak State College (B, NR)
De Montfort University (M, NR)
Excelsior College (B, NR)
Murdoch University (B, NR)
Open University and Open College
(B, NR)
Thomas Edison State College (B, NR)
University of Bradford (M-D, NR)
University of Kent at Canterbury
(M-D, SR)
University of Melbourne (M-D, NR)
University of South Africa (B-M-D, NR)

Chemistry Education
University of South Africa (M, NR)
See also **Science Education**

Children's Literature
University of Southern Queensland
(M, NR)

Chinese Language and Literature
University of Melbourne (M-D, NR)
University of New England (B-M, NR)

Church History
University of South Africa (B-M-D, NR)
University of Wales—Lampeter (M, NR)

Civil Engineering
Auburn University (M, SR)
Colorado State University (M, NR)
Kansas State University (M, NR)
Thomas Edison State College (B, NR)
University of Idaho (M, NR)
University of Melbourne (M-D, NR)
University of Southern Queensland
(B-M, NR)

Classics
University of Kent at Canterbury
(M-D, SR)
University of Melbourne (M-D, NR)
University of New England (B-M-D, NR)
University of South Africa (B-M-D, NR)
University of Wales—Lampeter
(M-D, NR)
University of Waterloo (B, NR)
See also **Ancient History**
See also **Greek**
See also **Latin**

Clinical Psychology
Fielding Institute (D, SR)
Union Institute (D, SR)
University of South Africa (M, NR)
See also **Counseling**
See also **Psychology and Behavioral
Science**

Commerce
See also **Business and Commerce (General)**

Communication
Caldwell College (B, SR)
Capital University (B, SR)
Charles Sturt University (M-D, NR)
Charter Oak State College (B, NR)
Edith Cowan University (B, NR)
Excelsior College (B, NR)
Jones International University (M, NR)
Murdoch University (B, NR)
Regent University (M-D, NR)
Rensselaer Polytechnic Institute (M, NR)
Texas Tech University (M, NR)
Thomas Edison State College (B, NR)
University of Bradford (M-D, NR)
University of Kent at Canterbury
(M-D, SR)
University of Leicester (M, NR)
University of Maryland (B, NR)
University of Melbourne (M-D, NR)
University of New England (B-M-D, NR)
University of Northern Iowa (M, NR)
University of Phoenix (B, NR)
University of South Africa (B-M-D, NR)
University of South Australia (B, NR)
University of Southern Queensland
(B-M, NR)

Communication Management
University of South Australia (B-M, NR)
See also **Telecommunications and
Telecommunications Management**

Community Studies
Central Michigan University (B, NR)
De Montfort University (M, NR)
Deakin University (M, NR)
Thomas Edison State College (B, NR)

Comparative Literature
California State University—Dominguez
Hills (M, NR)
Charter Oak State College (B, NR)
Excelsior College (B, NR)
University of Kent at Canterbury
(M-D, SR)
University of South Africa (B-M-D, NR)

Comparative Religion
See also **Religious Studies**

Complementary Health
Charles Sturt University (B, NR)

Computer-Aided Design (CAD)
See also **Industrial Computing**

**Computer Engineering and Computer
Engineering Technology**
Excelsior College (B, NR)
Georgia Institute of Technology (M, NR)
National Technological University
(M, NR)
University of Idaho (M, NR)
University of Southern Queensland
(B-M, NR)
See also **Electrical Engineering**
See also **Software Engineering**
See also **Systems Engineering**

B = Bachelor's • M = Master's • D = Doctorate • NR = Nonresident • SR = Short Residency

Computer Information Systems
Athabasca University (B-M, NR)
Baker College (M, NR)
Caldwell College (B, SR)
Charles Sturt University (B-M-D, NR)
Charter Oak State College (B, NR)
City University (B-M, NR)
Columbia Union College (B, NR)
Deakin University (M, NR)
Edith Cowan University (B-M, NR)
Excelsior College (B, NR)
Harvard University (B-M, SR)
ISIM University (M, NR)
National Technological University
  (M, NR)
New Jersey Institute of Technology
  (B-M, NR)
Nova Southeastern University (M-D, SR)
Open University (B-M-D, NR)
Regis University (M, NR)
Rensselaer Polytechnic Institute (M, NR)
Rochester Institute of Technology (M, SR)
St. Mary-of-the-Woods College (B, SR)
Thomas Edison State College (B, NR)
University of Bradford (M-D, NR)
University of London (B, NR)
University of Maryland (B-M, NR)
University of Melbourne (M-D, NR)
University of Phoenix (B-M, NR)
University of South Africa (B-M, NR)
University of South Australia (B, NR)
University of Southern Queensland
  (M, NR)
See also **Computer Science**
Computer-Mediated Communication
Regent University (M, NR)
Texas Tech University (M, NR)
See also **Internet Studies**
Computer Networking
City University (B, NR)
University of Southern Queensland
  (B, NR)
See also **Computer-Mediated
  Communication**
See also **Internet Studies**
See also **Telecommunications and
  Telecommunications Management**
Computer Programming
See also **Software Engineering**
Computer Science
Auburn University (M, SR)
Capital University (B, SR)
Charter Oak State College (B, NR)
  Colorado State University (M, NR)
Columbia University (M-S, NR)
Murdoch University (B, NR)
National Technological University
  (M, NR)
New Jersey Institute of Technology
  (B-M, NR)
Northwood University (B, SR)
Nova Southeastern University (M-D, SR)
Rensselaer Polytechnic Institute (M, NR)
Stanford University (M, NR)
Thomas Edison State College (B, NR)

University of Illinois at Urbana-Champaign
  (M, NR)
University of Kent at Canterbury
  (M-D, SR)
University of Maryland (B, NR)
University of Melbourne (M-D, NR)
University of New England (B-M-D, NR)
University of South Africa (B-M-D, NR)
University of Southern Queensland
  (B, NR)
University of Texas (M, NR)
Conflict Resolution and Peace Studies
California State University—Dominguez
  Hills (M, NR)
Nova Southeastern University (M-D, SR)
University of Bradford (M-D, NR)
University of New England (M, NR)
Construction
Thomas Edison State College (B, NR)
University of Melbourne (M-D, NR)
University of Southern Queensland
  (B, NR)
See also **Contracting and Building**
Continuing Education
See also **Adult and Continuing Education**
Contracting and Building
University of Southern Queensland
  (B, NR)
See also **Architecture**
See also **Construction**
Copyright Law
See **Intellectual Property Law**
Counseling
Athabasca University (M, NR)
Charles Sturt University (M, NR)
City University (M, NR)
Prescott College (B-M, SR)
University of Melbourne (M-D, NR)
University of Sarasota (M-D, SR)
University of South Africa (M, NR)
University of South Australia (M, NR)
University of Southern Queensland
  (M, NR)
See also **Clinical Psychology**
See also **Pastoral Counseling**
See also **Psychology and Behavioral
  Science**
Creative Writing
See also **Writing**
Criminal Justice and Law Enforcement
Bellevue University (B, NR)
Caldwell College (B, SR)
Charles Sturt University (B-M-D, NR)
Charter Oak State College (B, NR)
Edith Cowan University (B, NR)
Empire State College (B, NR)
Judson College (B, NR)
St. Joseph's College (B, SR)
University of Leicester (M, NR)
University of Melbourne (M-D, NR)
University of South Africa (B-M-D, NR)
Upper Iowa University (B, NR)
Washington State University (B, NR)
See also **Criminology, Forensic
  Psychology, and Criminal Intelligence**
See also **Forensics**

B = Bachelor's • M = Master's • D = Doctorate • NR = Nonresident • SR = Short Residency

Criminal Law
University of South Africa (M, NR)
Criminology, Forensic Psychology, and Criminal Intelligence
Capital University (B, SR)
Charles Sturt University (M, NR)
University of Kent at Canterbury (M-D, SR)
University of Leicester (M, NR)
University of South Africa (B-M-D, NR)
See also **Criminal Justice**
Crisis Management
Charles Sturt University (B, NR)
Empire State College (B, NR)
Thomas Edison State College (B, NR)
University of Leicester (M, NR)
Cultural Studies
See **Anthropology**
Curriculum Design
City University (M, NR)
Deakin University (M, NR)
Nova Southeastern University (M, SR)
University of Sarasota (M-D, SR)
University of Southern Queensland (M, NR)
See also **Education**
Death Studies
See **Thanatology**
Defense Management
University of New England (M, NR)
Dentistry
University of London (M, NR)
See also **Orthodontics and Prosthodontics**
Development Studies and Sustainable Agriculture
De Montfort University (M, NR)
Deakin University (M, NR)
Murdoch University (M, NR)
University of Bradford (M-D, NR)
University of London (M, NR)
University of Melbourne (M-D, NR)
University of New England (B-M, NR)
University of South Africa (B-M-D, NR)
University of Southern Queensland (M, NR)
University of Waterloo (B, NR)
See also **Rural Development**
Developmental Psychology
Edith Cowan University (B-M-D, NR)
Fielding Institute (D, SR)
Salve Regina University (M, SR)
Diaconology
See **Divinity**
See **Ministry**
Dietetics
See **Nutrition**
Digital Preservation
University of Glasgow (M, NR)
Diplomacy
See **Conflict Resolution and Peace Studies**
See **Intelligence Science**
See **International Relations**
Direct Marketing
See **Marketing**
Disability Studies
Edith Cowan University (B, NR)
University of Kent at Canterbury (M-D, SR)

Distance Education
Athabasca University (M, NR)
Deakin University (M, NR)
Nova Southeastern University (M-D, SR)
University of London (M, NR)
University of Maryland (M, NR)
University of Southern Queensland (M, NR)
Divinity
University of London (B, NR)
Drama and Theater Studies
Charles Sturt University (M-D, NR)
Thomas Edison State College (B, NR)
University of Kent at Canterbury (M-D, SR)
University of Melbourne (M-D, NR)
University of New England (B-M-D, NR)
E-Business
See **E-Commerce**
E-Commerce
Bellevue University (B, NR)
University of Maryland (M, NR)
University of Southern Queensland (M, NR)
Economics
Capital University (B, SR)
Charter Oak State College (B, NR)
Deakin University (M, NR)
Eastern Oregon University (B, NR)
Excelsior College (B, NR)
Murdoch University (B, NR)
Thomas Edison State College (B, NR)
University of Kent at Canterbury (M-D, SR)
University of London (B-M, NR)
University of Melbourne (M-D, NR)
University of New England (B-M-D, NR)
University of South Africa (B-M-D, NR)
University of Waterloo (B, NR)
Editing and Publishing
University of Southern Queensland (M, NR)
Education
Capella University (M-D, NR)
Charles Sturt University (B-M-D, NR)
City University (M, NR)
De Montfort University (M, NR)
Deakin University (B-M, NR)
Eastern Oregon University (M, SR)
Edith Cowan University (B-M-D, NR)
George Washington University (M, NR)
Judson College (B, NR)
Murdoch University (B-M, NR)
Naropa University (M, SR)
Norwich University (M, SR)
Nova Southeastern University (B-M-D, SR)
Open University (B-M-D, NR)
Prescott College (M, SR)
Regent University (M, NR)
St. Joseph's College (B-M, SR)
Stephens College (B, SR)
Thomas Edison State College (B, NR)
University of Bradford (M-D, NR)
University of Illinois at Urbana-Champaign (M, NR)
University of Maryland (M, NR)

Education (continued)
  University of Melbourne (M-D, NR)
  University of New England (B-M-D, NR)
  University of Northern Iowa (M, NR)
  University of Phoenix (M, NR)
  University of Sarasota (M-D, SR)
  University of South Africa (B-M-D, NR)
  University of South Australia (B-D, NR)
  University of Southern Queensland
    (B-M-D, NR)
  University of Texas (M, NR)
  Walden University (M-D, NR)
Educational Leadership and Administration
  City University (M, NR)
  Edith Cowan University (M-D, NR)
  Fielding Institute (D, SR)
  Nova Southeastern University (M-D, SR)
  Regent University (M, SR)
  University of Northern Iowa (M, NR)
  University of Sarasota (M-D, SR)
  University of South Africa (B-M-D, NR)
  University of Southern Queensland
    (M-D, NR)
Educational Psychology
  University of South Africa (B-M-D, NR)
Educational Technology
  City University (M, NR)
  Edith Cowan University (M-D, NR)
  George Washington University (M, NR)
  Nova Southeastern University (M-D, SR)
  University of Northern Iowa (M, NR)
  University of Southern Queensland
    (M, NR)
  University of Texas (M, NR)
  Walden University (M, NR)
Electrical Engineering
  Colorado State University (M-D, NR)
  Columbia University (M-S, NR)
  Kansas State University (M, NR)
  National Technological University
    (M, NR)
  Rensselaer Polytechnic Institute (M, NR)
  Rochester Institute of Technology (B, SR)
  Stanford University (M, NR)
  University of Bradford (M-D, NR)
  University of Idaho (M, NR)
  University of Illinois at Urbana-
    Champaign (M, NR)
  University of Southern Queensland
    (B-M, NR)
  University of Texas (M, NR)
  See also **Computer Engineering**
  See also **Electronics**
Electromechanical Engineering
  See **Robotics**
Electronic Commerce
  See **E-Commerce**
Electronics
  Excelsior College (B, NR)
  Thomas Edison State College (B, NR)
  University of Kent at Canterbury
    (M-D, SR)
  University of New England (B, NR)
  University of Southern Queensland
    (B-M, NR)
  See also **Electrical Engineering**
Elementary Education
  See **Primary Education**
Emergency Management
  See **Crisis Management**

Emergency Medical Services
  Charles Sturt University (B, NR)
Engineering (General)
  Auburn University (M, SR)
  Kansas State University (M, NR)
  Stanford University (M, NR)
  Texas Tech University (M, NR)
  University of Illinois at Urbana-
    Champaign (M, NR)
  University of Melbourne (M-D, NR)
  University of Southern Queensland
    (B-M, NR)
Engineering Management
  Columbia University (M, NR)
  National Technological University (M, NR)
  New Jersey Institute of Technology
    (M, NR)
  Syracuse University (M, SR)
  Texas Tech University (M, NR)
  University of Idaho (M, NR)
  Washington State University (M, NR)
Engineering Science
  Murdoch University (B, NR)
  Open University and Open College
    (B, NR)
  Rensselaer Polytechnic Institute (M, NR)
  University of Illinois at Urbana-
    Champaign (M, NR)
English Language and Literature
  Burlington College (B, SR)
  Caldwell College (B, SR)
  Capital University (B, SR)
  Excelsior College (B, NR)
  Judson College (B, NR)
  Murdoch University (B, NR)
  St. Mary-of-the-Woods College (B, SR)
  Stephens College (B, SR)
  Thomas Edison State College (B, NR)
  University of Kent at Canterbury
    (M-D, SR)
  University of London (B, NR)
  University of Maryland (B, NR)
  University of Melbourne (M-D, NR)
  University of New England (B-M-D, NR)
  University of Northern Iowa (M, NR)
  University of South Africa (B-M-D, NR)
  University of Southern Queensland (B, NR)
  University of Wales—Lampeter
    (M-D, NR)
  University of Waterloo (B, NR)
**Environmental Economics, Engineering,
    and Management**
  Auburn University (M, SR)
  Charles Sturt University (B-M-D, NR)
  Colorado State University (M, NR)
  De Montfort University (B-M, NR)
  Deakin University (M, NR)
  Georgia Institute of Technology (M, NR)
  Rochester Institute of Technology
    (B-M, SR)
  University of Kent at Canterbury
    (M-D, SR)
  University of London (M, NR)
  University of Maryland (B-M, NR)
  University of South Africa (M, NR)
  University of Southern Queensland
    (B-M, NR)
  See also **Environmental Law**
  See also **Environmental Studies**
  See also **Public Health**

B = Bachelor's • M = Master's • D = Doctorate • NR = Nonresident • SR = Short Residency

Environmental Law
De Montfort University (M, NR)
University of Kent at Canterbury
(M-D, SR)
Environmental Studies
Prescott College (M, SR)
Thomas Edison State College (B, NR)
University of Kent at Canterbury
(M-D, SR)
University of London (M, NR)
University of Melbourne (M-D, NR)
University of Waterloo (B, NR)
See also **Environmental Economics,**
Engineering, and Management
Epidemiology
University of London (M, NR)
Ethics
Charles Sturt University (M-D, NR)
University of South Africa (B-M-D, NR)
See also **Bioethics**
See also **Moral Theology**
Ethnomusicology
University of New England (B-M, NR)
European Studies
University of Bradford (M-D, NR)
University of Kent at Canterbury
(M-D, SR)
University of Melbourne (M-D, NR)
University of New England (B-M, NR)
Evangelism
University of South Africa (B-M-D, NR)

Family Studies
Edith Cowan University (B, NR)
Laurentian University (B, NR)
Feminist Law
University of Kent at Canterbury (M, SR)
Film Studies
Burlington College (B, SR)
University of Kent at Canterbury
(M-D, SR)
University of Melbourne (M-D, NR)
Finance
American College (M, SR)
Charles Sturt University (M-D, NR)
City University (M, NR)
Golden Gate University (M, NR)
Nova Southeastern University (M, SR)
Thomas Edison State College (B, NR)
University of Leicester (M, NR)
University of London (B-M, NR)
University of Melbourne (M-D, NR)
University of New England (B-M, NR)
University of Sarasota (M, SR)
University of South Australia (B, NR)
University of Southern Queensland
(B-M, NR)
See also **Accounting**
See also **Taxation**
Fire Science Service, Management,
and Training
Charter Oak State College (B, NR)
Colorado State University (B, NR)
Eastern Oregon University (B, NR)
Empire State College (B, NR)
Thomas Edison State College (B, NR)
University of Maryland (B, NR)
Upper Iowa University (B, NR)

Food Industry and Restaurant Management
See **Food Science**
See **Hospitality, Food Industry, and**
Restaurant Management
See **Wine Science**
Food Law
De Montfort University (M, NR)
Food Science
Charles Sturt University (B-D, NR)
University of Melbourne (M-D, NR)
Foreign Languages and Literature (General)
Murdoch University (B, NR)
Open University (B-M-D, NR)
University of Bradford (M-D, NR)
University of Melbourne (M-D, NR)
University of South Africa (B-M-D, NR)
University of Southern Queensland
(B, NR)
See also **[Language] Language and**
Literature (e.g., French Language
and Literature)
See also **Applied Linguistics**
See also **Comparative Literature**
Forensic Psychology
See **Criminology, Forensic Psychology,**
and Criminal Intelligence
Forestry
Thomas Edison State College (B, NR)
University of Melbourne (M-D, NR)
French Language and Literature
Charter Oak State College (B, NR)
University of London (B, NR)
University of Melbourne (M-D, NR)
University of New England (B-M, NR)
University of South Africa (B-M-D, NR)
University of Waterloo (B, NR)

Gender and Women's Studies
Edith Cowan University (B, NR)
Laurentian University (B, NR)
Murdoch University (B, NR)
University of Bradford (M-D, NR)
University of Kent at Canterbury
(M-D, SR)
University of Melbourne (M-D, NR)
University of New England (B-M, NR)
University of South Africa (B, NR)
See also **Feminist Law**
See also **Sexuality**
General Studies
Athabasca University (B, NR)
Brigham Young University (B, SR)
Capital University (B, SR)
Charter Oak State College (B, NR)
City University (B, NR)
Columbia Union College (B, NR)
Indiana University (B, NR)
Murdoch University (B, NR)
Murray State University (B, SR)
Open University and Open College
(B, NR)
Texas Tech University (B, NR)
University of Southern Queensland
(B, NR)
Genetic Counseling
Charles Sturt University (M, NR)
Genetics
University of Melbourne (M-D, NR)

B = Bachelor's • M = Master's • D = Doctorate • NR = Nonresident • SR = Short Residency

Geographic Information Systems
Charles Sturt University (B, NR)
University of Melbourne (M-D, NR)
University of Southern Queensland
(B-M, NR)
Geography
Charter Oak State College (B, NR)
University of London (B-M, NR)
University of Melbourne (M-D, NR)
University of New England (B-M, NR)
University of South Africa (B-M-D, NR)
University of Wales—Lampeter
(M-D, NR)
University of Waterloo (B, NR)
Geological Engineering
University of Idaho (M, NR)
Geology
Charter Oak State College (B, NR)
Excelsior College (B, NR)
University of Melbourne (M-D, NR)
Geomatics
See **Geographic Information Systems**
German Language and Literature
Charter Oak State College (B, NR)
Queens University (B, NR)
University of Kent at Canterbury
(M-D, SR)
University of London (B, NR)
University of Melbourne (M-D, NR)
University of New England (B-M, NR)
University of South Africa (B-M-D, NR)
Gerontology
Charles Sturt University (B-M, NR)
Edith Cowan University (B, NR)
Laurentian University (B, NR)
St. Mary-of-the-Woods College (B, SR)
Thomas Edison State College (B, NR)
Gifted Education
University of South Africa (B-M-D, NR)
See also **Special Education**
Greek Language and Literature
University of Melbourne (M-D, NR)
University of New England (B-M, NR)
University of South Africa (B-M-D, NR)
Guidance Counseling
City University (M, NR)
University of Sarasota (M, SR)
University of South Africa (M, NR)
University of Southern Queensland
(M, NR)

Health Care
Baker College (M, NR)
California College for Health Sciences
(B-M, NR)
Empire State College (B, NR)
Golden Gate University (M, NR)
Rochester Institute of Technology (M, SR)
St. Joseph's College (B-M, SR)
Thomas Edison State College (B, NR)
University of London (M, NR)
University of Sarasota (M, SR)
University of South Africa (M, NR)
University of Southern Queensland
(M, NR)
Walden University (D, SR)

Health Communication Systems
Stephens College (B, SR)
University of Southern Queensland
(M, NR)
Health Education
University of South Africa (M, NR)
Health Psychology
University of Kent at Canterbury
(M-D, SR)
Health Science
Athabasca University (M, NR)
Central Michigan University (B, NR)
Charles Sturt University (B-M-D, NR)
Deakin University (M-D, NR)
Edith Cowan University (M, NR)
George Washington University (B, NR)
Nova Southeastern University (M, SR)
Open University and Open College
(B, NR)
University of Kent at Canterbury
(M-D, SR)
University of South Africa (B-M-D, NR)
Hebrew Bible
University of London (B, NR)
University of South Africa (B-M-D, NR)
Hebrew Language and Literature
University of Melbourne (M-D, NR)
University of South Africa (B-M-D, NR)
History
Caldwell College (B, SR)
California State University—Dominguez
Hills (M, NR)
Charles Sturt University (M-D, NR)
Charter Oak State College (B, NR)
Excelsior College (B, NR)
Judson College (B, NR)
Murdoch University (B, NR)
Open University and Open College
(B, NR)
Queens University (B, NR)
Thomas Edison State College (B, NR)
University of Kent at Canterbury
(M-D, SR)
University of London (B, NR)
University of Maryland (B, NR)
University of Melbourne (M-D, NR)
University of New England (B-M-D, NR)
University of South Africa (B-M-D, NR)
University of Wales—Lampeter
(M-D, NR)
University of Waterloo (B, NR)
Hospitality, Food Industry, and Restaurant
Management
Charles Sturt University (B, NR)
University of London (M, NR)
See also **Food Science**
See also **Tourism**
See also **Wine Science**
Human Development
See also **Developmental Psychology**
Human Factors Psychology
University of Idaho (M, NR)

Human Resource Management
Baker College (B-M, NR)
Bellevue University (B, NR)
Charles Sturt University (M, NR)
Colorado State University (M, NR)
St. Mary-of-the-Woods College (B, SR)
Thomas Edison State College (B, NR)
University of Illinois at Urbana-
Champaign (M, NR)
University of Leicester (M, NR)
University of Sarasota (M, SR)
University of Southern Queensland
(B-M, NR)
Upper Iowa University (B, NR)

Human Science
Saybrook Graduate School (M-D, SR)

Human Services
Capella University (M-D, SR)
Charles Sturt University (B, NR)
Charter Oak State College (B, NR)
Empire State College (B, NR)
Prescott College (B, SR)
St. Mary-of-the-Woods College (B, SR)
Upper Iowa University (B, NR)
Walden University (D, SR)

Humanities
California State University—Dominguez
Hills (M, NR)
City University (B, NR)
Laurentian University (M, SR)
Prescott College (M, SR)
St. Mary-of-the-Woods College (B, SR)
Thomas Edison State College (B, NR)
University of Maryland (B, NR)
University of Melbourne (M-D, NR)
See also **Liberal Arts**

Individualized Major
Antioch University (M, SR)
Burlington College (B, SR)
Capital University (B, SR)
Charter Oak State College (B, NR)
Eastern Illinois University (B, NR)
Empire State College (B, NR)
Goddard College (B-M, SR)
Governors State University (B, NR)
Judson College (B, NR)
National Technological University
(M, NR)
Norwich University (M, SR)
Rensselaer Polytechnic Institute (M, NR)
Rochester Institute of Technology (M, SR)
Skidmore College (B, SR)
Stephens College (B, SR)
Southwestern Adventist University (B, SR)
Union Institute (B-D, SR)
University of Wisconsin—Superior (B, SR)
Western Illinois University (B, NR)
See also **Interdisciplinary Studies**

Indonesian Language and Literature
University of Melbourne (M-D, NR)
University of New England (B-M, NR)
University of Southern Queensland
(B, NR)

Industrial Administration
See **Industrial Management**

Industrial Computing
University of Melbourne (M-D, NR)
University of Southern Queensland
(B, NR)

Industrial Engineering
Auburn University (M, SR)
Colorado State University (M-D, NR)
Georgia Institute of Technology (M, NR)
University of Northern Iowa (B-M, NR)

Industrial Hygiene
Colorado State University (M, NR)
See also **Occupational Health**

Industrial Management
Baker College (M, NR)
Central Michigan University (B, NR)

Industrial Psychology
University of South Africa (B-M-D, NR)

Industrial Relations
See **Labor Studies and Industrial
Relations**

Infectious Diseases
University of London (M, NR)

Information Science
See **Library and Information Science**

Instructional Technology
See **Educational Technology**

Instrumentation
Excelsior College (B, NR)
University of Southern Queensland
(B-M, NR)

Insurance and Insurance Law
Regis University (B, NR)
See also **Risk Management**

Intellectual Property Law
University of South Africa (M, NR)

Intelligence Studies
Charles Sturt University (M, NR)
See also **International Relations**

Interdisciplinary Studies
Athabasca University (M, NR)
Edith Cowan University (D, NR)
Empire State College (B, NR)
University of Alabama (B, SR)
See also **General Studies**
See also **Humanities**
See also **Liberal Studies**

International Business
Baker College (M, NR)
Caldwell College (B, SR)
Charles Sturt University (M, NR)
National Technological University
(M, NR)
Thomas Edison State College (B, NR)
University of London (M, NR)
University of Maryland (M, NR)
University of New England (M, NR)
University of Phoenix (M, NR)
University of Sarasota (M, SR)
University of Southern Queensland
(M, NR)
University of Texas (M, SR)

International Communication
University of South Africa (B-M-D, NR)

B = Bachelor's • M = Master's • D = Doctorate • NR = Nonresident • SR = Short Residency

International Law
De Montfort University (M, NR)
Deakin University (M, NR)
Regent University (M, SR)
University of Leicester (M, NR)
University of South Africa (M, NR)
International Relations
Salve Regina University (M, SR)
University of Kent at Canterbury
(M-D, SR)
University of London (B, NR)
University of South Africa (B-M-D, NR)
University of Southern Queensland
(B, NR)
University of Wales—Lampeter (M, NR)
See also **Conflict Resolution and
Peace Studies**
See also **Intelligence Studies**
Internet Studies
City University (B, NR)
Investment Law
Deakin University (M, NR)
Islamic Studies
University of Melbourne (M-D, NR)
University of New England (M, NR)
University of South Africa (B, NR)
University of Wales—Lampeter
(M-D, NR)
Italian Language and Literature
University of Kent at Canterbury
(M-D, SR)
University of London (B, NR)
University of Melbourne (M-D, NR)
University of New England (B-M, NR)
University of South Africa (B-M-D, NR)

Japanese Language and Literature
University of Melbourne (M-D, NR)
University of New England (B-M, NR)
Jewish Studies
University of London (B, NR)
University of Melbourne (M-D, NR)
University of South Africa (B-M-D, NR)
Journalism
Charles Sturt University (M, NR)
Deakin University (B, NR)
Regent University (M, NR)
St. Mary-of-the-Woods College (B, SR)
Thomas Edison State College (B, NR)
University of Southern Queensland
(B, NR)

Kinesiology
University of Texas (M, NR)
See also **Physical Education**

Labor Studies and Industrial Relations
Charles Sturt University (M, NR)
Empire State College (B, NR)
Indiana University (B, NR)
Thomas Edison State College (B, NR)
University of Kent at Canterbury
(M-D, SR)
University of Leicester (M, NR)
Latin American Studies
University of London (B, NR)

Latin Language and Literature
University of Melbourne (M-D, NR)
University of New England (B-M, NR)
University of South Africa (B-M-D, NR)
See also **Classics**
Law
Charles Sturt University (M, NR)
De Montfort University (M, NR)
Deakin University (B-M, NR)
Open University (B-M-D, NR)
Regent University (M, NR)
Stephens College (B, SR)
University of Kent at Canterbury
(M-D, SR)
University of Leicester (M, NR)
University of London (B-M, NR)
University of Melbourne (M-D, NR)
University of New England (B-M-D, NR)
University of South Africa (B-M-D, NR)
University of Southern Queensland
(M, NR)
See also **Agriculture Law**
See also **Business Law**
See also **Criminal Justice and Law
Enforcement**
See also **Criminal Law**
See also **Environmental Law**
See also **Feminist Law**
See also **Food Law**
See also **Insurance and Insurance Law**
See also **Intellectual Property Law**
See also **International Law**
See also **Investment Law**
See also **Legal Psychology**
See also **Philosophy of Law**
See also **Taxation**
See also **Trade Law**
Law Enforcement
See **Criminal Justice and Law
Enforcement**
Leadership
Antioch University (D, SR)
Baker College (M, NR)
Bellevue University (B-M, NR)
Regent University (M-D, NR)
University of Sarasota (D, SR)
University of South Africa (M-D, NR)
University of Southern Queensland
(M-D, NR)
Upper Iowa University (M, NR)
See also **Educational Leadership and
Administration**
See also **Management**
Legal Psychology
University of Leicester (M, NR)
Leisure Studies
Charles Sturt University (B, NR)
Edith Cowan University (M, NR)
University of Luton (M-D, NR)
Liberal Arts
Excelsior College (A-B, NR)
Harvard University (B-M, SR)
Norwich University (B, SR)
Prescott College (B, SR)
Syracuse University (A-B, SR)

B = Bachelor's • M = Master's • D = Doctorate • NR = Nonresident • SR = Short Residency

Liberal Studies
Charter Oak State College (B, NR)
Empire State College (M, SR)
Excelsior College (M, NR)
St. Joseph's College (B, SR)
Salve Regina University (B, SR)
Skidmore College (M, SR)
Thomas Edison State College (B, NR)
University of Iowa (B, NR)
University of Northern Iowa (B, NR)

Library and Information Science
Charles Sturt University (M-D, NR)
Edith Cowan University (M, NR)
Nova Southeastern University (M-D, SR)
Syracuse University (M, SR)
University of Illinois at Urbana-
   Champaign (M, SR)
University of Northern Iowa (M, NR)
University of South Africa (B-M-D, NR)

Linguistics
Edith Cowan University (M, NR)
University of Melbourne (M-D, NR)
University of New England (B-M-D, NR)
University of South Africa (B-M-D, NR)
See also **Applied Linguistics**

Literacy Education
City University (M, NR)
Edith Cowan University (M-D, NR)
Indiana University (M, NR)
University of Texas (M, NR)

Literary Theory
University of South Africa (B-M-D, NR)
See also **Comparative Literature**

Logistics, Decision Sciences, and
   Operations Management
Charles Sturt University (M, NR)
Thomas Edison State College (B, NR)
University of Southern Queensland
   (B, NR)
Walden University (D, SR)
See also **Project Management**

Management
Bellevue University (B, NR)
Caldwell College (B, SR)
Capital University (B, SR)
Charles Sturt University (B-M-D, NR)
City University (B-M, NR)
Colorado State University (M, NR)
Edith Cowan University (B, NR)
Empire State College (B, NR)
Northwood University (B, SR)
Prescott College (B, SR)
Regent University (M, SR)
Regis University (B, NR)
Rensselaer Polytechnic Institute (M, NR)
Salve Regina University (M, SR)
Thomas Edison State College (M, SR)
University of Bradford (M-D, NR)
University of Kent at Canterbury
   (M-D, SR)
University of London (B-M, NR)
University of Maryland (B-M, NR)
University of Melbourne (M-D, NR)
University of Phoenix (B, NR)
University of Sarasota (B, SR)
University of South Africa (B-M-D, NR)
University of South Australia (D, NR)

University of Southern Queensland
   (B-M, NR)
Upper Iowa University (B, NR)
Walden University (D, SR)
See also **Business Administration**

Management Information Systems
Bellevue University (B, NR)
Deakin University (M, NR)
Judson College (B, NR)
Nova Southeastern University (M, SR)
University of London (B, NR)
University of Maryland (B-M, NR)
See also **Business Information Systems**
See also **Technology Management**

Manufacturing and Manufacturing
   Engineering
Excelsior College (B, NR)
National Technological University
   (M, NR)
Rensselaer Polytechnic Institute (M, NR)
Thomas Edison State College (B, NR)
University of Melbourne (M-D, NR)
University of South Australia (M, NR)
Washington State University (B, NR)

Manufacturing Management
University of South Australia (M, NR)

Marketing
Baker College (M, NR)
Caldwell College (B, SR)
Charles Sturt University (B-M, NR)
City University (B-M, NR)
Deakin University (M, NR)
Edith Cowan University (B, NR)
Golden Gate University (M, NR)
Northwood University (B, SR)
Nova Southeastern University (M, SR)
St. Mary-of-the-Woods College (B, SR)
Syracuse University (M, SR)
Thomas Edison State College (A-B, NR)
University of Leicester (M, NR)
University of Melbourne (M-D, NR)
University of New England (M, NR)
University of Sarasota (M, SR)
University of Southern Queensland
   (B-M, NR)
Upper Iowa University (B, NR)

Mass Communication and Media Studies
University of Bradford (M-D, NR)
University of Leicester (M, NR)
University of Melbourne (M-D, NR)
University of Southern Queensland
   (B-M, NR)
See also **Communication**
See also **Internet Studies**

Materials Engineering
Auburn University (M, SR)
Columbia University (M, NR)
National Technological University
   (M, NR)
Thomas Edison State College (B, NR)
University of London (M, NR)

Mathematics
Charles Sturt University (B, NR)
Charter Oak State College (B, NR)
Excelsior College (B, NR)
Murdoch University (B, NR)
Open University and Open College
(B, NR)
St. Mary-of-the-Woods College (B, SR)
Thomas Edison State College (B, NR)
University of Bradford (M-D, NR)
University of Kent at Canterbury
(M-D, SR)
University of London (B, NR)
University of Melbourne (M-D, NR)
University of New England (B-M-D, NR)
University of South Africa (B-M-D, NR)
University of Southern Queensland
(B, NR)

Mathematics Education
Edith Cowan University (M-D, NR)
University of Idaho (M, NR)
University of Melbourne (M-D, NR)
University of Northern Iowa (M, NR)
University of South Africa (M, NR)

Mechanical Engineering
Auburn University (M, SR)
Colorado State University (M-D, NR)
Columbia University (M-S, NR)
Excelsior College (B, NR)
Georgia Institute of Technology (M, NR)
National Technological University
(M, NR)
Rensselaer Polytechnic Institute (M, NR)
Rochester Institute of Technology (B, SR)
Thomas Edison State College (B, NR)
University of Bradford (M-D, NR)
University of Idaho (M, NR)
University of Illinois at Urbana-
Champaign (M, NR)
University of Melbourne (M-D, NR)
University of Southern Queensland
(B-M, NR)

Media Arts
University of Melbourne (M-D, NR)
See also **Mass Communication and Media
Studies**

Medical Ethics
See **Bioethics**

Medical Imaging
Charles Sturt University (B-M, NR)
See also **Dental Radiology**
See also **Radiology**

Medieval Studies
University of Kent at Canterbury
(M-D, SR)
University of Melbourne (M-D, NR)
University of Waterloo (B, NR)

Mental Health
Charles Sturt University (B, NR)
Thomas Edison State College (B, NR)
University of Kent at Canterbury
(M-D, SR)
University of Sarasota (M, SR)
University of South Africa (M, NR)

Metallurgical Engineering
Murdoch University (B, NR)
University of Idaho (M, NR)

Meteorology
University of Melbourne (M-D, SR)

Microbiology and Molecular Biology
University of Kent at Canterbury
(M-D, SR)
University of Melbourne (M-D, NR)
University of New England (B-M, NR)

Microelectronics
Rensselaer Polytechnic Institute (M, NR)

Midwifery
University of Southern Queensland
(M, NR)

Mining
University of Idaho (M, NR)
University of Southern Queensland
(B, NR)

Ministry
Charles Sturt University (M, NR)
St. Joseph's College (M, SR)
St. Mary-of-the-Woods College (M, SR)
See also **Divinity**
See also **Evangelism**
See also **Pastoral Counseling**
See also **Religious Education**

Molecular Biology
See **Microbiology and Molecular Biology**

Moral Theology
University of South Africa (B-M-D, NR)

Museum Studies
University of Leicester (M, NR)

Music
California State University—Dominguez
Hills (M, NR)
Excelsior College (B, NR)
Judson College (B, NR)
Norwich University (M, SR)
Open University and Open College
(B, NR)
University of New England (B-M-D, NR)
University of South Africa (B-M-D, NR)

Music Education
Edith Cowan University (M-D, NR)
Judson College (B, NR)
University of Northern Iowa (M, NR)

New Testament Studies
University of London (B, NR)
University of South Africa (B-M-D, NR)

Nonprofit Management
Regis University (M, NR)
See also **Organizational Management**

Nuclear Engineering
Excelsior College (B, NR)
Thomas Edison State College (B, NR)

B = Bachelor's • M = Master's • D = Doctorate • NR = Nonresident • SR = Short Residency

Nursing
    Athabasca University (B, NR)
    California State University—Dominguez
       Hills (B-M, NR)
    Capital University (B, SR)
    Charles Sturt University (B, NR)
    Deakin University (M-D, NR)
    Eastern Oregon University (B, SR)
    Edith Cowan University (B-M-D, NR)
    Excelsior College (A-B-M, NR)
    Indiana University (M, NR)
    Laurentian University (B, NR)
    Open University and Open College
       (B, NR)
    St. Joseph's College (B-M, SR)
    Salve Regina University (B, SR)
    Syracuse University (M, SR)
    Thomas Edison State College (B, NR)
    University of Melbourne (M-D, NR)
    University of Phoenix (B-M, NR)
    University of South Africa (M, NR)
    University of South Australia (B, NR)
    University of Southern Queensland
       (B-M, NR)
Nutrition
    Central Michigan University (M, NR)
    Deakin University (M-D, NR)
    Thomas Edison State College (B, NR)

Occupational Health
    Edith Cowan University (M-D, NR)
    Nova Southeastern University (M-D, SR)
    University of London (M, NR)
    University of Southern Queensland
       (M, NR)
    See also **Industrial Hygiene**
    See also **Occupational Safety**
Occupational Psychology
    See **Industrial Psychology**
Occupational Safety
    Edith Cowan University (M-D, NR)
    University of Southern Queensland
       (M, NR)
    See also **Industrial Hygiene**
    See also **Occupational Health**
Old Testament
    See **Hebrew Bible**
Oncology
    University of Bradford (M-D, NR)
Open and Distance Education
    See **Distance Education**
Optical Engineering
    Excelsior College (B, NR)
    National Technological University
       (M, NR)
Organizational Development
    Fielding Institute (M-D, SR)
    Saybrook Graduate School (M-D, SR)
    University of Leicester (M, NR)
Organizational Management
    Charter Oak State College (B, NR)
    Regent University (M, NR)
    Thomas Edison State College (B, NR)
    University of Phoenix (M, NR)
    See also **Management**
    See also **Nonprofit Management**

Organizational Psychology
    Kansas State University (M, NR)
    University of London (M, NR)
Orthodontics and Prosthodontics
    University of London (M, NR)

Palliative Care
    Edith Cowan University (M, NR)
Paralegal Studies
    St. Mary-of-the-Woods College (B, SR)
    University of Maryland (B, NR)
Pareschatology
    University of Wales—Lampeter (M, NR)
Pastoral Counseling
    University of Sarasota (D, SR)
    University of South Africa (M-D, NR)
Peace Studies
    See **Conflict Resolution and Peace Studies**
Penology
    University of South Africa (B-M-D, NR)
Petroleum Engineering
    Texas Tech University (M, NR)
Pharmacy
    De Montfort University (M, NR)
    University of Bradford (M-D, NR)
    University of Melbourne (M-D, NR)
    University of South Australia (B, NR)
    Washington State University (D, SR)
Philosophy
    Capital University (B, SR)
    California State University—Dominguez
       Hills (M, NR)
    Charter Oak State College (B, NR)
    Eastern Oregon University (B, NR)
    Excelsior College (B, NR)
    Murdoch University (B, NR)
    St. Mary-of-the-Woods College (B, SR)
    Stephens College (B, SR)
    Thomas Edison State College (B, NR)
    University of Kent at Canterbury
       (M-D, SR)
    University of London (B, NR)
    University of Melbourne (M-D, NR)
    University of New England (B, NR)
    University of South Africa (B-M-D, NR)
    University of Wales—Lampeter
       (M-D, NR)
    University of Waterloo (B, NR)
Philosophy of Education
    University of South Africa (M-D, NR)
Philosophy of Law
    University of Kent at Canterbury
       (M-D, SR)
    University of South Africa (M, NR)
Physical Education
    Eastern Oregon University (B, NR)
    Edith Cowan University (M-D, NR)
    University of Melbourne (M-D, NR)
    See **Kinesiology**
Physical Therapy
    Indiana University (M, NR)
    Nova Southeastern University (M-D, SR)
    University of Melbourne (M-D, NR)
    See also **Therapeutic Recreation**

B = Bachelor's • M = Master's • D = Doctorate • NR = Nonresident • SR = Short Residency

Physics
Charter Oak State College (B, NR)
Excelsior College (B, NR)
Georgia Institute of Technology (M, NR)
Murdoch University (B, NR)
Thomas Edison State College (B, NR)
University of Kent at Canterbury
(M-D, SR)
University of Melbourne (M-D, NR)
University of South Africa (B-M-D, NR)

Polish Language and Literature
University of Melbourne (M-D, NR)

**Political Science, Public Policy, and Social
Policy**
Caldwell College (B, SR)
Capital University (B, SR)
Charles Sturt University (B-M-D, NR)
Charter Oak State College (B, NR)
Eastern Oregon University (B, NR)
Empire State College (B, NR)
Excelsior College (B, NR)
Murdoch University (B, NR)
Queens University (B, NR)
Regent University (M, SR)
Thomas Edison State College (B, NR)
University of Kent at Canterbury
(M-D, SR)
University of London (B, NR)
University of Melbourne (M-D, NR)
University of New England (B-M-D, NR)
University of South Africa (B-M-D, NR)
University of Wales—Lampeter
(M-D, NR)

Polymer Science and Engineering
De Montfort University (M, NR)

Portuguese Language and Literature
University of Melbourne (M-D, NR)
University of South Africa (B-M-D, NR)

Practical Theology
Regent University (M, SR)
St. Mary-of-the-Woods College (M, SR)
University of South Africa (B-M-D, NR)

Preprimary Education
Charles Sturt University (B, NR)
Edith Cowan University (M-D, NR)
Nova Southeastern University (B, SR)
St. Mary-of-the-Woods College (B, SR)
University of South Africa (B, NR)
University of South Australia (B, NR)

Primary Education
Charles Sturt University (B, NR)
Judson College (B, NR)
Murdoch University (B-M, NR)
Nova Southeastern University (B, SR)
St. Mary-of-the-Woods College (B, SR)
University of Leicester (M, NR)
University of Northern Iowa (B, NR)
University of South Africa (B, NR)

Professional Studies
See **Applied and Professional Studies**

Project Management
City University (M, NR)
George Washington University (M, SR)
Henley Management College (M, NR)
National Technological University
(M, NR)
University of Bradford (M-D, NR)
University of Melbourne (M-D, NR)
University of Pretoria (M, NR)
University of South Africa (M, NR)
University of South Australia (M, NR)
University of Southern Queensland
(M, NR)

Psychology and Behavioral Science
Burlington College (B, SR)
Caldwell College (B, SR)
California State University—Dominguez
Hills (M, NR)
Capella University (M-D, SR)
Capital University (B, SR)
Charles Sturt University (B-M-D, NR)
Charter Oak State College (B, NR)
City University (M, NR)
Columbia Union College (B, NR)
Edith Cowan University (B. NR)
Excelsior College (B, NR)
Judson College (B, NR)
Kansas State University (M, NR)
Laurentian University (B, NR)
Open University and Open College
(B, NR)
Prescott College (M, SR)
Queens University (B, NR)
St. Mary-of-the-Woods College (B, SR)
Saybrook Graduate School (M-D, SR)
Stephens College (B, SR)
Thomas Edison State College (B, NR)
University of Idaho (M, NR)
University of Kent at Canterbury
(M-D, SR)
University of Leicester (M, NR)
University of Maryland (B, NR)
University of Melbourne (M-D, NR)
University of New England (B, NR)
University of South Africa (B-M-D, NR)
University of Southern Queensland
(B, NR)
University of Waterloo (B, NR)
Walden University (M-D, SR)
See also **Clinical Psychology**
See also **Counseling**

Public Administration
Central Michigan University (B-M, NR)
Golden Gate University (B-M, NR)
Regent University (M, SR)
Thomas Edison State College (B, NR)
University of London (M, NR)
University of South Africa (B-M-D, NR)
Upper Iowa University (B, NR)

Public Health
Charles Sturt University (B, NR)
Edith Cowan University (M, NR)
Murdoch University (M, NR)
University of London (M, NR)
University of Melbourne (M-D, NR)

B = Bachelor's • M = Master's • D = Doctorate • NR = Nonresident • SR = Short Residency

Public Order
University of Leicester (M, NR)
See also **Criminal Justice and Law Enforcement**
Public Relations
Capital University (B, SR)
Deakin University (B, SR)
University of Northern Iowa (M, NR)
University of Southern Queensland (B-M, NR)

Quality Assurance and Engineering
California State University—Dominguez Hills (B-M, NR)
Rensselaer Polytechnic Institute (M, NR)

Radiology
Georgia Institute of Technology (M, NR)
Thomas Edison State College (B, NR)
University of London (M, NR)
See also **Medical Imaging**
Real Estate
Thomas Edison State College (B, NR)
Religion and International Relations
University of Wales—Lampeter (M, NR)
Religious Education
Edith Cowan University (M-D, NR)
Judson College (B, NR)
Regent University (M, SR)
Religious Studies
Caldwell College (B, SR)
Capital University (B, SR)
Charter Oak State College (B, NR)
Columbia Union College (B, NR)
Judson College (B, NR)
Laurentian University (B, NR)
Thomas Edison State College (B, NR)
University of Kent at Canterbury (M-D, SR)
University of New England (B-M-D, NR)
University of South Africa (B-M-D, NR)
University of Wales—Lampeter (M-D, NR)
University of Waterloo (B, NR)
Respiratory Care
California College for Health Sciences (B, NR)
Charles Sturt University (M, NR)
Columbia Union College (B, NR)
Open University and Open College (B, NR)
Risk Management
University of Leicester (M, NR)
See also **Insurance and Insurance Law**
Robotics
Excelsior College (B, NR)
University of Southern Queensland (B-M, NR)
Rural Development
Charles Sturt University (M, NR)
University of London (M, NR)
University of Melbourne (M-D, NR)
University of New England (B, NR)
University of South Africa (B, NR)
See also **Development Studies and Sustainable Agriculture**

Rural Health
University of Southern Queensland (M, NR)
Russian Language and Literature
University of Melbourne (M-D, NR)
University of South Africa (B-M-D, NR)

Science Education
Edith Cowan University (M-D, NR)
Nova Southeastern University (B, SR)
University of Melbourne (M-D, NR)
University of South Africa (M, NR)
Secondary Education
Judson College (B, NR)
Murdoch University (M, NR)
Nova Southeastern University (B, SR)
University of South Africa (B, NR)
Security Management
University of Leicester (M, NR)
Semitic Languages and Literature
University of South Africa (B-M-D, NR)
See also **Arabic Language and Literature**
See also **Hebrew Language and Literature**
Sexuality
Laurentian University (Cert., NR)
Social Sciences
Caldwell College (B, SR)
Charles Sturt University (B-M, NR)
City University (B, NR)
Edith Cowan University (M, NR)
Kansas State University (B, NR)
Syracuse University (M, SR)
University of Maryland (B, NR)
University of New England (B, NR)
University of South Africa (B-M-D, NR)
University of South Australia (M, NR)
Upper Iowa University (B, NR)
Washington State University (B, NR)
Social Work
Capital University (B, SR)
Charles Sturt University (B-M-D, NR)
Curtin University of Technology (B, SR)
Laurentian University (B, NR)
University of Kent at Canterbury (M-D, SR)
University of Melbourne (M-D, NR)
University of South Africa (B-M-D, NR)
Sociolinguistics
University of South Africa (M, NR)
Sociology
Caldwell College (B, SR)
Capital University (B, SR)
Charter Oak State College (B, NR)
Edith Cowan University (B, NR)
Excelsior College (B, NR)
Laurentian University (B, NR)
Murdoch University (B, NR)
Open University and Open College (B, NR)
Thomas Edison State College (B, NR)
University of Kent at Canterbury (M-D, SR)
University of Leicester (M, NR)
University of London (B, NR)
University of Melbourne (M-D, NR)
University of New England (B-M, NR)
University of South Africa (B-M-D, NR)
University of Waterloo (B, NR)

B = Bachelor's • M = Master's • D = Doctorate • NR = Nonresident • SR = Short Residency

Software Engineering
Kansas State University (M, NR)
Murdoch University (B-M, NR)
National Technological University
(M, NR)
Rochester Institute of Technology (M, SR)
Texas Tech University (M, NR)
University of Maryland (M, NR)
University of Melbourne (M-D, NR)
University of Southern Queensland
(B, NR)

Spanish Language and Literature
Charter Oak State College (B, NR)
University of Kent at Canterbury
(M-D, SR)
University of London (B, NR)
University of Melbourne (M-D, NR)
University of South Africa (B-M-D, NR)
See also **Catalan Language and Literature**
See also **Latin American Studies**

Special Education
Charles Sturt University (M, NR)
Edith Cowan University (B-M-D, NR)
Nova Southeastern University (B, SR)
St. Mary-of-the-Woods College (B, SR)
University of Northern Iowa (M, NR)
University of South Africa (B-M-D, NR)
University of Southern Queensland
(M, NR)

Spirituality
University of South Africa (M-D, NR)

**Sport, Sport Sociology, and Sport
Management**
Edith Cowan University (M, NR)
University of Leicester (M, NR)

Statistics
Colorado State University (M, NR)
Murdoch University (B, NR)
Rochester Institute of Technology (M, SR)
University of Kent at Canterbury
(M-D, SR)
University of London (B, NR)
University of Melbourne (M-D, NR)
University of New England (M, NR)
University of South Africa (B-M-D, NR)
University of Southern Queensland
(B, NR)

Surveying
Thomas Edison State College (B, NR)
University of Southern Queensland
(B, NR)

Systematic Theology
University of South Africa (B-M-D, NR)

Systems Engineering
Colorado State University (M-D, SR)
National Technological University
(M, NR)
Rensselaer Polytechnic Institute (M, NR)
University of Southern Queensland
(B-M, NR)

Systems Management
National Technological University
(M, NR)
Texas Tech University (M, NR)
University of Maryland (M, NR)

Taxation
Golden Gate University (M, NR)
Regent University (M, NR)
University of South Africa (M, NR)

Teaching
Charles Sturt University (B, NR)
De Montfort University (M, NR)
Edith Cowan University (B-M-D, NR)
University of Maryland (M, NR)
University of South Africa (B-M-D, NR)
University of Southern Queensland
(M, NR)
See also **Education**

**Teaching English as a Second or Foreign
Language**
Deakin University (M, NR)
University of Southern Queensland
(M, NR)
University of Texas (M, NR)

Technical Writing
Texas Tech University (M, NR)
See also **Writing**

Technology Management
Colorado State University (M, NR)
University of Maryland (M, NR)
University of Phoenix (M, NR)
University of Southern Queensland
(B, NR)
University of Waterloo (M, NR)
See also **Engineering Management**
See also **Systems Management**
See also **Telecommunications and
Telecommunications Management**

**Telecommunications and
Telecommunications Management**
City University (B, NR)
Golden Gate University (M, NR)
Murdoch University (M, NR)
Syracuse University (M, SR)
University of Maryland (M, NR)

Thanatology
University of Wales—Lampeter (M, NR)

Theater Studies
See **Drama and Theater Studies**

Theology and Theological Studies
Charles Sturt University (B-M, NR)
Columbia Union College (B, NR)
Murdoch University (B, NR)
Regent University (M, SR)
St. Mary-of-the-Woods College
(B-M, SR)
University of Kent at Canterbury
(M-D, SR)
University of South Africa (B-M-D, NR)
University of Wales—Lampeter
(M-D, NR)

Therapeutic Recreation
Indiana University (M, NR)
See also **Leisure Studies**
See also **Physical Therapy**

Trade Law
Deakin University (M, NR)

Transpersonal Studies
Burlington College (B, SR)
Naropa University (M, SR)

Transportation Management
Thomas Edison State College (B, NR)
University of South Africa (B, NR)

B = Bachelor's • M = Master's • D = Doctorate • NR = Nonresident • SR = Short Residency

Ukrainian Language and Literature
    University of Melbourne (M-D, NR)
Urban Ministry
    University of South Africa (M-D, NR)
    See also **Evangelism**

Veterinary Science
    Charles Sturt University (B, NR)
    Kansas State University (B, NR)
    Murdoch University (M, NR)
    University of London (M, NR)
    University of Melbourne (M-D, NR)

Women's Studies
    See **Gender and Women's Studies**
Writing
    Antioch University (M, SR)
    Burlington College (B, SR)

    Goddard College (M, SR)
    Norwich University (M, SR)
    University of Melbourne (M-D, NR)

Xhosa Language and Literature
    University of South Africa (B-M-D, NR)

Youth Studies and Youth Work
    De Montfort University (M, NR)
    Edith Cowan University (B, NR)
    Nova Southeastern University (M-D, SR)

Zoology
    University of Melbourne (M-D, NR)
    University of New England (M, NR)
Zulu Language and Literature
    University of South Africa (B-M-D, NR)

Index

A

Abraham Lincoln University, 149
Acadia University, 29
Accreditation, 16–23
ACE. *See* American Council on Education
ACT (American College Testing Program), 14
Advanced Placement examinations, 35
Alabama, unaccredited schools in, 162
American College, 46
American College Testing Program. *See* ACT
American Council on Education (ACE), 38, 43
American Education Research Corporation, 41
Antioch University, 47
Arizona, unaccredited schools in, 163
Associate's degrees, 7
Athabasca University, 29, 48
Auburn University, 49

B

Bachelor's degrees, 7
Baker College, 50
Bellevue University, 51
Brigham Young University, 28, 52
British-American University School of Law, 149, 150
Burlington College, 53

C

CAEL. *See* Council for Adult and Experiential Learning
Caldwell College, 54
California, unaccredited schools in, 163
California College for Health Sciences, 55
California State University—Dominguez Hills, 56
Capella University, 57
Capital University, 58
Central Michigan University, 59
Chancellorates, 8
Charles Sturt University, 60–61
Charter Oak State College, 28, 62
CHEA. *See* Council for Higher Education Accreditation
City University, 63
Clarkson College, 64
CLEP. *See* College-Level Examination Program
College Board. *See* College Entrance Examination Board
College Entrance Examination Board, 14, 30
College-Level Examination Program (CLEP), 30–31
Colorado State University, 28, 65

Columbia Union College, 66
Columbia University, 67
Concord University School of Law, 149
Connecticut Board for State Academic Awards, 62
Correspondence courses, 27–29
Council for Adult and Experiential Learning (CAEL), 37
Council for Higher Education Accreditation (CHEA), 17
Credit bank, 43–44
Curtin University of Technology, 29

D

DANTES (Defense Activity for Non-Traditional Education Support), 34–35
De Montfort University, 68
Deakin University, 29, 69
Degree Consulting Services, 153
Degrees, 7–9
DETC. *See* Distance Education and Training Council
Distance Education and Training Council (DETC), 19
Doctorates, 8

E

Eastern Illinois University, 70
Eastern Oregon University, 71
Edith Cowan University, 29, 72
Education Evaluators International, 42
Educational Credential Evaluators, 41
Educational Records Evaluation Service, 42
Educational Testing Service, 34
Empire State College, 73
Employment, credit for, 36
Entrance examinations, 14–15
Equivalency examinations, 30–35
Examinations
    entrance, 14–15
    equivalency, 30–35
    preparing for, 15, 33
Excelsior College, 74
Excelsior College Credit Bank, 43–44
Excelsior College Examinations, 31–32

F

Fielding Institute, 75
Florida, unaccredited schools in, 164
Foreign Academic Credential Service, 42
Foreign academic experience, 41–42

G

GAAP. *See* Generally Accepted Accreditation Principles
Generally Accepted Accreditation Principles (GAAP), 17

George Washington University, 76
Georgia Institute of Technology, 77
Global Education Group, 42
Goddard College, 78
Golden Gate University, 79
Governors State University, 80
Graduate Record Examination (GRE), 14–15, 34
Graduate School of America. *See* Capella University
GRE. *See* Graduate Record Examination

H

Harvard University, 81
Hawaii, unaccredited schools in, 164
Henley Management College, 82
Heriot-Watt University, 83
Higher education agencies, 154–161
Hobbies, credit for, 36
Homemaking, credit for, 36
Honorary degrees, 9

I

Indiana University, 28, 84
Institutionalized students, 169–73
International Consultants of Delaware, 42
International Credential Evaluation Service, 42
International Credentialing Associates, 42
International Education Research Foundation, 42
International Qualifications Assessment Service, 42
Iowa, unaccredited schools in, 164
ISIM University, 85

J

James Cook University, 29
Jones International University, 86
Joseph Silny & Associates, 42
Judson College, 87

K

Kansas State University, 88

L

Laurentian University, 89
Law apprenticeship, 150
Law degrees, 149–50
Law School Admission Test (LSAT), 15
Leicester Polytechnic. *See* De Montfort University
Life-experience learning, 36–40
Life-experience portfolio, 37–38
Louisiana State University, 28
Louisiana, unaccredited schools in, 164–65
LSAT. *See* Law School Admission Test